The Open University

A103

AN INTRODUCTION TO
THE HUMANITIES

Resource Book 3

The Open University
Walton Hall, Milton Keynes MK7 6AA

First published 1998

Edited, designed and typeset by The Open University.

Printed and bound by Scotprint Ltd., Musselburgh, Scotland.

ISBN 0 7492 8712 8

This text is a component of the Open University course A103 *An Introduction to the
Humanities*. Details of this and other Open University courses are available from Course
Enquiries Data Service, PO Box 625, Dane Road, Milton Keynes MK1 1TY; telephone
+ 44 - (0)1908 858585.

17177B/a103rb3i1.1

Contents

(Note that extracts E3 to E23 are not referred to in the course material for Study Week 22 but have been included for use at Summer School.)

Section A STUDYING RELIGION

A1 Eileen Barker, 'Transcendental Meditation (TM)'

From E. Barker (1989) *New Religious Movements: A Practical Introduction*, London, HMSO, pp.213–14, footnotes omitted.

Transcendental meditation (TM)

Transcendental Meditation is a technique for deep relaxation and revitalization which develops the inner potential of energy and intelligence that form the basis of all success in life. TM is practised for twenty minutes morning and evening whilst sitting comfortably in a chair with the eyes closed ... [TM] is practised by people of every age, education, culture and religion. TM requires no belief or any great commitment. More than three million people all over the world practise TM.

[*From* Corporate Development Programme: An Introduction to Transcendental Meditation, *leaflet distributed by Maharishi Corporate Development International, London*]

Maharishi Mahesh Yogi (1911–) graduated in physics from Allahabad University in 1940 before studying for thirteen years with his spiritual master, Guru Dev (1869–1953), who had rediscovered, from Hindu Scriptures, the technique that is known as transcendental meditation. In 1958 Maharishi brought TM to the West.

To be taught the basic technique, which involves concentration on a mantra, costs £165. This covers an introductory presentation, an hour-long personal instruction and three further instruction meetings that last one and a half hours. Those who go on to the more advanced TM–Sidhi course pay about £1,200 for a weekend course, two weeks of evening courses and, later, a two-week course at one of the movements Academies, when they can be taught the widely publicised levitation or 'flying' technique during which the person, cross-legged, hops about and, if successful, manages to jump onto a pile of mattresses.

The movement produces an abundance of literature describing both the achievements of TM and Vedic Science 'the science of life according to pure knowledge', and the movement's plans for implementing such ambitious projects as world peace, the reduction of world poverty and the achievement of perfect health. Associated with TM are numerous other organisations promoting various ventures. Maharishi Corporate Development International provides not only courses for business executives, but also a number of in-company programmes. In the United States, Maharishi International University, founded in 1971, offers over a thousand students undergraduate, master's and doctoral programmes.

[...] most meditators continue with 'ordinary lives'. There have, however, been negative reports in the media about the dependency that some people are said to develop on either the techniques or the movement itself. Other reports have questioned some of the claims that scientists have made about the efficacy of the techniques.

A2 Denise Denniston and Peter McWilliams, 'What TM is'

From D. Denniston, P. McWilliams and B. Geller (illus.) (1975) *The TM Book: How to Enjoy the Rest of Your Life*, Michigan, Versemonger Press, pp.13–16, 19–23, 26–7, 32–3, 35–6, 38–9, 44–7, footnotes and illustrations omitted.

What TM is not

TM does not involve religious belief

TM is not a religion? I've heard it was just some Westernized form of Hinduism.

No, no – it's absurd to assume that just because TM comes from India it must be some Hindu practice. Italy is considered a Catholic country. Galileo, an Italian, discovered that the earth is round. The fact that the earth is round is no more connected with the Catholic Church than TM is connected with the Hindu religion. TM is a scientific discovery, a technique, which happens to come from India. As with all scientific discoveries, it works everywhere because it involves the basic laws of nature. TM does not involve any religious belief or practice – Hindu or otherwise. Just like bathing always works to get you clean, TM is a universally applicable *technique* for getting the most out of life.

Isn't Maharishi a monk?

Yes, he is. Many great scientists and thinkers are men of profound religious convictions. Gregor Mendel, who discovered the laws of genetics, was himself a Jesuit priest. Einstein often spoke of his 'cosmic religious sense'. A scientist's personal religious beliefs have no bearing on the validity of his contributions to science.

Does TM conflict with any form of religion?

No. People of any religion practice TM. In fact, they find the increased clarity of mind brought about through TM greatly broadens the comprehension and enhances the appreciation of their individual religious practices. Priests practice TM, rabbis practice TM, ministers practice TM, and they recommend TM to their congregations. [...]

What about atheists?

Atheists enjoy TM and for the same reason the devoutly religious enjoy it – it involves no dogma, belief or philosophy. The technique is purely scientific and produces scientifically verifiable results.

But doesn't meditation have something to do with knowing God? Doesn't that make TM essentially a religious practice?

TM has something to do with knowing *anything*. It makes the mind more orderly, gives the body deep rest, and improves the coordination between the two. This means that with clear awareness we can focus sharply and succeed in activity – whatever our activity may be. [...]

No special diet

Aren't most meditators vegetarians?

Some are. Many aren't. But then, a lot of nonmeditators are vegetarians. The point is, there are no dietary restrictions or recommendations involved with TM.

No daily ration of brown rice?

Nope.

I can still eat Big Macs?

You can eat anything you want.

This is sounding better and better.

No special clothing

No funny clothes?

No.

How about sandals? Some meditators wear sandals.

And some wear Sneakers, or Hush Puppies, or Gucci's. We get all kinds. People who practice TM grow to express their own unique individuality, and this is reflected in their life style, self expression, and, of course, their clothing. [...]

TM is not contemplation

What is contemplation?

Contemplation is thinking *about* something (a problem, a philosophical idea) or just letting the mind wander from one idea to the next with no particular direction.

Isn't that what people mean by meditation?

Many do, yes. They say 'I am meditating' on this or that thought. Some call quiet reflection 'meditation,' while others glorify their day-dreams with the title 'meditation.'

Transcendental Meditation (TM) is a very specific technique, very different from any of these sorts of 'meditation'.

No change of life style

No change of life style?

There is no need to change in any way to start TM. There are no pleasures you must abandon, nor any new traditions you must uphold.

So my life would go on without change.

Without *forced* change. Life is always changing. The TM program produces remarkably rapid growth. Your life will continue to change naturally, in the direction of more strength, more effectiveness, and more enjoyment. But remember, you're in full control of your own growth – it's your responsibility every step of the way.

There is no need to change anything to start TM?

Right.

What TM is

Now that I know what TM is not, tell me what it is.

Let's give you a complete definition first; then we can analyze it point by point.

But please remember that TM is an experience, and like any experience it is hard to describe or define. No matter how clearly or cleverly we might describe a strawberry, for instance, you would still have only an abstract idea of the strawberry. But when you see a strawberry, feel a strawberry, and taste a strawberry, then the experience becomes very real. So with that in mind –

> Transcendental Meditation is a simple, natural, effortless technique that allows the mind to experience subtler and subtler levels of the thinking process until thinking is transcended and the mind comes into direct contact with the source of thought. [...]

The source of thought. What's that?

Have you ever had the feeling that thoughts don't just spring to mind fully formed?

I've never thought about it.

Consider it for a moment. Do thoughts simply pop into the mind, fully formed, or do they seem to come from somewhere deep within the mind, existing at some abstract, more subtle level before they become totally clear?

Well, they're not just there. I guess they do seem to come from someplace.

They seem to come from somewhere within us.

All these thoughts come from one source: a field of pure energy deep within the mind.

You're getting a bit abstract, aren't you?

Let us be abstract just a minute longer, because what we want to find out is what the source of thought is really like.

Every thought has some meaning, some direction. Even a nonsensical thought or a thought in a dream makes some kind of sense to us – we recognize it as a picture, as words, as an emotion, or as an idea. This means that every thought has some kind of intelligent purpose or direction. We don't think at random because thoughts themselves contain intelligence.

So now we know one thing about the source of thought – it has to be creative, a reservoir of intelligence. Every bit of intelligence that we display in our daily lives reflects the intelligence contained in our thoughts.

Also, we experience thousands of thoughts every day – they just keep coming and coming. So they must be coming from a virtually unlimited source of energy.

The source of thought, then, is the source of millions of individual bundles of creativity, intelligence, and energy.

Some people don't seem to display as much intelligence as they might.

Right. We all display different degrees of intelligence in different kinds of activity. That's why we're talking about TM – all of us want to display *maximum* intelligence in *everything* we do. Thinking is the basis of action, action is the basis of achievement, and achievement makes us feel fulfilled.

This still seems abstract ...

Consider it from the objective point of view. According to physics, everything that exists is built up of layers of energy, one inside another. Einstein demonstrated that matter is just another form of energy with his equation '$E = mc^2$.' Also, we notice that in all creation, from the growth of the plants to the movement of the planets, there is great order, or intelligence. Since thoughts also exist, they must be made of the most basic form of energy as well. And they have their source, or basis, in the same field of creative intelligence and energy that underlies all creation.

What does this have to do with TM?

The regular practice of the Transcendental Meditation technique taps this field of energy within ourselves, bringing it out to fully enhance our lives. We tap the source of intelligence, and daily we are more intelligent. We tap the source of energy, and daily we are more energetic. We tap the source of creativity, and daily we are more creative. So Transcendental Meditation is a process by which one contacts this source of pure creativity and intelligence at the basis of the thinking process, allowing this creative intelligence to be expressed in greater clarity of mind, greater efficiency of action, and increasing fulfilling achievements in daily life.

TM is effortless

'Easy' and 'effortless'?

Anything that is natural *must* be easy and effortless. It is easy to talk, to eat, to sleep, to enjoy our friends – and because it is so easy it's also effortless. The same is true of TM. Once the technique is learned, the process flows – easily and effortlessly.

Ah! There's the catch! 'Once the technique is learned.' Just how many years does it take to learn this technique?

Years? Days. Hours, actually. Four two-hour sessions with a qualified teacher of TM, and that's it.

And then I do TM whenever I want?

No. TM is practiced twice a day, morning and evening, for 15–20 minutes each time. It's preparation for activity. We sit comfortably anywhere we happen to be: propped up in bed, on a train, in the office, in your living room, anywhere. [...]

The Transcendental Meditation program fits into your life something like this:

You wake in the morning wishing that sleep would have worked a little better. You begin your morning TM and contact the source of creative intelligence. By the time your TM is finished you feel refreshed, awake, alive. As the day wears on and this feeling of freshness wears off, you begin to feel less efficient, more tired. Time for the early-evening period of TM. The deep rest of TM dissolves any stress accumulated during the day and the contact with creative intelligence enlivens the mind. After TM you are ready to engage in a full evening of enjoyable activities.

Our days are structured in cycles with a period of rest (night's sleep) and a period of activity (the day and evening). TM adds two additional periods of revitalizing rest – making the entire structure of activity more flexible and more enjoyable.

A3   John Bowker, 'I live by faith: the religions described'

From J. Bowker (1983) *Worlds of Faith: Religious Belief and Practice in Britain Today*, London, Ariel Books, pp.24–48.

[A] Hinduism

[...] Hinduism is not a single, simple religion: it's a coalition of many different teachings and practices; it's a religion without a founder or a founding figure (such as Jesus or Muhammad), but it does have many teachers (gurus), many holy men and women, who have their own succession of disciples. The uniformity of Hinduism is much more in the way society is organised than it is in religious belief. In fact, that's the point that was made to me most often by Hindus, that Hinduism is *not* a religion! It's a *dharma*, to use their word: a way of life leading to the goal; and it's only one way among many. Dr Gokal, a consultant renologist at a Manchester hospital, explained this:

> Hinduism is a way of life, rather than a religion. And I think if you practise religion and base it along those lines, then all religions seem to blend into one. The principles of Hinduism are no different in reality from Christianity or Islam or Buddhism. The basis seems to be honesty, being unselfish, caring for others, and trying to bring about a betterment of mankind. If you can achieve that, then you are a good person. So the whole aim in life should be to attain oneness with the Almighty; and if you can achieve that oneness and unity, then the Hindu philosophy says that you don't have to come back to this earth time and time again: you achieve it, and that's it. You have achieved the utmost.

Already we have picked up two key points in Hinduism. The first is what the goal is: it is to achieve unity with the Almighty – or in the Hindu term, *Brahman*. Some Hindus regard *Brahman* as the personal God from whom all things are derived and to whom the divine within us can relate; others regard *Brahman* as beyond any idea or concept of God, being itself eternal, self-existent, impersonal, but still the origin and end of all things. Since the abiding, eternal reality is already within us, as *atman*, soul, the purpose of our life must be to realise what is already the case, namely, that you (what you really and essentially *are*) are *Brahman*. The goal of life is to realise – or bring into reality as a matter of fact – our union with *Brahman*.

The second key point is that it may take a long time to do that. Dr Gokal referred to the fact that when you have achieved that 'oneness and unity', you no longer have to return to this earth; but if you don't achieve it, then [...] you may have to be reborn millions of times. That's why Dr Gupta, a Hindu who has now returned to India, emphasised the importance of following the example of holy teachers *in practice* – thinking and arguing about it leads nowhere. Hinduism is a *practical* philosophy leading to enlightenment and union with the One:

> I was born in a family where my parents used to practise all the religious rituals; my father used to wake up early in the morning (we always preferred to wake up early in the morning), and he used to read an epic called *Ramayana*. So in my life I have been greatly influenced by *Ramayana* and the *Gita* [the *Gita* is part of another epic, the *Mahabharata*, and it is the holy book held in greatest reverence by most Hindus], and I've also come in contact with many saints and holy men – and I listened to them very carefully. So now I'm coming to the conclusion that if I want to search out all these things, then I'm going to spend my whole life without coming to any conclusion. So it's better to follow what has been practised by others, and I believe that I *must* practise.

I asked him what the point of the practice is – where is it all leading? He answered:

> I believe that if I've done any good deeds in my life, then I'll be reborn as a human being. It has been said in Hinduism that there are 84,000, if I'm not wrong – or 840,000 – different kinds of living creatures on this earth, some in the water, some that can fly. And according to our deeds, we have to pass through these. This is a cycle. But there are some who do good deeds: they may bypass all this. Otherwise we have to go through the cycle. The main aim of this whole life, as I trust, and as it has been said in the *Bhagavad-Gita* and in all the religious books, is to attain Enlightenment; and if we can achieve that, we won't come back. So first of all, I must detach myself from all my possessions. Even though I have the possessions, if anybody wants this jacket, if I give it without any feeling that I am giving anything, then it means I'm totally detached from it. But if I'm giving it and I'm saying, 'Oh, I'm giving it', it still means I've not reached to that state. When I reach *that* state, then I've passed one stage; but then there are further stages, and then I must find my eternal Master, who can guide me; because without the Master, it's impossible to achieve Enlightenment. You can reach to a certain stage, but he is the only one who can guide you properly.
>
> So Hinduism is so simple – and so difficult. But those who are ignorant, and know only a few norms of the religion and their followings, well, someone has said, 'Truthfulness is the only Hinduism.' So if that person follows that, throughout his life, and is truthful, then I think he has at least achieved something – rather than a person who knows he must be honest, he must be truthful, he must be well-behaved, and he must not hurt anybody, while he is not practising. So the important point is, you *must* practise. So if you inspect the basics of any religion, they will come out the same. But the only necessity is, you must practise.

So Hinduism offers many different ways, leading through many different lives, to Enlightenment and union with *Brahman*; and to attain that union is *moksha* – release from our attachment to this world and to the constant succession of rebirth:

> *Moksha* emanates from the cycle of birth and death. I don't want to be born again. This is my last journey in the world, and I never want to come back. I'll be one with God, and I have that positive thinking that I am sure he would want me to be with him. He would never send me back now, because this world is full of miseries and so on. *I* am not miserable, but I don't want to come back to this world. There is far more happiness with him, and I hope I will attain that.

We shall hear much more about *moksha* and Hindu practices later on. At the moment, we need simply to recognise that Hinduism does not claim to be the *only* way leading to the goal; but it is *all*-embracing, as Mr Singh explained to me in Leeds:

> Hinduism is not a religion, in the same sense in which Christianity is a religion, Islam is a religion, and even Buddhism is a religion. Hinduism really doesn't mean the religion of a group of people: it's supposed to mean the religion of human beings. In human beings, there is the element of

wonder at this universe – the creation, and the creator, and the self. Therefore, Hinduism deals with these fundamental things. The other things are just accessory to it, you see. They are involved with life, because life has got so many aspects. But this basic aspect, of this spiritualism, that is – well, you may say, it's Hinduism. But it's not confined to Hinduism, because it is also in Christianity, it is in Islam, it is in all other religions. But in Hinduism *this* is the *basic* thing. Therefore, the main point in Hinduism is about the self and the creator, how this universe has come into being, what is at the back of this, and how it is related to our own self. And the realisation of this unity of the soul with that force that has created all this universe, *this* is the main topic of religion, this is the main subject.

[B] Buddhism

Buddhism began historically in the sixth centuryBC, as (in part) a protest against a prevailing tendency in Indian religion at that time to rely on sacrifices and rituals to ensure one's successful progress through life. The term 'Buddha' means 'Enlightened One'.

So the main point of departure for Buddhism is the Enlightenment of Gautama – his deep realisation of what are known as The Four Noble Truths: the truth that nothing (absolutely nothing) can escape the condition of transience, suffering and decay (no matter how long anything lasts, it will one day disappear); the truth of how this suffering (which in Pali is called *dukkha*) originates; the truth of how *dukkha* nevertheless can cease; and the truth of the path that leads to the ceasing of *dukkha* – the eight-runged ladder of Buddhist belief and action, which leads beyond the bondage of *dukkha*.

The Four Noble Truths and the Eightfold Path combine with the Five Precepts (five mainly ethical principles) to make the most basic summary of what Buddhism involves, as Dr Fernando explained to me. Dr Fernando is a dentist in North London who lived originally in Sri Lanka. Like the Hindus, he stressed that Buddhism is a practical path, and that the Buddha's purpose was simply to show us the *dharma* (in Pali, the *dhamma*), the path to follow which will lead the way out of our bondage to suffering and death:

> The Buddha was only a teacher. He showed us the Way. We call Buddhists, the observers of the *dhamma*. The *dhamma* is the doctrine. It's a practical philosophy – a philosophy that has to be practised. The Five Precepts are meant for the layman [as opposed to the *bhikkus*, the Buddhist monks]; but to understand this, we must first understand the Four Noble Truths. The Buddha enunciated four of them. The first is, that there is sorrow in the world, from the time of birth to the time of death; there *are* moments of happiness, but they are just gilded sorrow. Then the cause of this sorrow (it's really stress: you can use the word 'sorrow' for want of a better term, but I would use the word 'stress'), this stress is there from the time you are born. So the second truth is the cause of sorrow. Now, like a physician, the Buddha is diagnosing this so-called affliction. He knows *what* it is, but now he wants to know what the cause is. What causes sorrow? There must be a

cause; and you can't attack the problem unless you know the cause. And the cause, according to him, is *tanha* – that is in Pali: for want of a better term you may call it 'craving', which includes all these emotions like hatred, anger, lust, envy, jealousy, quickness of temper. They are all included under *tanha*. In Buddhism the main thing is moderation, not to carry anything to excess.

So up to this stage, people have described it as a very pessimistic view. But it's *not* a pessimistic view. Even if it is pessimistic at this stage, when you discuss the other two Truths, it becomes the most optimistic philosophy one could ever find; because now he discusses the *destruction* of the sorrow: for any energy to flow, there must be a motivating force; it is *tanha* which is this motivating force (in driving our lives), according to the Buddha. If you remove that force – that causative factor – then the energy must lose its momentum and come to a standstill. That is what we could understand as *nirvana.*

Of course, it's a question what exactly *nirvana*, the ultimate goal for Buddhists, is – and Dr Fernando had something to say about that. But before pursuing that question, I asked him to tell me what the Fourth Noble Truth is:

The fourth is – and it's the most optimistic – how to destroy this so-called sorrow; and that is by establishing oneself on the Eightfold Path; and that is, right understanding, right thought, right speech, right action, right livelihood, right effort, right mindfulness and right concentration. The first one that I mentioned, right understanding, is the most important, because without the right understanding you will never observe the other seven. Now the right understanding leads us to the Five Precepts: because of this understanding, they are not *laws*. Through a right understanding, one says to oneself, I resolve – I make a resolution – not to take life, because the life is precious to the person who has it – maybe it's a little insect: to us he's an insect, like the Lilliputians who were almost insects to Gulliver, but Gulliver was himself an insect in another land. They're all relative terms, but life is still important: life was important to Gulliver when he was among the Lilliputians, and life was still important to him when he was in the land of the giants; but still it was the same Gulliver. So however mean, however small, the animal may seem, life to that animal is as important and precious as it is to us.

The second precept is, I resolve not to take anything that does not belong to me. If you take two people: one may not steal because he fears the consequences of being caught in the act or of a prison sentence; the other will not steal even if the opportunity presents itself and he knows that he will never be caught – but he still will not steal, because he knows it doesn't rightly belong to him. Both people are not committing the act of stealing, but one is with a different motive: and here we come to the *motive*, which is very, very important – the *motive*.

The third is, I resolve not to indulge in excessive sensual pleasure – not adultery: in excessive sensual pleasures – that is, the five senses – anything in excess. Even where sexual behaviour is concerned, indulging in excessive sexual pleasure with one's own wife is not conducive to mental culture.

In the fourth one, I resolve not to tell lies, to deceive, to slander, to cause ill-will between two people by spreading rumours.

The fifth is, I resolve not to indulge in intoxicants. Now if I've been asked to take a bit of whisky or brandy – a capful every night – I'm not taking a delight in it, but to me it is a medicine, and I do so. It is not an absolute prohibition: it's something I must be in control of.

So the key-point here is discipline and control; and it's leading, as Dr Fernando said, to the final goal of *nirvana*. But he couldn't say what *nirvana* is, because the Buddha couldn't talk about it either:

He never discussed what *nirvana* was. He never told us what *nirvana* was, because he couldn't describe it. It is something that one can only experience, never describe. By what words can you describe the indescribable? He said, 'I can only show you the way. It is something that you must experience for yourself'; and by reasoning, you experience it. So he didn't say that *nirvana* is a state which does exist, neither did he say it does not exist.

Twewang Topgyal comes from a very different kind of Buddhism. He is a refugee from Tibet; and Tibetan Buddhism, as we shall see, is very different from Sri Lankan Buddhism. But he too said exactly the same, when I asked him if he could tell me what this final goal of *nirvana* is:

I won't be able to tell you exactly what it is like, because I've not been there. I can just give you my picture, or what I would like to see it as. *Nirvana* is the ultimate goal which every Buddhist aspires to reach. It is a state of being, I would like to think. It is the end of all sorrow, it is the total end of ignorance, and it is the sort of stage where you become all-knowing. Apart from that – how one would feel or anything like that – I can't really elaborate. That's just how I would like to see *nirvana* as being.

There are two main kinds of Buddhism. Theravada (also known as Hinayana) is found mainly in Sri Lanka and South-East Asia, sticking closely to the so-called Pali Canon, the collected teachings of the Buddha; and Mahayana, which is a term covering a multitude of different developments of Buddhism, with more elaborate rituals, a greater number of sacred texts (many of which are also believed to have come from the Buddha), more gods and demons, and also more ways of approaching Enlightenment, embracing the extremes of Tantric and Zen Buddhism. From his Tibetan background, Twewang Topgyal tried to explain the different emphases in Buddhism – and he also went on to warn about the dangers of Tibetan Tantric Buddhism, which is a kind of commando raid on truth:

Basically there are two parts in Buddhism. One is a much more sure sort of way, but it is a much more gradual process. The other one is a bit dangerous, if all the circumstances and if all the combinations do not work correctly, and that is the Tantric Buddhism. It was originally started by the Indian guru called Padmasambhava in Tibet. And the other part was mainly started by someone called Tsongkhapa who was a Tibetan religious teacher. This came much later than the Tantric practice, and of course in terms of actual practice, there are a lot of differences: for instance, Tantric practitioners are quite often married, quite often they drink alcoholic drinks, and so on, which is totally prohibited in the other way of practising. It is said that someone who is practising in the Tantric way of Buddhism is like someone climbing through the inside of a bamboo pole: it's a sort of one-way tunnel, and once you fall down, you will go right down. I think what it basically means is that the practitioner needs to reach a certain sort of level in order to put it into right practice. Now what does tend to happen is that because the Tantric rules of practice are quite liberal, to a layman, therefore there are quite a number of fakes, if you like, or malpractices, which do originate from all that.

So there are many different interpretations of Buddhism. But where they all agree (and here they are simply following the Buddha) is in *rejecting* the Hindu belief (which we've just heard described) that there is a soul, or *atman* within us, which endures through death, and which is reborn until it attains *moksha*, release. For Buddhists, there is *nothing* which is permanent, not even a soul. On the other hand, there *is* a continuing flow or process of change, in which the present stage immediately gives rise to the next stage, and so on, with the direction of that change being controlled by strict laws. So what the organisation of energy (which is at present 'you' or 'me') does, at any moment, influences what that flow of energy will become at some later date – even beyond death. In *that* sense there is rebirth in Buddhism, but there is no self – no soul – riding along through the process of change: there is only the process itself.

So the idea of no-self, which is called in Pali *anatta*, is one great difference between Hindus and Buddhists. But where, in contrast, they *agree* (and so also does our third religion, Sikhism) is in maintaining that the whole process of rebirth, or of reappearance, is controlled by a strict rule or law of reward and punishment. This is called *karma* (or by Buddhists in Pali, *kamma*). *Karma* means that any good you do in this life will be rewarded in whatever future form you reappear, and any evil you do will be punished, maybe by going to a place of torment and pain, or by coming back to this earth as an animal.

Kunvergi Dabasia is a Hindu, living in Coventry, and he described, very briefly, how the kind of life you now live depends on what you have done in previous lives:

> It depends what kind of *karma* you have done in a previous life: if you have done good *karma* then you won't be suffering. But if you have done very bad *karma*, then you'll be suffering. And if you are doing good *karma* in this life, then you'll be having a good life in the coming life – say, if your *karma* is good, you *might* come back as a human being. But if your *karma* is very bad, then you might be going to be an animal.

[C] Sikhism

So *karma* and rebirth (or in the case of Buddhists, reappearance) lie at the very root of Hindu and Buddhist lives – and the same is true of Sikhs.

Sikhism also began in India, as a kind of reforming movement. It is based on the teaching of ten gurus, beginning with Guru Nanak, who died in 1539. Gurbachan Singh Sidhu, a Sikh living in Coventry, explained to me that a guru is a teacher: 'Prayer establishes a relation with God and a relation with our guru. Guru is the teacher, and by this word we mean, the person who brings us from darkness to light.'

Sikhs place much emphasis on the way they combine different religions: 'We are a combination of all the religions,' said Gurcharan Singh Kundi, echoing the verse of Guru Nanak: 'There is neither Hindu nor Muslim, so whose path shall I follow? I shall follow God's path. God is neither Hindu nor Muslim, and the path which I follow is God's.' 'Mind you,' he then went on to say, 'but we are also different from other religions, because of our preaching, and because that's what our gurus said.'

Two things stand out as making the Sikh different. The first is the reverence they have for their Holy Book which they regard as a *living guru.* The second is the set of five items which the fully commited Sikh must wear, the five Ks, so called because each of them begins with the letter K. (The most distinctive sign of a Sikh, to the outsider, is the turban, though in fact the obligation is to wear the hair uncut: the turban comes in as a part of that, because it is necessary to keep the hair tidy.)

Let's look at these in turn. First, the living guru: before the tenth guru, Guru Gobind Singh, died, he said that after him there would be no further guru except the living guru, which is the collection of holy writings known as the Guru Granth Sahib. This holy book is deeply revered, and it is attended to and treated (both in the home and in the *gurdwara*, or temple) as a living reality, as Gurcharan Singh Kundi explained to me, when I talked to him in Leeds:

> We take our Holy Book as a living guru. It's not a Holy *Book.* Christians take the Holy Book as a Holy Book; Hindus take the Holy Book as a Holy Book; and Muslims take their Quran as a Holy Book. But we take our Holy Book as a living guru. We respect him as a living guru. Now when you go to a Sikh temple our Holy Book will be above the congregation. It won't be on the same level. It's always at a special place in our congregation. In the morning – as in the Army there is a reveille in the morning – so we, at night, take our Holy Book: we close it, we call it *santokh*, and then we take it to the bed, a special place. In the morning, again we bring our Holy Book and put it on the throne; because that itself is a throne. Where our Holy Book is, where we place our Holy Book, that is a throne of a king. So anything which is said from, or read from, our Holy Book, it's taken that these are the actual words of our guru. Because our tenth guru (when they departed from us), his answer was, 'After me, there won't be any guru, and the Holy Book will be your living guru.' So we have faith that the Holy Book is our guru.

I wondered how a Sikh actually goes about consulting this living guru, and he went on to tell me:

> The way we go is this: when we go to a temple, we bow – the same mark of respect – and then we go behind and ask somebody (if there is

somebody on the seat already), we ask them to give a *wak*; 'wak' means, to read the first paragraph of the Holy Book. And that paragraph would definitely coincide with what you had in your mind, because that is the answer.

I asked him if it is the first paragraph that his eye falls on. He said:

Yes, the first paragraph from the left hand side. Some people take it from the right hand side – you know, the bottom right. Some take it from the left. So if the paragraph has started, he turns his page back. And these words – again, it's a question of faith – are exactly what you want.

Then our conversation went on:

'But supposing they're not what you want: can you argue with the living guru? Can you disagree with the advice that is given?'

'No, we don't have to disagree, because guru is a guru.'

'So he has authority over your choice?'

'Definitely. Because nothing could happen otherwise: if the guru wants he can make things happen. That's our belief. I mean, even the wind won't blow unless the Almighty wants it to blow. The rain won't go unless the Almighty wants the rain. So everything is in his hands.'

By immersing themselves in the teaching of the living guru, Sikhs believe that they approach the highest in what Surinder Singh Hyare called 'the easiest way':

Sikhism is the way for perfection, just like all other religions are. But Sikhism is something which has been brought to bear much more on *all* sides of human being, physical, intellectual, and spiritual. This Holy Book is made in the words of the saints – saints who were the fruits of humanity, I can say – the best. Their words are written in poetry; and those we sing in temples and at home. So in a way, the physical side is the best way, because we start from that. But mentally and spiritually also, we get the company of the best. So we approach to the highest in an easy way, not in a forceful way, but easily, just starting from the family.

The second distinctive mark of the Sikhs are the five Ks. They, with prayer, are the mark of what Amritpal Singh Hunjan called 'the practical Sikh':

A real practical Sikh is supposed to get up in the morning, say about five or six, to say his prayers. In the evenings, he says his prayers again before going to bed. In the same way, a practical Sikh is supposed to have the five Ks – that is the shorts (that's one of them); and he's supposed to have the steel bangle. He is not supposed to cut his hair, and the fourth one is the *kangh*; and the *kirpan*, that's the fifth – the sword, the small dagger. All these are important. The *kesh*, that is, the hair, identifies a person's spiritual heritage. The *kara*, that's the steel bangle, is supposed to prevent someone from doing bad deeds: it reminds a person that he ought not to do bad deeds with his right hand. The shorts [*kachha*] come from the time when Sikhs were soldiers and the shorts were worn by the Sikhs as a soldier's uniform, really. And the *kirpan* is because in those days, olden ages, when

Sikhism was still in the process of being formed, the Sikhs were under threat from the Muslims. So they had to wear this *kirpan* for protection; and the comb (that's the *kangh*) is to remind a person that he's supposed to comb his hair and keep it healthy.

From this one can see what a deep emotional issue it is for a Sikh to be asked to give up one of these marks and messages of his faith – his dagger, for example, because it is an offensive weapon (or could be, in the meaning of the Act); or even more to the point, if he is asked to shave off his beard, cut his hair and abandon his turban, if he is to get a job. Here are two Sikhs, describing what it felt like when they were required to do exactly that. The first is Amrik Singh Dhesi, who had great trouble in finding work, though now he works for British Telecom:

When I came here in 1961, there were not many people living here. And the jobs' problem was difficult at that time. Whenever we go to the factories for any employment, they looked at our turban and they used to refuse to give us the jobs. And the people who were already living here, they were telling the same stories to the new chaps coming here. So only my uncle was living here at that time, so he suggested, 'You will have to cut your hair.' I waited for a month, I was very, very hesitant to get it cut. Before I got my hair cut, I asked my uncle, 'I must get my photograph taken'; and here's the photograph, taken at that time. I saved my hair. When I cut it, it's still there – I'm still keeping it. I was crying all day on that day I got my hair cut. I did not like it, but that's the thing that happened.

The second is the same Gurcharan Singh Kundi who described Sikhism as a combination of all different religions. He too had to get his hair cut in order to get a job – but it wasn't easy:

I went to the barber five times, and every time I came out: five times. There's no lie in it. But the conditions were such that I couldn't do any job. And I thought of the only way to earn more, and that was on the buses. I had to have my hair cut so that I can get my family, and I can achieve my objectives of coming to England.

'But then,' I asked him, 'on the sixth time when you went to the barber, what did you feel? What did you feel when your hair was cut?' He said:

I have no words to express how I felt at that time. But on the other hand, I had no choice, I had to do it.

But at least in Sikhism, you can always find your way back. And this again is a basic point about Sikhism. No matter how often you fail or abandon the five Ks, you can always come back into the full commitment and practice of faith, through a ceremony of initiation – or of new beginnings – which is known as the *amrit* ceremony. Harbans Singh Sagoo used to be an air traffic controller in East Africa, but now he is a garage owner in Leeds. He described the *amrit* ceremony to me, and told me something also of the basic vows that are made:

The *amrit* ceremony is conducted by Five Beloved Ones, as we call them, or Panj Pyare. They are people who have already been baptised, and are usually the elders in the community. The ceremony takes place in the presence of the Holy Granth. Members of the public who are ready for initiation get together inside the prayer hall of the temple, where the ceremony is to take place. The Panj Pyare, or the five Beloved Ones, together with two other attendants, and one person in the presence of the Holy Granth, get together round a steel bowl into which water is poured; then specially prepared sweet things (they are called *patasse*; they are special sweets that are prepared for the occasion) are poured into the water by the Panj Pyare, and they use a dagger to stir the water. Then five morning prayers of the Sikhs are said turn by turn. The first prayer that is said, is the *Japji*, the second one is called *Japji*, which is Guru Gobind Singh's writing; then the third one is *Sawaiyas*, and then the *Chaupai*, and finally the *Anand*. Those are the five prayers that are said, and the *amrit* is then ready to be distributed among the initiates. And the initiates partake by sipping the *amrit* five times, and uttering the words: *wahi Guru, wahi Guruka Khalsa, wahi Guruki fateh*, meaning that the *Khalsa*, the Community of the Pure, belongs to the guru, and the victory is the guru's. And the *amrit* is also sprinkled into the eyes and into the top of the hair. This is to purify and sanctify the body and the soul, so that you see, you think, and you do good. And the five Ks of the Sikhs are essential – the wearing of the five Ks is essential before the ceremony starts – the five Ks are of course, the *kesh* which is the unshorn hair, the *kangh*, which is a little wooden comb, the *kara*, which is a steel bracelet that a Sikh wears on his wrist; and then the *kirpan*, which is a small sword-like thing, and the *kachha*, which is a special type of breeches. And then the *amrit* is distributed to all the initiates, at the end of which the four vows are taken. They are basically the 'don'ts'; one of the 'don'ts' is that they will never cut their hair from any part of their body: they are not to eat anything that is fish, meat or eggs; they don't drink anything that's alcoholic, and they don't make use of tobacco in any form; and the fourth 'don't', of course, is that they never commit adultery. And apart from that, the *Gur Mantra*, which is the word '*wahi guru*', is given to them for devotional purposes, and the *Mur Mantra* is given to them as the basic formula. And they are asked to repeat that on a regular basis. They are also advised that the five prayers that were said during the preparation of the *amrit* are to be said regularly as part of the early morning devotion. People who are not in a position to read, or people who are not conversant with Punjabi, can devote a similar amount of time, which works out to about maybe two and a half hours a day, by merely repeating the *Mur Mantra*, or the *Gur Mantra*, which is the word '*wahi guru*'.

[D] Judaism

The three religions which we have looked at so far all belong together: there are strong differences between them, and some of their beliefs contradict each other – for example, is there an immortal soul within us, or (as Buddhists say) is there 'no-self'? Is there One who is the source and creator of the whole universe? To that last question, Hindus (in general) and Sikhs say, Yes; Buddhists say, No (although most Buddhists believe that there are gods to whom they can pray: but the gods are themselves part of the process of change and decay within the universe).

So there are differences between these three religions. But despite the differences, they belong to the same general outlook; and historically, as we've seen, Buddhism and Sikhism are derived from the Hindu tradition – in fact, Hindus regard Buddhism, not as 'another religion', but as one of three *nastika* (unorthodox) *darsanas* (interpretations of the Indian tradition).

Our three other religions, Judaism, Christianity and Islam, also belong together in the same kind of way: they have sharp (all too often murderous) disagreements about life and belief, but they share the same general outlook; and both Christianity and Islam are (*historically*) derived from Judaism – though both Christianity and Islam would claim *theologically* that they are also derived from the particular initiative of God.

Jews believe that Judaism goes back to the original creative act of God: 'In the beginning God created,' says the opening verse of Jewish Scripture, Genesis (*Bereshith*) i.1. Genesis goes on, in the early chapters, to describe how men and women have become separated from God and divided against each other. It then tells how God began to heal those separations and divisions by entering into a covenant (a bond of commitment and trust), first with Noah, then 'with Abraham and his descendants for ever'. The terms and conditions of this agreement were finally summed up and entrusted to Moses.

So the Jews see themselves as chosen by God to keep the terms and conditions of the covenant (or at the very least to live in the spirit of the covenant agreement) as a kind of pledge or demonstration – a demonstration in miniature of how *all* human beings should live with each other, and with God, until the day will eventually come when, as their own prophets put it, 'the knowledge of the Almighty will cover the earth as the waters cover the sea.'

Therefore, at the very root of Judaism is this sense of being called by God to undertake his mission on behalf of the whole world, as a Jewish husband and wife, Mr and Mrs Dresner, explained to me:

> *Mrs Dresner*: We are chosen for a purpose of carrying out a mission which he has shown us throughout history. The mission is the responsibility of upkeeping his laws despite the suffering and the non-understanding of the reasons behind them. It's a mission of faith.

> *Mr Dresner*: Specifically, it's been the role of the Jewish people, by way of the Ten Commandments, to form the corner-stone of the Western civilisation – in a sense, with the rule of law. The Ten Commandments have formed the basis of legal systems in Western society – and I think that's been a very valuable contribution.

Both Mr and Mrs Dresner referred there to 'commandments' and 'laws'. That is a reminder that the covenant people (the restored and restoring community under God) has to keep *its* side of the agreement, and that includes specific commands and prohibitions. All this is summarised in the term 'Torah', which is often translated as 'Law', but which covers much more than that: it is the term applied to the *whole* of the Pentateuch (the first five books of Scripture), and it is sometimes also applied to the whole of Scripture itself. So Torah is guidance and instruction, which *includes* specific laws and commands. The basic point of this is *holiness* – which means, being separated from all that contaminates and corrupts in order to be close to God. Mr Jack Schild (who was born in Galicia, but who came to this country when he was four, and is now retired) emphasised that 'holiness' is the basic reason for Torah as Law:

> The Bible says, 'I want the children of Israel to be holy, as I am holy', you see. God was supposed to have said that to Moses. He wants the children of Israel, his chosen people, to be holy as he is holy. So from that point of view of holiness, it's believed that the various foods that we're not supposed to eat, and some foods that we *are* supposed to eat, are commanded because of holiness: some animals are clean animals (those that are cloven footed, or cloven hoofed right along, and they chew the cud, those are considered the clean animals), and the others are unclean animals. So the question of holiness is basic; and also there is another reason for the Law. We believe that the Law was passed in order to keep the Jewish people – prevent the Jewish people – from assimilating. It was a kind of fence against assimilation. But actually the main reason is the holiness. It's a lot to do with holiness, you see.

But of course Torah (written Scripture) doesn't cover *every* detail of life. So written Torah was extended in what is known as *Torah shebe'al peh* – Torah transmitted by word of mouth. This 'Oral Torah' is collected in Mishnah and Talmud – collections of interpretations of Torah made by Jewish teachers, or Rabbis. *Some* Jews believe that Oral Torah was *also* entrusted to Moses on Mount Sinai, but that it was only gradually made public, as the changing circumstances made it necessary.

In addition to that, some Jews (a much smaller number) also believe that a third form of Torah was given to Moses on Mount Sinai, the mystical meaning of Torah, which is preserved in what is known as the Kabbalah. One of the forms of organised Judaism, in which this belief is held, is Lubavitch Hasidism. The Lubavitch Hasidim are Jews who are carefully observant of Torah in its traditional form; and one of them, Mr Douber Klein (who is a teacher at a Hasidic, though not Lubavitch, school), described these expressions of Torah:

> When Moses went to heaven to receive the Torah, there were revealed to him all the different aspects of the Torah: first of all, the written Torah, as we can see it today, as it is written in Hebrew, in the sacred text. Secondly, he was given the laws which are known as the Oral Torah. These laws are a deeper explanation of matters which, in the written Torah, are very scantily expressed. For instance, in the written Torah it is explained that the Jewish people shall make a sign on their hands, and between their eyes. It is not explained in very much more detail what this sign should be. The Oral Torah explains that this sign takes the form of what are known as *tefillin*, or

phylacteries, and it explains in exact detail how these phylacteries are to be made, and in exactly what position on the arm and head they are to be placed. So therefore it is obvious that the Oral Torah is an essential part of the Torah for our practical purposes. As well as receiving the Oral Torah, which later on was written down in the form of the Mishnah and the Talmud, Moses was also given the mystical explanation of the Torah, which has come down in the form of Kabbalah and Hasidic philosophy.

There are other Jews (in Liberal, Progressive, or Reform Judaism) who do not accept so strong or so extensive a view of revelation, but who would hold that the interpretations of the instructed teachers (the rabbis), which end up in Talmud, are precisely that – interpretations for particular circumstances; and they would argue that this process of interpreting Judaism and making it relevant for life must continue. One Jew, who has moved from the Orthodox to the Reform community, saw the point about *change*, and of Torah remaining relevant for life, as the key issue:

> The idea that Judaism has been the same for thousands of years is historically false. It's had to change, because society has changed. And although it's very much a religion with a strong legalistic basis, even that legal framework has changed. What Reform Judaism is attempting to do is to maintain that change, out into the twentieth century. Certainly I think it's fair to say that in the early days of reform in Judaism (and we're now talking of the last century, and of Germany, particularly), it almost became a secularisation. Reform Judaism now is much more in the mainstream of the historical pattern of Judaism, but with a strong emphasis on trying to make Jewish law and Jewish practice and worship consistent with the environment in which most people live. And because it's doing that, for people who take their Reform Judaism seriously, it's possible to be a Jew, and a thinking Jew, seven days a week.

His wife added:

> I have a great respect for people who honestly keep the laws because they feel that this is a way of preserving a Jewish identity. But as far as I'm concerned myself, it's only a part of Judaism; it's not the whole of Judaism. And if you talk about survival, you have to talk also about, survival for what? The point of Judaism is not just to survive, but to survive for something. And I believe that the laws that have grown up – if you start off with a central ethical concept, the laws grew up as a fence to preserve that central ethical concept, and that central belief in one God. And, yes, they're important to ensure continuity. But you mustn't lose sight of the central message, by making your fences too high.

So Judaism, like Hinduism and Buddhism, is not a single, or simple, thing. But all Jews are agreed that they are *Jews*, and that they live under the command to be holy, even as God is holy; and to be holy, as we've already seen briefly, means being separated from all that is contaminating or unclean – everything, in other words, which might destroy the bond (the covenant) between God and his people. Putting it more positively, the purpose of Judaism is the sanctification – the making holy – of both life and time. This is how Mrs Dresner put it:

For me, Judaism is the practice of an ancient tradition which involves the sanctification (if it's not too difficult a word) of time and of certain aspects of life itself, so that you are living your life in some sort of relationship with your past and with God. There's a lot more to it than that, obviously, but I think that it's summed up in that way, that it sanctifies and makes holy a certain area of your life.

So Judaism, is a *practical* religion, worked out in life (especially in the family), and it's much less concerned with theological or philosophical problems, as both Mr and Mrs Levy explained, when I asked them the rather philosophical question, of how they could reconcile the evil and suffering in the world with their belief in God as a wise creator:

> *Mr Levy*: Judaism is not a very theological religion, in the sense that thinking about God and trying to work out the nature of God is in fact very unJewish. Moses attempted to understand God, and was told fairly forcibly that even for him there wasn't any way in which he would know the nature of God; and so Jews don't spend much time trying to fathom out the nature of God. They tend to accept that there is a God. *Some* of us philosophise about the nature of God, but more about the creation process.

> *Mrs Levy*: Judaism doesn't actually distinguish between God and the Devil, and have a sort of theological system, as it were. God is the creator, and he created the world as it is: and why, I don't know, but I accept that basically all the suffering and all the evil must be compensated. That there is a purpose to living, I accept that; and having accepted that, then I have a responsibility to act in a certain way.

So above all else, Judaism is immersed in its past – in its history – through which God has laid his claim upon his people and entrusted his covenant to them. As Stuart Dresner summarised Judaism: 'Judaism is an ethical way of life, set in the particular historical context of the Jewish people.'

It is, therefore, inconceivable for a Jew to betray his or her past, because to do so would mean that they were betraying God. Many Jews made this point to us, but this is how Mrs Jacobs put it:

> Judaism is my inheritance. If I'm going to hand down an inheritance, the Jews have got to keep on going – otherwise, what a terrible waste of suffering for all those thousands of years, if we're going to allow ourselves to disappear – through lack of effort, through lack of faith, through lack of love. I mean, what would God say? What would Abraham say? What a let-down!

[E] Christianity

But one break in that chain of inheritance has been Christianity. Many of the early Christians were originally Jews: and Paul understood what had happened in the life (and death) of Jesus as God's way of extending the family of Abraham – in other words, of bringing all the nations into the promise of blessing, which God had made to Abraham long ago:

'In your seed shall all the nations of the earth be blessed, because you have obeyed my voice.' (Gen/Ber. xxiii.18)

So Christianity really began as an interpretation of Judaism – an interpretation of what God had intended the faith of his people to be. But it was an interpretation which saw in Jesus a decisive action of God, through and within a human life, restoring the connection between God and human beings. In other words, it was a renewal or an extension of the covenant – a new testament.

But the interpretation of Jesus was made in Jewish terms in ways which few Jews could accept. Jesus was claimed to be the promised Messiah, or (in Greek) *Christos*, Christ; and he was seen to be, in a unique way, the Son of God, the effective action of God in dealing with sin, and in reconciling the world to himself.

So Christianity divided from Judaism and became a religion of redemption from sin and of atonement with God, passing from death and through death into life. A Christian doctor in Basingstoke explained to me why Jesus was – and is – necessary in dealing with the fact of sin:

> If I do something wrong, I want to say 'Sorry' to God. Because I'm such a miserable sinner, because I do so many things wrong, I'm far apart from God, so I'm sort of not on speaking terms with God, really: God is just too good for me. So I can't even begin to say that I'm sorry. I need somebody to go through, and that's what Jesus is. He's somebody who's identified with your sins, through death. What did he say? This is my body which is broken for you. He didn't need to do it. In the garden of Gethsemane before it, he was really struggling, because he realised that's what God was asking him to do; but he realised how hard it was going to be for himself, because it was going to mean pain and suffering of the biggest kind for him. But he did it so that we could reach God through him.
>
> So if I sin, the point is that he's already paid the price of all the sins that are going to be committed in the world. He's not confined to time: so the fact that I sin today can still be transferred to that atonement. So for us, that's what Jesus is, a way of getting your 'sorry' message across.

For another Christian, this basic point (about the seriousness of sin and of the way in which Jesus brings people back to God) is summarised in a reflection on prayer which she keeps by her bed:

> O the comfort, the inexpressible comfort, the feeling safe with a person, having neither to weigh thoughts nor measure words, but pour them out, just as they are, chaff and grain together, knowing that a faithful hand will take and sift them, keep what is worth keeping, and then with a breath of kindness, blow the rest away.

For Christians, therefore, Christ makes manifest, not only the character of God as love, but also the reality of God in human form, and in the Spirit of love which continues from him. As a result there is an urgency among Christians to share the message of that love and that redemption with others, as this young Pentecostal Christian makes clear:

In this period of time, God is now showing love towards mankind. The Bible tells us, 'For God so loved the world that he sent his only begotten Son.' Now God sent his Son because of his love for mankind. When man fell into sin, God did not have to send his Son, he did not have to do anything, OK? It's because of his love, his compassion. He could not let man die, so he sent his Son. It's because of his love. Now he said, 'I have provided the sacrifice, I have provided the way for you to live a life in the spirit.' And in every day, like even by just talking to you now and sharing the Gospel with you, God is saying, 'Listen to me, I'm calling you, I love you.' And from the very time he sent his Son, he's saying, 'I love you: listen to me.' Christianity is the love of God: that's what it is. The love of God: that's what Christianity means.

There are, of course, many different interpretations of the meaning and practice of Christianity – Protestants, Roman Catholics, Anglo-Catholics, Pentecostalists and so on; but the same basic point comes through them all, that Christianity is (or should be) the translation of the love of God – of God who is love – into this life and this world. And Christians have the sense that God, having participated in human life in the person of Christ, is able to share in their own lives, helping and encouraging them into this life of love, which will keep them safe beyond death. This is how another Pentecostal Christian (who came to this country from the West Indies twenty years ago and who has suffered much during her life) saw it:

I am a Christian because I'm living in this life, and there's a lot of suffering, a lot of insults, a lot of grief, a lot of pain. And since I know that there's a life after this, I would love to know that after this life, I will live a comfortable life – no suffering, no pain, no torment, and the tear will be wiped away. To me, Christianity is knowing that the Lord is always with me: he knows the sorrow, the fears, the burden, the joy; because, you see, Christianity is not just pure joy. Sometimes there is sadness. But when you are experiencing sadness and little hardships, the joy of knowing that God is with you covers all the sorrow. I really wouldn't exchange this life for anything else. Sometimes I don't feel well, but I don't worry about it – I don't think about it; because Jesus has suffered more than this – and it says, If you suffer with him, you shall reign with him.

[F] Islam

Islam is derived from the call of God to Muhammad to be his prophet, to be one who warns people and calls them back to the truth, that they and all people and all created things come from God and depend on God for their life and being. It is his duty also to warn people that their lives are returning to God who will judge them by an exact balance according to their good and evil deeds.

For the Muslim, Muhammad (who lived in Arabia from 586–632CE) is the last of the prophets, the seal of the prophets, through whom the Quran, the uncorrupted revelation, has been transmitted into the world. There have been many previous prophets – Moses and Jesus among them – all with the same message. So Islam is connected to Judaism and

Christianity, in the sense that God has sent a prophet to every nation. But Islam is different, in the sense that Muslims believe that they are the only community which has preserved the message of God (the Quran) in a pure and uncorrupted form. Mr Abdul Rahman, a taxi driver in Coventry, talked to me about this:

> From Adam to Jesus, every prophet has preached this religion which is called Islam. Of course, there was no name for it at that time. Then the last prophet came, when the prophet of Islam went on pilgrimage to Mecca. And he called everybody (about 140,000, I suppose, but I don't know what was the right figure) all Muslims in front of him; and then Gabriel came, and he read this verse to the prophet: *alyaum* (that means, today) *akmaltu* (has been completed) *lakum* (upon you) this religion. So 'Today this religion has been completed and you have done your duty. And it is my will that I have named this religion for you, and the next future world; and this religion will be called Islam.' It's not that the earlier prophets have been rejected. They *have* been rejected by the people that never listened to them, but they have never been rejected by God. They did their duty. It's like building a house: one person comes and he builds the walls, and he's called, bricklayer. The next comes and he builds the window, and he's called the carpenter. Then the glazier, then the roof-tiler and everything; so everybody is called by a different name. Adam came with a different duty. Noah came with a different duty. They were doing a chapter, you know. We say they have done a chapter. The Bible does not tell all those things in detail which the Quran does. Those books were for their own time, and Quran is for the whole time until the end – the end of the world.

So Islam is the one – and same – religion which God has always intended, and to which he has continually called men and women through his prophets. Indeed, those earlier prophets foresaw Muhammad as the final prophet and talked about him – a point which Hajji Cassim Mohammad made, while also emphasising that there cannot be another prophet:

> God sent his messengers at different times to different nations. Islam is not a new way of life, it is the same old way of life, the same religion of Abraham, the same way of life coming down, Judaism, Islam, right down the line. God sent thousands of prophets. In the Holy Quran God says so (and we believe that the Holy Quran is the word of God, and God does not tell lies). In Deuteronomy, God, speaking to Moses, said, 'I will raise the prophet from among thy brethren, and he shall not speak of himself, but what he shall hear, that he shall speak, for I, God, shall put my words into his mouth.' Now this prophet, we believe, is the holy prophet Muhammad. The holy prophet Muhammad was an unlettered prophet. He did not know how to read or write. He was untaught by man, but he was taught by God; the angel Gabriel taught him. In all the religious Scriptures the advent of the holy prophet Muhammad was foretold; and in Deuteronomy, it's very, very clear. Muslims believe that the person referred to there is the holy prophet Muhammad. There is no doubt about it. In the Holy Quran, God says, 'I am its author, I am its protector: no one can change it.' 1400 years have passed, not even one *ayat* [verse], not even one word in the Holy Quran, has changed. How has God managed to protect it? He caused the Muslims to

memorise the whole Quran by heart. God has sent his final messenger as a seal of the prophets. And he has sent his final message, the Holy Quran. So there is no more need for any more messages, or any more prophets. What the holy prophet did say was that, after me, reformers will come, *mujaddids*, who will come at different times simply to correct you when you drift away from that straight path. So there is no need for any further prophets or books, because the message is complete.

It follows that Muslims must live their lives as the Quran instructs and encourages them – with the help of what are known as *hadith*: they are the records describing what Muhammad did and said, which can, so to speak, illustrate the Quran, and give practical guidance to the ways in which Muslims should behave.

The word *Sunni* means that I am following the thing that the prophet has done in his life: the movement of his body (what he has done by his hand, by his foot, by his eyes, mouth, ears, anything), following the movement of his body is called *sunna*. The word he has said from his mouth is called *hadith*. His sayings are called *hadith*, his movements are called *sunna*. So we are following both things.

That attention to detail explains why many Muslims emphasise (like some of the Jews speaking of Judaism) that Islam is not a religion, it's a way of life. As Cassim Mohammad put it, 'We don't refer to Islam as a religion. It's a way of life. The Holy Quran refers to Islam as a *din*, and a *din* is a way of life.'

That way of life is summarised in what are known as the **Five Pillars of Islam** – the five fundamental affirmations and practices. Mr Mohammed Ali, who works as a guard for British Rail, and who is a member of an interfaith dialogue council, told me what the Five Pillars are:

The first of the Five Pillars is the *Kalima*: that is, *La Ilaha illa Allah, waMuhammad rasul Illah* – it is to say, There is no God but God, and Muhammad is his Apostle. The second is the prayer, the five-times-a-day prayer, which I start in the early morning when I get up. It's the most important thing in our life, prayer: prayer keeps us away from lots of things – from all bad things, and bad thoughts. And the third is the fasting [during daylight hours] which we do for a month; I do it anyway, and most of my family does, and most of the brothers and Muslims I know, we all do – regardless of time or anything: this last year we have to keep fast over 18 hours in a day; that's the longest we have. And then the next Pillar is the *Zakat* [almsgiving]: so if we have £1000, £25 is for the poor people. It's 2% of our earnings – and it's not much. It's like a tax. And then the fifth one is the *hajj*, the pilgrimage – that is, whoever goes to the blessed place (Mecca), that's the *hajj*, and they are purified.

Although Islam emphasises the unity of God and the unity of all life and all creation as derived from God, Islam itself is divided into two main communities, the Sunni and the Shia'. The Sunni claim to follow the *sunna*, or path of the prophet, without adding any new practice or teachings. The Shia' are the party of Ali – the word *shia'* means 'party'; and the Shia' are those who believe that Ali, Muhammad's son-in-law, should have succeeded him, on the grounds, as one Shiite Muslim put it, that it is the close family of a person which knows him best.

The political implications of the Sunni/Shia' divide can still be serious, as we can see in Iran and Iraq. Nevertheless, virtually all Muslims, Sunni and Shia', say that they are Muslim first and foremost – and that being Sunni or Shia' is more a matter of lifestyle and inherited history than it is of being a true or false Muslim.

A4   Eileen Barker, 'New religious movements: definitions, variety and numbers'

From E. Barker (1989) *New Religious Movements: A Practical Introduction*, London, HMSO, app.II, pp.145–50, footnotes edited.

Problems with definitions

Most of the movements referred to as part of the current wave of new religious movements are *new* in that they have become visible in their present form since the Second World War; and most are *religious* in the sense that either they offer a religious or philosophical world-view, or they claim to provide the means by which some higher goal such as transcendent knowledge, spiritual enlightenment, self-realisation or 'true' development may be obtained. The term is, thus, used to cover groups that might provide their members with ultimate answers to fundamental questions (such as the meaning of life or one's place in the nature of things).[1]

There is, however, no general agreement over precisely what constitutes a religion. Some definitions, by referring to belief in a god, could exclude Buddhism; others are so all-encompassing that they could include ideologies such as Marxism. Even more disagreement surrounds definitions of 'new religious movements' or 'cults'. In an attempt to address the question as to whether or not the Church of Scientology is a religion, Bryan Wilson listed 20 different characteristics, some, but not all, of which would have to be present for a movement to qualify as a religion. He found 11 of these clearly present in Scientology, 5 clearly absent, and the presence of the remaining 4 characteristics arguable.[2]

Those who object to the term 'new religious movement' frequently do so on the grounds that NRMs are not *real* religions, the assumption often being that religions are seen as 'good', so movements such as ISKCON (the International Society for Krishna Consciousness, popularly known as the Hare Krishna movement) or the Unification Church (popularly known as the Moonies), both of which, by *any* dictionary definition, would be religions, may be denied the label by their opponents. On the other hand, some of the NRMs see religion in negative terms as either a divisive or a lifeless institution, and they do not, therefore, wish to be associated with the term – even if their movement would be covered by most definitions of religion.

There are, moreover, numerous vested interests, both religious and secular, that make any drawing of precise boundaries a contentious and risky exercise. The disagreements over usage of these terms often lead to sterile arguments, in which different groups merely assert their definition in order to make a particular point because of the associations, benefits or restrictions implied by their own or others' understanding of the term. For example, being defined as a religion may mean that an NRM can claim tax exemption; but it may also mean that it is not allowed to be taught in American public schools as a consequence of the First Amendment to the United States' Constitution.[3]

The Church of Scientology has fought in the courts (successfully in Australia) to be registered as a religion for the purposes of taxation. Transcendental Meditation (TM) has fought in a New Jersey court in an (unsuccessful) attempt to prove that it is *not* a religion but, rather, a technique which might be taught in the state schools. TM describes itself as 'a technique for deep relaxation and revitalisation which develops the inner potential of energy and intelligence that forms the basis of all success in life', and it points out that one can belong to any or to no religion and still practise TM. The Brahma Kumaris (Raja Yoga) provide another example of a movement that would rather not be labelled a religion; they prefer to be seen as a spiritual or educational movement. Ananda Marga, which is against all religions in so far as these are seen as artificial barriers that divide humanity, describes itself as a socio-spiritual organisation. Graduates of the Forum or Exegesis are likely to insist that these are not religious organisations, but that they transcend or go beyond religion in so far as religion is associated with dogma and empty ritual. Raëlians have referred to their movement as an atheistic religion.

Some of the movements will deny that they are 'new' when their novelty is rooted in a traditional religion. For example, ISKCON devotees consider theirs to be an ancient and a traditional religion. So far as their vedic beliefs and ritual practices are concerned, this is undoubtedly true. None the less, the *organisation*, set up in the West by Srila Prabhupada, is a new organisation that has exhibited several of the characteristics of an NRM since its inception.

Sometimes controversy arises over whether or not one should include groups that have, generally speaking, come to be considered 'respectable', but about which anxious enquiries are, none the less, made to an organisation such as INFORM. Should one, as is sometimes done, label Freemasons, or the numerous professional people (teachers, journalists, lawyers, and writers) who are involved in secret Gurdjieffian groups, cultists or members of NRMs? It has been pointed out that the United Reformed Church (which was formed in 1972 as a union between the Presbyterian Church of England and the Congregational Union of

England and Wales) could be called a new religious movement – although few would dream of doing so. And, although most Westerners would consider *Western* Krishna devotees to be members of an NRM, they might be less certain whether to label as 'cultists' the far larger number of worshippers in ISKCON temples in Britain who are drawn from the Asian community and are regarded as little more or less than members of one Hindu tradition among many by most of their fellow Asians. ISKCON is, indeed, a respected member of the National Council of Hindu Temples. The point at issue here is that, explicitly or implicitly, *respectability* or 'cause for concern' are sometimes drawn into the *definition* of what constitutes an NRM (or 'cult'). [...]

Among the better-known of the movements that fall slightly less ambiguously into the general category under consideration are the Ananda Marga, the Bhagwan Rajneesh movement, the Children of God (Family of Love, Heaven's Magic), the Divine Light Mission (Elan Vital), Sahaja Yoga, the Church of Scientology and the Unification Church (the 'Moonies'). Then there is the New Age movement, which, when broadly defined, includes at its 'psycho-spiritual' wing, the Human Potential movement. Paul Heelas has termed many of the groups to be found in such categories the 'self-religions' in that they see the self as the ultimate locus of the Ultimate, and the ego, or some equivalent, as standing in the way of realising the self's true potential.[4] These groups may draw from a number of diverse sources such as the teachings of Jung, Gurdjieff, Alan Watts and, more recently, L. Ron Hubbard, as well as from various traditions of the East (certain kinds of Buddhism in particular). Examples of these very different groups would be Arica, the Emin, Emissaries of Divine Light, Exegesis (which no longer offers seminars to the public but has developed into Programmes Ltd.), Findhorn, the Forum (a later development of *est*), Insight/MSIA, Primal Therapy, Psychosynthesis, some versions of Rebirthing, the School of Economic Science, Self Transformation (now referred to as the Bellin Partnership), Silva Mind Control, TOPY and a great variety of 'growth centres', encounter, therapeutic, self-development and holistic healing groups.

There are numerous Witches' covens, and pagan, occult and 'magick' movements. Satanism, while itself not exactly a new religion, has been viewed as a cult in recent years, and there are a number of satanic NRMs. There are, furthermore, several groups or organisations that, although still linked to one or other of the mainstream religions, have been thought to exhibit certain sectarian or 'cult-like' characteristics; several Christian groups (Protestant and Catholic) fall into this last category, especially some of those of a more fundamentalist nature that place the winning of converts high among their priorities.

But while attempts to define too precisely what is or is not an NRM are undoubtedly foolhardy, the term should be used within common-sense boundaries. It would clearly be unhelpful to consider Jainism, The Society of Friends, Friends of the Earth or the Wimbledon Pigeon

Fanciers Association to be either a 'cult' or an NRM. Those who wish to know more about a mainstream religion, such as Jainism, Islam or Zoroastrianism, that has long been established in other societies but is relatively new to Westerners, might seek further information from the religion's own representatives, or from the Inter Faith Network.

Numbers of movements

The actual number of NRMs in Britain depends upon the definition used (see the previous section), but a figure of around five hundred is not unreasonable. Claims have been made that there are up to 5,000 'cults' in North America, but no one has produced a list of these movements, and anyone who tried to do so would undoubtedly be using a very broad definition – a figure somewhere between 1,500 and 2,000 might be more realistic. [...]

Counting members in Britain

An obvious problem, which is related to that discussed in the previous sections, arises when one tries to estimate the total numbers of people involved in NRMs: a decision has to have been made as to what constitutes an NRM. Furthermore, even when one is attempting to count the number of members of a particular NRM, it is important to recognise the enormous diversity in the degree and type of membership that the movements may demand of their followers.

Most NRMs (like most mainstream Churches) have different 'layers' of membership, ranging from full-time service (equivalent to a priesthood), to active followers (similar to devout lay members of a congregation), with yet others who may be classified as constituting a mildly involved band of sympathisers. Another complication is that some people, especially those who have pursued a course with more than one of the self-religions, are quite likely to be counted several times as they move from one path to another. Bearing these problems in mind, what follows can be no more than a tentative attempt to give some idea of the membership of the movements in so far as such information is available.

In Britain, it is unlikely that any of the NRMs has succeeded, at any one time, in accumulating more than a few hundred members who devote their whole lives to working for their movement. It is impossible to estimate the number of people who, while living in their own homes and employed in an 'outside' job are deeply committed, and devote almost all of their spare time to a particular group or movement – rather like, in some ways, the elders or those who organise or devotedly attend the functions of their local church. If, however, an estimate were to be made, it would be likely to be somewhere in the tens of thousands. A greater number of people maintain a more peripheral relationship, which may, none the less, be of considerable importance in their lives. An even greater number will have come into contact with one or other of the movements for a short, transitory period. It is not impossible for members to change the level of their involvement according to their personal circumstances – for example, student (CARP) members of the Unification Church could become either full-time or associate members upon completing their studies.

There could be a million or so people who have, minimally, 'dabbled in' or 'flirted with' one or other of the movements in Britain at some time during the past quarter century. If one were to accept the claim that there is 'a conservative estimated population of over 250,000 Witches/Pagans throughout the UK and many more hundreds of thousands of people with a serious interest in Astrology, Alternative Healing Techniques and Psychic Powers',[5] and if one were to count such people as members of NRMs, the total could be considerably greater.

[1] See McGuire, M. and Kantor, D. (1989) *Ritual Healing in Suburban America*, New Brunswick, Rutgers University Press.

[2] 'Scientology: a secularized religion?' in Bryan R. Wilson (1990) *The Social Dimensions of Sectarianism*, Oxford University Press.

[3] 'Congress shall make no law respecting an establishment of religion, or prohibiting the free exercise thereof: or abridging the freedom of speech, or of the press; or the right of the people peaceably to assemble, and to petition the Government for a redress of grievances.'

[4] Heelas, P. (1982) 'Californian self-religions and socialising the subjective' in E. Barker (ed.) *New Religious Movements: A Perspective for Understanding Society*, New York and Toronto, Edwin Mellen Press, p.69ff.

[5] *The Occult Census: Statistical Analysis and Results*, The Sorcerer's Apprentice Press, 1989, p.3.

A5 Ninian Smart, 'The nature of a religion and the nature of secular worldviews'

From N. Smart (1989) *The World's Religions: Old Traditions and Modern Transformations*, Cambridge University Press, pp.10–25.

[A] The nature of a religion

In thinking about religion, it is easy to be confused about what it is. Is there some essence which is common to all religions? And cannot a person be religious without belonging to any of the religions? The search for an essence ends up in vagueness – for instance in the statement that a religion is some system of worship or other practice recognizing a transcendent Being or goal. Our problems break out again in trying to define the key term 'transcendent.' And in answer to the second question, why yes: there are plenty of people with deep spiritual concerns who do not ally themselves to any formal religious movement, and who may not themselves recognize anything as transcendent. They may see ultimate spiritual meaning in unity with nature or in relationships to other persons.

It is more practical to come to terms first of all not with what religion is in general but with what *a* religion is. Can we find some scheme of ideas which will help us to think about and to appreciate the nature of the religions?

Before I describe such a scheme, let me first point to something which we need to bear in mind in looking at religious traditions such as Christianity, Buddhism or Islam. Though we use the singular label 'Christianity,' in fact there is a great number of varieties of Christianity, and there are some movements about which we may have doubts as to whether they count as Christian. The same is true of all traditions: they manifest themselves as a loosely held-together family of subtraditions. Consider: a Baptist chapel in Georgia is a very different structure from an Eastern Orthodox church in Romania, with its blazing candles and rich ikons: and the two house very diverse services – the one plain, with hymns and Bible-reading, prayers and impassioned preaching; the other much more ritually anchored, with processions and chanting, and mysterious ceremonies in the light behind the screen where the ikons hang, concealing most of the priestly activities. Ask either of the religious specialists, the Baptist preacher or the Orthodox priest, and he will tell you that his own form of faith corresponds to original Christianity. To list some of the denominations of Christianity is to show something of its diverse practice – Orthodox, Catholic, Coptic, Nestorian, Armenian, Mar Thoma, Lutheran, Calvinist, Methodist, Baptist, Unitarian, Mennonite, Congregationalist, Disciples of Christ – and we have not reached some of the newer, more problematic forms: Latter-Day Saints, Christian Scientists, Unificationists, Zulu Zionists, and so forth.

Moreover, each faith is found in many countries, and takes color from each region. German Lutheranism differs from American; Ukrainian Catholicism from Irish; Greek Orthodoxy from Russian. Every religion has permeated and been permeated by a variety of diverse cultures. This adds to the richness of human experience, but it makes our tasks of thinking and feeling about the variety of faiths more complicated than we might at first suppose. We are dealing with not just traditions but many subtraditions.

It may happen, by the way, that a person within one family of subtraditions may be drawn closer to some subtradition of another family than to one or two subtraditions in her own family (as with human families; this is how marriage occurs). I happen to have had a lot to do with Buddhists in Sri Lanka and in some ways feel much closer to them than I do to some groups within my own family of Christianity.

The fact of pluralism inside religious traditions is enhanced by what goes on between them. The meeting of different cultures and traditions often produces new religious movements, such as the many black independent churches in Africa, combining classical African motifs and Christianities. All around us in Western countries are to be seen new movements and combinations.

Despite all this, it is possible to make sense of the variety and to discern some patterns in the luxurious vegetation of the world's religions and subtraditions. One approach is to look at the different aspects or dimensions of religion.

The practical and ritual dimension

Every tradition has some practices to which it adheres – for instance regular worship, preaching, prayers, and so on. They are often known as rituals (though they may well be more informal than this word implies). This *practical* and *ritual* dimension is especially important with faiths of a strongly sacramental kind, such as Eastern Orthodox Christianity with its long and elaborate service known as the Liturgy. The ancient Jewish tradition of the Temple, before it was destroyed in 70 CE, was preoccupied with the rituals of sacrifice, and thereafter with the study of such rites seen itself as equivalent to their performance, so that study itself becomes almost a ritual activity. Again, sacrificial rituals are important among Brahmin forms of the Hindu tradition.

Also important are other patterns of behavior which, while they may not strictly count as rituals, fulfill a function in developing spiritual awareness or ethical insight; practices such as yoga in the Buddhist and Hindu traditions, methods of stilling the self in Eastern Orthodox mysticism, meditations which can help to increase compassion and love, and so on. Such practices can be combined with rituals of worship, where meditation is directed towards union with God. They can count as a form of prayer. In such ways they overlap with the more formal or explicit rites of religion.

The experiential and emotional dimension

We only have to glance at religious history to see the enormous vitality and significance of experience in the formation and development of religious traditions. Consider the visions of the Prophet Muhammad, the conversion of Paul, the enlightenment of the Buddha. These were seminal events in human history. And it is obvious that the *emotions* and *experiences* of men and women are the food on which the other dimensions of religion feed: ritual without feeling is cold, doctrines without awe or compassion are dry, and myths which do not move hearers are feeble. So it is important in understanding a tradition to try to enter into the feelings which it generates – to feel the sacred awe, the calm peace, the rousing inner dynamism, the perception of a brilliant emptiness within, the outpouring of love, the sensations of hope, the gratitude for favors which have been received. One of the main reasons why music is so potent in religion is that it has mysterious powers to express and engender emotions.

Writers on religion have singled out differing experiences as being central. For instance, Rudolf Otto (1869–1937) coined the word 'numinous'. For the ancient Romans there were *numina* or spirits all around them, present in brooks and streams, and in mysterious copses, in mountains and in dwelling-places; they were to be treated with awe and a kind of fear. From the word, Otto built up his adjective, to refer to the feeling aroused by a *mysterium tremendum et fascinans*, a mysterious something which draws you to it but at the same time brings an awe-permeated fear. It is a good characterization of many religious experiences and visions of God as Other. It captures the impact of the prophetic experiences of Isaiah and Jeremiah, the theophany through which God appeared to Job, the conversion of Paul, the overwhelming vision given to Arjuna in the Hindu Song of the Lord (*Bhagavadgita*). At a gentler level it delineates too the spirit of loving devotion, in that the devotee sees God as merciful and loving, yet Other, and to be worshipped and adored.

But the numinous is rather different in character from those other experiences which are often called 'mystical'. Mysticism is the inner or contemplative quest for what lies within – variously thought of as the Divine Being within, or the eternal soul, or the Cloud of Unknowing, emptiness, a dazzling darkness. There are those, such as Aldous Huxley (1894–1963), who have thought that the imageless, insight-giving inner mystical experience lies at the heart of all the major religions.

There are other related experiences, such as the dramas of conversion, being 'born again', turning around from worldly to otherworldly existence. There is also the shamanistic type of experience, where a person goes upon a vision quest and acquires powers to heal, often through suffering himself and vividly travelling to the netherworld to rescue the dying and bring them to life again. Shamans are common to many small-scale societies and peoples that make their living by hunting, but many of the marks of the shamanistic quest have been left upon larger religions.

The narrative or mythic dimension

Often experience is channeled and expressed not only by ritual but also by sacred narrative or myth. This is the third dimension – the *mythic* or *narrative*. It is the story side of religion. It is typical of all faiths to hand down vital stories: some historical; some about that mysterious primordial time when the world was in its timeless dawn; some about things to come at the end of time; some about great heroes and saints; some about great founders, such as Moses, the Buddha, Jesus, and Muhammad; some about assaults by the Evil One; some parables and edifying tales; some about the adventures of the gods; and so on. These stories often are called myths. The term may be a bit misleading, for in the context of the modern study of religion there is no implication that a myth is false.

The seminal stories of a religion may be rooted in history or they may not. Stories of creation are before history, as are myths which indicate how death and suffering came into the world. Others are about historical events – for instance the life of the Prophet Muhammad, or the execution of Jesus, and the enlightenment of the Buddha. Historians have sometimes cast doubt on some aspects of these historical stories, but from the standpoint of the student of religion this question is secondary to the meaning and function of the myth; and to the believer, very often, these narratives *are* history.

This belief is strengthened by the fact that many faiths look upon certain documents, originally maybe based upon long oral traditions, as true scriptures. They are canonical or recognized by the relevant body of the faithful (the Church, the community, Brahmins and others in India, the Buddhist Sangha or Order). They are often treated as inspired directly by God or as records of the very words of the Founder. They have authority, and they contain many stories and myths which are taken to be divinely or otherwise guaranteed. But other documents and oral traditions may also be important – the lives of the saints, the chronicles of Ceylon as a Buddhist nation, the stories of famous holy men of Eastern Europe in the Hasidic tradition, traditions concerning the life of the Prophet (*hadith*), and so forth. These stories may have lesser authority but they can still be inspiring to the followers.

Stories in religion are often tightly integrated into the ritual dimension. The Christian Mass or communion service, for instance, commemorates and presents the story of the Last Supper, when Jesus celebrated with his disciples his forthcoming fate, by which (according to Christians) he saved humankind and brought us back into harmony with the Divine Being. The Jewish Passover ceremonies commemorate and make real to us the events of the Exodus from Egypt, the sufferings of the people, and their relationship to the Lord who led them out of servitude in ancient Egypt. As Jews share the meal, so they retrace the story. Ritual and story are bound together.

The doctrinal and philosophical dimension

Underpinnnng the narrative dimension is the *doctrinal* dimension. Thus, in the Christian tradition, the story of Jesus' life and the ritual of the communion service led to attempts to provide an analysis of the nature of the Divine Being which would preserve both the idea of the Incarnation (Jesus as God) and the belief in one God. The result was the doctrine of the Trinity, which sees God as three persons in one substance. Similarly, with the meeting between early Christianity and the great Graeco-Roman philosophical and intellectual heritage it became necessary to face questions about the ultimate meaning of creation, the inner nature of God, the notion of grace, the analysis of how Christ could be both God and human being, and so on. These concerns led to the elaboration of Christian doctrine. In the case of Buddhism, to take another example, doctrinal ideas were more crucial right from the start, for the Buddha himself presented a philosophical vision of the world which itself was an aid to salvation.

In any event, doctrines come to play a significant part in all the major religions, partly because sooner or later a faith has to adapt to social reality and so to the fact that much of the leadership is well educated and seeks some kind of intellectual statement of the basis of the faith.

It happens that histories of religion have tended to exaggerate the importance of scriptures and doctrines; and this is not too surprising since so much of our knowledge of past religions must come from the documents which have been passed on by the scholarly elite. Also, and especially in the case of Christianity, doctrinal disputes have often been the overt expression of splits within the fabric of the community at large, so that frequently histories of a faith concentrate upon these hot issues. This is clearly unbalanced; but I would not want us to go to the other extreme. There are scholars today who have been much impressed with the symbolic and psychological force of myth, and have tended to neglect the essential intellectual component of religion.

The ethical and legal dimension

Both narrative and doctrine affect the values of a tradition by laying out the shape of a worldview and addressing the question of ultimate liberation or salvation. The law which a tradition or subtradition incorporates into its fabric can be called the *ethical* dimension of religion. In Buddhism for instance there are certain universally binding precepts, known as the five precepts or virtues, together with a set of further regulations controlling the lives of monks and nuns and monastic communities. In Judaism we have not merely the ten commandments but a complex of over six hundred rules imposed upon the community by the Divine Being. All this Law or Torah is a framework for living for the Orthodox Jew. It also is part of the ritual dimension, because, for instance, the injunction to keep the Sabbath as a day of rest is also the injunction to perform certain sacred practices and rituals, such as attending the synagogue and maintaining purity.

Similarly, Islamic life has traditionally been controlled by the Law or *Shari'a*, which shapes society both as a religious and a political society, as well as the moral life of the individual – prescribing that he should pray daily, give alms to the poor, and so on, and that society should have various institutions, such as marriage, modes of banking, etc.

Other traditions can be less tied to a system of law, but still display an ethic which is influenced and indeed controlled by the myth and doctrine of the faith. For instance, the central ethical attitude in the Christian faith is love. This springs not just from Jesus' injunction to his followers to love God and their neighbors: it also flows from the story of Christ himself who gave his life out of love for his fellow human beings. It also is rooted in the very idea of the Trinity, for God from all eternity is a society of three persons, Father, Son and Holy Spirit, kept together by the bond of love. The Christian joins a community which reflects, it is hoped at any rate, the life of the Divine Being, both as Trinity and as suffering servant of the human race and indeed of all creation.

The social and institutional dimension

The dimensions outlined so far – the experiential, the ritual, the mythic, the doctrinal, and the ethical – can be considered in abstract terms, without being embodied in external form. The last two dimensions have to do with the incarnation of religion. First, every religious movement is embodied in a group of people, and that is very often rather formally organized – as Church, or Sangha, or *umma*. The sixth dimension therefore is what may be called the *social* or *institutional* aspect of religion. To understand a faith we need to see how it works among people. This is one reason why such an important tool of the investigator of religion is that subdiscipline which is known as the sociology of religion. Sometimes the social aspect of a worldview is simply identical with society itself, as in small-scale groups such as tribes. But there is a variety of relations between organized religions and society at large: a faith may be the official religion, or it may be just one denomination among many, or it may be somewhat cut off from social life, as a sect. Within the organization of one religion, moreover, there are many models – from the relative democratic governance of a radical Protestant congregation to the hierarchical and monarchical system of the Church of Rome.

It is not however the formal officials of a religion who may in the long run turn out to be the most important persons in a tradition. For there are charismatic or sacred personages, whose spiritual power glows through their demeanor and actions, and who vivify the faith of more ordinary folk – saintly people, gurus, mystics and prophets, whose words and example stir up the spiritual enthusiasm of the masses, and who lend depth and meaning to the rituals and values of a tradition. They can also be revolutionaries and set religion on new courses. They can, like John Wesley, become leaders of a new denomination, almost against their will; or they can be founders of new groups which may in due course emerge as separate religions – an example is Joseph Smith II, Prophet of the new faith of Mormonism. In short, the social dimension of religion includes not only the mass of persons but also the outstanding individuals through whose features glimmer old and new thoughts of the heaven towards which they aspire.

The material dimension

This social or institutional dimension of religion almost inevitably becomes incarnate in a different way, in *material* form, as buildings, works of art, and other creations. Some movements – such as Calvinist Christianity, especially in the time before the present century – eschew external symbols as being potentially idolatrous; their buildings are often beautiful in their simplicity, but their intention is to be without artistic or other images which might seduce people from the thought that God is a spirit who transcends all representations. However, the material expressions of religion are more often elaborate, moving, and highly important for believers in their approach to the divine. How indeed could we understand Eastern Orthodox Christianity without seeing what ikons are like and knowing that they are regarded as windows onto heaven? How could we get inside the feel of Hinduism without attending to the varied statues of God and the gods?

Also important material expressions of a religion are those natural features of the world which are singled out as being of special sacredness and meaning – the river Ganges, the Jordan, the sacred mountains of China, Mount Fuji in Japan, Eyre's [sic] Rock in Australia, the Mount of Olives, Mount Sinai, and so forth. Sometimes of course these sacred landmarks combine with more direct human creations, such as the holy city of Jerusalem, the sacred shrines of Banaras, or the temple at Bodh Gaya which commemorates the Buddha's Enlightenment.

Uses of the seven dimensions

To sum up: we have surveyed briefly the seven dimensions of religion which help to characterize religions as they exist in the world. The point of the list is so that we can give a balanced description of the movements which have animated the human spirit and taken a place in the shaping of society, without neglecting either ideas or practices.

Naturally, there are religious movements or manifestations where one or other of the dimensions is so weak as to be virtually absent: nonliterate small-scale societies do not have much means of expressing the doctrinal dimension; Buddhist modernists, concentrating on meditation, ethics and philosophy, pay scant regard to the narrative dimension of Buddhism; some newly formed groups may not have evolved anything much in the way of the material dimension. Also there are so many people who are not formally part of any social religious grouping, but have their own particular worldviews and practices, that we can observe in society atoms of religion which do not possess any well-formed social dimension. But of course in forming a phenomenon within society they reflect certain trends which in a sense form a shadow of the social dimension (just as those who have not yet got themselves a material dimension are nevertheless implicitly storing one up, for with success come buildings and with rituals ikons, most likely).

If our seven-dimensional portrait of religions is adequate, then we do not need to worry greatly about further definition of religion. In any case, I shall now turn to a most vital question in understanding the way the world works, namely to the relation between more or less overtly religious systems and those which are commonly called secular: ideologies or worldviews such as scientific humanism, Marxism, Existentialism, nationalism, and so on. In examining these worldviews we shall take on some of the discussion about what count as religious questions and themes. It is useful to begin by thinking out whether our seven-dimensional analysis can apply successfully to such secular worldviews.

[B] The nature of secular worldviews

Nationalism

Although nationalism is not strictly speaking a single worldview or even in itself a complete worldview, it is convenient to begin with it. One reason is that it has been such a powerful force in human affairs. Virtually all the land surface of the globe, together with parts of the world's water surface, is now carved up between sovereign states. Nationalism has given shape decisively to the modern world, because its popularity in part stems from the way in which assembling peoples into states has helped with the processes of industrialization and modern bureaucratic organization. Countries such as Britain, France, the United States, Germany, and Italy pioneered the industrial revolution, and the system of national governments spread from Western to Eastern Europe after World War I and from Europe to Asia, Africa, and elsewhere after World War II. Ethnic identity was sometimes demarcated by language and therefore cultural heritage, sometimes by religion, sometimes both, and sometimes simply by shared history. Examples of each of these categories can be seen in the cases of Germany (shared language), the two parts of Ireland (distinctive religion), Poland (both distinctive language and religion), and Singapore (shared history of Chinese, Malay, and other linguistic groups). Colonialism often helped to spread nationalism by reaction: the British conquest of India fostered an Indian nationalism, and there are signs of national awakening in parts of the Soviet Union, once colonized by Tsarist Russia, and in Tibet, conquered by China.

The nation-state has many of the appurtenances of a religion. First of all (to use the order in which we expounded the dimensions of religion in the previous section), there are the *rituals* of nationhood: speaking the language itself; the national anthem; the flying and perhaps saluting of the flag; republic and memorial days, and other such festivals and holidays; the appearance of the Head of State at solemn occasions; military march-pasts; and so on. It is usual for citizens to make secular pilgrimages to the nation's capital and other significant spots –

Washington (the Lincoln Memorial, the Vietnam Memorial, the White House, and so on); Plymouth Rock; Mount Rushmore; natural beauties exhibiting 'America the Beautiful'. Memorials to the nation's dead are of special significance, and often religious language is used about the sacrifices of the young on the altar of national duty.

The experiential or *emotional* side of nationalism is indeed powerful – for the sentiments of patriotism, pride in the nation, love of its beauties and powers, and dedication to national goals, can be very strong. Especially in times of national crisis, such as war, such sentiments rise to the surface. But they are reinforced all the time by such practices as singing the national anthem and other patriotic songs.

The *narrative* dimension of nationalism is easily seen, for it lies in the history of the nation, which is taught in the schools of the country, and which in some degree celebrates the values of the great men and women of the nation – for Italians, such great forebears as Julius Caesar (Giulio Cesare), Dante, Galileo, Leonardo, Garibaldi, Cavour, Verdi, Leopardi, Alcide de Gasperi and others. History is the narrative that helps to create in the young and in citizens at large a sense of identity, of belonging, of group solidarity.

Of *doctrines* nationalism is somewhat bereft, unless you count the doctrine of self-determination. But often, too, nations appeal to principles animating the modern state, such as the need for democracy and the rights of the individual in a freedom-loving nation, etc.; or a nation may appeal to the doctrine of a full-blown secular ideology, such as Marxism. Or it may hark back to the teachings of its ancestral religion, and so represent itself as guarding the truths and values of Christianity, or of Buddhism, or of a revived and revolutionary Islam.

The *ethical* dimension of nationalism consists in those values which are inculcated into citizens. Young people are expected to be loyal people, taxpayers, willing to fight if necessary for the country, law-abiding, and hopefully good family people (supplying thus the nation with its population). There is of course a blend between ethical values in general and the particular obligations to one's own kith and kin, one's fellow-nationals.

The *social* and *institutional* aspect of the nation-state is of course easily discerned. It culminates in a head of state who has extensive ceremonial functions – especially with monarchy, as in Britain, where the Queen is an important ritual object – and on whom sentiments of patriotism also focus. The state has its military services which also perform ceremonial as well as fighting tasks. There are the public schools, with the teachers imparting the treasured knowledge and rules of the nation. Even games come to play an institutional role; loyalty is expressed through Olympics and various other contests, and the ethos of the athlete comes to be blended with that of the ideal citizen. In some countries loyalty to religion or to a secular ideology blends with loyalty to one's nation, and those who do not subscribe to it are treated as disloyal. State occasions are shown on television, which itself comes to have a role in transmitting and focusing the values of the nation.

Finally, there is of course much *material* embodiment of the nation in its great buildings and memorials, its flag, its great art, its sacred land, its powerful military hardware.

In all these ways, then, the nation today is like a religion. If you have a relative who has died for a cause, it is not like the old days when he might have died for his religion, maybe at the stake; now he is most likely to have died for his country.

It is, then, reasonable to treat modern nationalism in the same terms as religion. It represents a set of values often allied with a kind of modernism, which is natural to the thinking of many of our contemporaries, and which stresses certain essentially modern concerns: the importance of economic development; the merits of technology; the wonders of science; the importance of either socialism or capitalism, or some mixture, in the process of modernization; the need for the state to look after the welfare of its citizens; the importance of universal education; and so on.

There are some growing limitations on nationalism: the fact that in many countries which were once reasonably homogeneous there are now increasing ethnic mixes, the growth of transnational corporations, the developing economic interdependence of nations, the impossibility of older ways of conceiving sovereignty in the context of modern warfare, and so on. But nevertheless, nationalism remains a very strong and alluring ingredient in the world, and many of the trouble spots are so because of unfulfilled ethnic expectations and ethnic rivalries – in Cyprus, Northern Ireland, Israel and Palestine, South Africa, Sri Lanka, Kurdistan, Afghanistan, and elsewhere.

The dimensions of Marxism

It is because Marxism has itself become more than a movement of ideas but has become embodied in many states that its analysis too needs to follow the general outlines I have sketched. It has a coherent set of *doctrines*, modified variously by leaders such as Stalin, Mao, Hoxha and Ceausescu; it has a *mythic* dimension in the analysis of historical events in accordance with the principles of the dialectic (so that then the history of the Russian Revolution or the German Democratic Republic gets fitted into a more general salvation-history of the human race). Its *rituals* combine with those of nationalism but have their own symbolisms, such as the widespread use of the colour red, the adoption of festivals such as May Day and the anniversary of the October Revolution, the adulation of the Party leader, etc. The *emotions* it encourages are those of patriotism, internationalism, and revolutionary commitment; its *ethics* those of solidarity; its *institutions* those of the Party; and its *artistic* style is that of socialist realism, which glorifies the ideals of the Party, state, and country, with more than a hint of that pietism which can characterize religious painting. Its music is heroic and rousing. State Marxism, then, has a distinctly religious-type function, and moves men by theory, symbols, rituals, and Party energy. Like many religions it may not ultimately prove to be successful, for the people may not be inwardly and deeply moved by the embodied values of Marxism as an ideology: indeed much evidence shows the hollowness of Marxism in a number of Eastern European countries, and even in the Soviet Union. It is always faced with the struggle against local patriotisms, against religions, against the humanist desire for freedom of enquiry, and so on.

Some other secular worldviews are less clearly like traditional religions in so far as they tend not to wield the symbols of power: for instance, scientific humanism, which is influential in one form or another among many intellectuals in the West, and which in rather inarticulate form expresses something of the worldview of ordinary folk in secularized circumstances. It holds to human and democratic values, and it stresses science as the source of knowledge. It repudiates the doctrines of religion, especially of Jewish and Christian theism. It sees human individuals as of ultimate value. But it does not, as I have said, embody itself in a rich way as a religious-type system. Its *rituals* are slight, beyond those which reinforce other aspects of modernity. Perhaps the modern passion for games and sports is one sign of a kind of persistence of interest in activities pursued according to ritual rules. Its *myths* are not extensive, beyond a feel for the clash between science and religion during the modern period from Galileo Galilei (1564–1642) onwards. Its *doctrines* can be complex, especially in the formulations of contemporary humanistic (analytical and linguistic) philosophy. Its profoundest *experiences* are maybe those of culture, such as music and the arts. Its *ethics* are generally speaking those of utilitarianism, which sees morality as maximizing happiness and minimizing suffering. Its *institutions* are found in secular education. Its *material* symbols are perhaps the skyscraper and the stadium. But it is hard to disentangle its manifestations from many other aspects of modern living.

Though to a greater or lesser extent our seven-dimensional model may apply to secular worldviews, it is not really appropriate to try to call them religions, or even 'quasi-religions' (which by implication demotes them below the status of 'real' religions). For the adherents of Marxism and humanism wish to be demarcated strictly from those who espouse religions – they conceive of themselves, on the whole, as antireligious. However, we have seen enough of the seven-dimensional character of the secular worldviews (especially nationalism and state Marxism) to emphasize that the various systems of ideas and practices, whether religious or not, are competitors and mutual blenders, and can thus be said to play in the same league. They all help to express the various ways in which human beings conceive of themselves, and act in the world.

A6 David R. Kinsley, 'Introduction: Benares'

From D.R. Kinsley (1982) *Hinduism: A Cultural Perspective*, New Jersey, Prentice-Hall, pp.2–9.

Even before the sun has risen, the streets and alleyways of Benares leading to the Ganges River swirl with devout pilgrims making their way to the broad steps that lead down into the river. By the time the sun is up the steps teem with pilgrims and devout residents taking ritual baths in Mother Ganges' sacred waters, which are believed to cleanse one of all sins. Small shops specializing in religious paraphernalia crowd the area around the steps and do a thriving business. Hundreds of priests whose task it is to aid pilgrims are setting up their large umbrellas against the heat of the sun, and by midday the steps leading to the river look as if they are overgrown with immense mushrooms.

Dawn also signals the beginning of activity in the thousands of temples and shrines throughout the city dedicated to the many gods and goddesses of the Hindu pantheon. In the impressive Vishvanath temple of the ascetic god Shiva, hereditary priests prepare to do *puja* (worship by personally waiting upon a deity), and devotees crowd the temple precincts to have a view of the image of the deity, a sight that is held to be auspicious, and to watch the colorful ceremony. Throughout the day devotees stream to the thousands of temples scattered all over Benares to worship their favorite god or goddess. The variety of images from which they can choose reflects the extraordinary richness through which the divine has revealed itself in the Hindu tradition.

Enshrined in these temples is a veritable kaleidoscope of divinity: Vishnu, the great heavenly king who descends to the world from time to time in various forms to maintain cosmic stability; Shiva, the ascetic god who dwells in yogic meditation in the Himalayas, storing up his energy so that he can release it periodically into the world to refresh its vigor; Krishna, the adorable cowherd god who frolics with his women companions in the idyllic forests of Vrindavana; Hanuman, the monkey god, who embodies strength, courage, and loyalty to the Lord Rama; Ganesha, the elephant-headed god who destroys all obstacles for his devotees; Durga, the warrior goddess who periodically defeats the forces of evil in order to protect the world; Kali, the black goddess who dwells in cremation grounds and is served with blood; and many more.

Dawn is a busy time at the cremation grounds on the Ganges too. A steady stream of funeral processions wends its way to a particular set of steps where several funeral pyres burn constantly. At the funeral grounds the stretcher-borne corpses are set down to await their turn in the purifying fires. The constant activity at this particular burning ground reflects the belief of pious Hindus that death in or near the Ganges at Benares results in *moksha*, the final liberation from the endless cycles of birth and rebirth that is the ultimate spiritual goal of most Hindus.

Thousands of devout Hindus, in their old age, come to die in Benares, and many funeral processions seem joyous, reflecting the auspicious circumstances of the person's death. As one watches the crackling fires consume the corpse, the rising tendrils of smoke suggest the soul's final and longed for liberation.

Benares is the center of several religious orders, and the city's population includes a great number of ascetics who have chosen to live in the holy city permanently or who are simply wandering through. It would not be unusual to see several of these holy men or women sitting in meditation around the steps. The burning ground itself is an auspicious site to perform meditation, as the funeral pyres remind the ascetics of the transcience of the worldly life they have renounced. The appearance of these renouncers is striking. Typical ascetics wear a minimum of clothes or are perhaps even naked. Their bodies are smeared with ashes, sometimes taken from the cremation grounds. Their hair is long and matted, indicating their utter neglect of bodily appearance, or their heads may be shaven. Their only possessions are a water pot and a staff. In the midst of a bustling city like Benares, which like all cities caters to the inexhaustible worldly desires of its populace with markets, cinemas, shops, and so on, the ascetics look like wayfarers from another world. They are a common sight in Benares, however, and remind one of the importance of world renunciation and asceticism in the Hindu tradition.

Before the day is over, a visitor to Benares will have witnessed many scenes common to the Hindu tradition: Brahmins performing ancient Vedic rituals; devotees from Bengal performing communal worship to Lord Krishna with much singing and dancing; students at Benares Hindu University consulting an astrologer to determine if the day on which their exams will be held will be auspicious; a low-caste pilgrim making an offering at the shrine of a beloved saint who is little known outside the pilgrim's own caste; a traditional pundit, or teacher, expounding the ethereal subtleties of Hindu philosophy to his students; a priest or storyteller animatedly telling stories from Hindu scriptures to groups of devotees in the precincts of a temple; and a pious person ritually worshipping a cow, many of which wander freely in the streets of Benares, perhaps in fulfillment of a vow to some deity for a favor granted in the past or expected in the future.

By the end of the day the visitor to Benares seeking to discern the essential outlines of the Hindu religious tradition probably will be very confused and tempted to conclude that Benares, with all its diversity, is not the best place to look for the essential ingredients of Hinduism. Indeed, Hinduism itself, like Benares, tends to defy neat analysis and description and leaves the impression that what happens in the name of Hinduism is chaotic. Hinduism, it seems, eludes and frustrates attempts to summarize it neatly because it offers exceptions or even contradictions to what at first might seem essential or generally true.

For example, many Hindus in Benares say that *ahimsa* (noninjury) is essential to the Hindu vision of reality, and they will be able to cite countless texts to support that view. They will mention Mahatma Gandhi as a recent example of the centrality of this theme in Hinduism, and possibly also the Hindu respect for cows and the emphasis on vegetarianism. You may be convinced that here, indeed, is an essential aspect of Hinduism. Thanking your informant, you will go on your way, only to come upon a temple of Kali or Durga, where worshippers are beheading a goat in sacrifice to the goddess. Or you might happen upon a copy of the *Artha Shastra* of Kautiliya, an ancient and authoritative text on Hindu political philosophy from around the fourth century AD. You will look in vain for Gandhian political principles in this book, because the *Artha Shastra* is consistently ruthless and cunning in its approach to seizing and holding power.

You might, on the other hand, be told by an ascetic in Benares that Hinduism involves essentially the renunciation of society and all egotistical desires and the achievement of liberation from the lures of the world. But before long you would find a group of orthodox Brahmins performing ancient rituals from the *Vedas*, also affirmed to be the essence of Hinduism, the explicit aim of which is the stability and welfare of the world, what the Hindus call *loka-samgraha*, one of the central teachings of Hinduism's most famous scripture, the *Bhagavad Gita*.

Who is right? The orthodox Brahmin who performs daily rituals prescribed by the ancient *Vedas*? The ascetic who performs no such rituals, who may even show disdain for them, and who denies any obligation to society? The low-caste farmer who daily praises the Lord Rama and celebrates his heroic exploits? The untouchable who makes a pilgrimage to Benares to honor a saint beloved by his or her entire caste but virtually unknown to most high-caste Hindus? Or the pious businessman who consults his astrologer before closing a deal? One must believe them all, it seems, for they are all Hindus undertaking common and acceptable Hindu practices. And this leads to our first generalizations about the Hindu religious tradition.

One cannot find the equivalent of a Hindu pope or an authoritative Hindu council in Benares. Historically Hinduism has never insisted upon the necessity of a supreme figure in religious matters and has never agreed upon certain articles of belief as essential for all Hindus. Throughout its long history, then, Hinduism, has been highly decentralized.

Another feature of Hinduism follows from this one, a feature reflected in both the caste system and the different paths one may take in the religious quest. Hinduism affirms in a variety of ways that people are different from one another and that these differences are both crucial and distinctive. People have different *adhikaras*, different aptitudes, predilections, and abilities. What is natural to one person is unnatural to another. So it is that different ways are made available to different types.

Some may have an aptitude for philosophy, and a path centering on knowledge is available for them. Others may be of a devotional aptitude, and so a path of devotion is appropriate for them. Over the centuries, then, Hinduism has accepted a variety of paths, spiritual techniques, and views of the spiritual quest that all succeed in helping man fulfill his religious destiny.

On the social level the Hindu emphasis on differences manifests itself in the caste system. Human differences are systematically arranged in hierarchical order, and people are segregated into specialized cohesive groups called castes. Social contact with other castes is carefully circumscribed in such a way that the religious beliefs and practices of a particular Hindu will often reflect his or her caste tradition and differ markedly from the religious practices of other castes. The philosophical ideas underlying the caste system are *karma*, the moral law of cause and effect according to which a person reaps what he or she sows, and *samsara*, rebirth according to the nature of a person's *karma*. The basic idea is that what a person is now is the result of all that one has done in the past, and what one will become in the future is being determined by all one's actions in the present. In effect, a person's present caste identity is only a brief scene in an endless drama of lives that will end only with *moksha*, liberation from this endless round of birth, death, and rebirth.

Hinduism also affirms that during one's life a person changes, and different kinds of activities are appropriate to various stages of life. Traditionally four stages have been described, with different obligations for each one. The ideal was designed primarily for men, and only very rarely did a woman follow the pattern. Ideally, a high-caste male is to pass through these stages in the following order: student, householder, forest recluse, and wandering holy man. As a student one's duty is to study his tradition, particularly the *Vedas* if he is a Brahmin. As a householder he is to foster a family, undertake an occupation appropriate to his caste, and perform rituals, usually Vedic rituals, that help insure the stability of the world. As a forest hermit, he is supposed to leave his home, retire to the forest with his wife, continue Vedic rituals, and meditate on those realities that will bring about liberation from the world and rebirth. Finally, he is to abandon even his wife, give up Vedic rituals, wander continually, begging his food, and strive for the knowledge that emancipates him from the cycles of rebirth. Although this pattern is not always followed, it affirms the tradition's liberality in permitting a variety of approaches in one's spiritual sojourn: study; supporting the world through rituals, work, and family life; meditation away from society; and renunciation of the world through extreme asceticism.

The Hindu insistence on differences between people, then, leads to the very common definition of Hinduism in sacred texts as *varna-ashrama-dharma*, which may be loosely translated as performing the duty (*dharma*) of one's stage of life (*ashrama*) and caste or social station (*varna*).

Hindus also have acknowledged that differences exist among the regional areas of the Indian subcontinent, and the Hindu Law Books accept as authoritative regional customs and peculiarities. These regional dissimilarities help us understand another aspect of the diversity of belief and practice among Hindus in Benares. Hindus from Tamilnad in the South have a cultural history that differs greatly from, say, Hindus from Bengal. Each region has its own vernacular tradition, its favorite gods and goddesses, its own distinctive customs and rituals. In Benares, where pilgrims from all over India congregate, these differences further complicate one's attempts to discern common themes, patterns, and beliefs. The history of Hinduism is, to a great extent, the record of what has gone on in the regions of India and is therefore marked by much diversity in belief and practice.

On the other hand, a strong, articulate, and authoritative tradition, called the Great, Sanskrit, or Aryan tradition, has counterbalanced this diversity by imposing upon it certain myths, beliefs, customs, and patterns of social organization. Dominated by a literate Brahmin elite, Hinduism over the centuries always has manifested a certain coherence because of the prestige of this tradition throughout India. Thus, Hinduism today is, as it always has been, the dynamic interaction of various regional traditions with an all-India tradition in which the particular beliefs and rituals of any given Hindu will be a combination. For orthodox Benares Brahmins, very little if any of the regional traditions may affect their brand of Hinduism. For low-caste Bengali peasants, on the other hand, very little of the Sanskrit tradition may be a part of their religion.

All this adds up to what one might call a liberal tendency in Hinduism that permits and even encourages men and women to undertake their religious sojourns in a variety of ways. Some things, to be sure, are encouraged for all Hindus: caste purity (intermarriage between castes is discouraged strongly), respect for Brahmins, and life-cycle rituals, for example. Certain ethical precepts also are encouraged for all, and certain underlying beliefs are accepted by most Hindus: *karma, samsara,* and *moksha,* for example. In Benares, then, we find very general parameters defining Hinduism that for the most part are provided by the Sanskrit tradition and that permit a great diversity of belief and practice. What goes on within these parameters, finally, may be summed up as representing four accents within the Hindu tradition:

1   *The Vedic Tradition.* Historically, the Aryans, who composed the *Vedas,* were foreigners who succeeded in superimposing on the indigenous peoples of India their language, culture, and religion. This Vedic religion is still dominant in living Hinduism and is best represented by the orthodox Brahmins. One of the central aims of this religion is the stability and welfare of the world, which is achieved through a great variety of rituals. In Benares today this accent is represented by those Brahmins who study the traditional Law Books and sponsor elaborate Vedic rituals.

2   *The Devotional Tradition.* The Hinduism of the majority of people in Benares is devotional, and this accent within the tradition goes all the way back to at least the time of the *Bhagavad Gita* (around 200BC). Devotion is of varying types and is directed to a great variety of gods and goddesses, but generally we can speak of three strands within this tradition: (*a*) devotion to Shiva or to one of his family; (*b*) devotion to Vishnu or to one of his *avataras* (incarnations), the two most popular of which in the Benares area are Krishna and Rama; and (*c*) devotion to one of the many manifestations of the Great Goddess, the Mahadevi. It is primarily against the background of the devotional tradition that Hindus will identify themselves as Shaiva (devotees of Shiva), Vaishnava (devotees of Vishnu), or Shakta (devotees of the Goddess). Devotion to all three manifestations of the divine is concerned with liberation from the cycle of endless births (*moksha*) or with eternal proximity to the deity in his or her eternal heaven.

3   *The Ascetic Tradition.* The several thousand ascetics in Benares are the living representatives of a tradition that is probably as ancient as the *Vedas* and that has been highly honored in Hinduism for over 2,500 years. The underlying assumptions of this tradition are that (*a*) life in the world is a hindrance to realizing one's spiritual destiny; (*b*) renunciation of society, including family ties, is necessary to realize one's spiritual essence; (*c*) various kinds of austerities are the necessary means of purifying oneself of both ignorance and attachments; and (*d*) the ultimate goal of this arduous path is complete liberation from the wheel of rebirth. There are various types of ascetics, ascetic orders, and spiritual exercises undertaken by ascetics. Generally, though, they all share these ideas and emphasize the importance of the individual's emancipation rather than one's obligations to the social order and its maintenance. In this respect there has often been a tension between the Vedic tradition and the ascetic tradition, a tension we shall return to later.

4   *The Popular Tradition.* This tradition refers to all those other rites and beliefs of Benares Hindus that do not fit neatly under the other three traditions. The sanctity of Benares itself, and of the River Ganges that flows through it, points to the central importance of sacred places and pilgrimage in the Hindu tradition. For Hindus the entire subcontinent bubbles with sacred places, where immediate access to sacred and purifying power is obtainable. Most prominent geographical features, such as mountains and rivers, are sacred and are the focal points of pilgrimage. Most cities contain famous temples and are also sacred centers. In addition to geographical sites and cities, some plants are held to be sacred. To the worshipers of Vishnu, the *tulasi* plant is particularly sacred, whereas to many devotees of the Goddess, it is the *bilva* tree. Time is punctuated by auspicious and inauspicious moments that are determined by the

movements of the stars, the planets, the sun, and the moon. Many Hindus are extremely sensitive to these rhythms and will undertake nothing of significance unless they have been assured by their astrologer that the time is auspicious. Most Hindus know precisely at what time they were born, because they, and their parents, need that information to determine the compatibility of marriage partners. We also include under the popular tradition the preoccupation many Hindus have with diet. Many Hindu scriptures give lists of pure and impure foods and characterize the different properties of foods according to the physical and spiritual effects they produce. The preoccupation of many Hindus and many Hindu scriptures with signs and omens is also part of the popular tradition, as are rituals that have to do with gaining control over enemies and members of the opposite sex. In short, the popular tradition refers to things that we might call magical or superstitious simply because we do not understand them fully; we are unable to do so because those who practice them cannot articulate in ways we can understand what these practices and beliefs mean to them or meant to their forefathers.

By way of concluding this introductory portrait of Hinduism, let me suggest an image that might be useful in thinking about its diversity. We all know someone who is a collector, who rarely throws anything away, whose possessions include the exquisite treasure, the tackiest bauble, the unidentifiable photograph, the neglected and dusty item, and the latest flashy gadget. The Hindu religious tradition has shown itself to be an incurable collector, and it contains in the nooks and crannies of its house many different things. Today this great collector may hold one or another thing in fashion and seem to be utterly fascinated by it. But very few things are ever discarded altogether, and this is probably one of the most interesting and distinctive features of Hinduism. Like a big family, with its diversity, quarrels, eccentricities, and stubborn loyalty to tradition, Hinduism is a religion that expresses the ongoing history of a subcontinent of people for over 3,500 years.

A7 Jaya Chaliha and Bunny Gupta, 'Durga Puja in Calcutta'

From Sukanta Chaudhuri (ed.) (1990) *Calcutta: The Living City*, Oxford University Press, vol.2, pp.331–3, 335–6.

Durga Puja in Bengal, Dussehra and Navaratri in other parts of India, celebrate the universal resurgence of the power of creation over destruction. The story goes that Mahishasur, the Buffalo Demon, ravaged the earth and was invincible. The gods, in dismay, combined their powers to create a beautiful sixteen-year-old maiden, and each placed his or her most potent weapon in one of her ten hands. Her return each year in the Bengali month of Ashwin (September–October) commemorates Rama's invocation of the goddess Durga before he went into battle with Ravana.

The traditional image of the Bengali Durga follows the iconographic injunctions of the Shastras. It is similar to the Durga of Aihole and of Mahabalipuram (seventh century). The tableau of Durga with her four children – Kartik, Ganesh, Saraswati and Lakshmi, representing respectively the Protector, the Initiator of the puja, Knowledge and the Provider – signifies the complete manifestation of the goddess. A later iconographic development, this tableau has turned Durga Puja into a family affair.

Preparations begin a month in advance. Processions and posters press the demand for Puja bonus, as the bread-winner has to meet many demands for new clothes and furbishings for the home. Pre-Puja bargain sales and exhibitions introduce the sartorial style for the coming year. Bengali newspapers and magazines publish voluminous 'numbers' or annuals – the springboard for many a budding author, besides their quantum of works by well-known writers.

Durga Puja is ushered in on Mahalaya, the first phase of the waxing moon in Ashwin. Thousands offer prayers to their ancestors at the city's river ghats. A special pre-dawn programme of readings from the Chandi and *Agamani* songs welcoming the goddess are relayed by All-India Radio. This traditional programme, conceived by Birendrakrishna Bhadra, has become an institution: a chorus of protests led to its restoration after a change was attempted one year.

The joyous atmosphere builds up as *dhakis* or drummers from the countryside collect at the stations and at important street corners. They beat their feathered drums to attract the community-puja organizers who come to engage the best performers they can find.

The first recorded Durga Puja seems to have been celebrated by Bhabananda, the ancestor of Maharaja Krishnachandra of Nadia, in or about 1606. In Krishnachandra's day, the Puja was a grand but private affair in the elegant *thakur dalan* (hall of the deity) of the palace built by his ancestor Rudra Ray. The family Puja of the Sabarna Choudhuris of Barisha dates back to 1610 – the oldest in Calcutta, and conducted even today in a highly traditional style.

Durga Puja broke free from the pillared cortiles at Guptipara in Hugli District when twelve angry young men were stopped from taking part in a household puja. They formed a twelve-man committee, which held the first public or community Durga Puja by subscription. Hence such pujas came to called *baroari* (*baro*, twelve: *yar*, friend). A plaque at Bindeshwaritala shrine dates the event in 1168 Saka (1761AD). But records are scant and the date controversial. The *Friend of India*, the monthly once published from Shrirampur, mentions 1790.

The word *sarbajanin* (for all men) came to be substituted for *baroari* at the time of the Indian National Congress held in Calcutta in 1910. The first community puja in Calcutta was held at Balaram Basu Ghat Road the same year. The celebration was used as a nationalist forum in religious guise. A pledge of solidarity was taken, and the country was identified with the goddess.

The fun and excitement of the old *baroari* puja took a serious turn in the early *sarbajanin*. Fencing with staves (*lathi khela*), yoga and drill display, provided moving demonstrations of a people preparing to fight for freedom. Swadeshi goods were sold in the stalls around the pandals (the awnings or temporary structures where the pujas are held). After Independence, martial arts of an international flavour have made their entry – jujitsu, karate etc. – but variety shows of song, dance and recitation are more popular. Many types of books, Marxist literature no less than popular fiction and children's fare, are prominently displayed.

Going back to earlier times, Durga Puja became the practice among the compradors, the new urban mercantile aristocracy in Calcutta. The accent changed. Nabakrishna Deb, patriarch of the Shobhabazar Raj, founded the family Puja and further used it to enhance his business interests. Thus began the tradition of business entertainment.

After his victory at Palashi (Plassey, in 1757) Clive [English soldier and colonial administrator] wanted a grand thanksgiving service; but the only church in town had been razed to the ground by Nawab Siraj-ud-Daula the year before. Clive consulted his *munshi*,' Offer your thanks at the Devi's feet at my Durga Puja,' the latter advised, 'But I am a Christian,' protested Clive, 'That can be managed,' smiled the wily 'Nubkissen'.

And so Clive came to Shobhabazar in the Black Town. A golden sofa was placed for him in the open quadrangle. The Durga Puja at 36 Raja Nabakrishna Street is still referred to as the Company Puja. 'Nubkissen' set a pattern for the Puja which became a fashion and a status symbol among the parvenu merchants. The number of sahibs attending the family puja became an index of prestige. Religious scruples fell by the wayside. The nautch girls were mostly from Muslim *gharanas*; and while they danced, the English guests dined on beef and ham from Wilson's Hotel, washed down with wine.

In those colonial-style merchant mansions, the northern side of the quadrangle – sometimes covered but often open – was the *thakur dalan*, where religious and social activities took place. Even today, on an auspicious day in August, clay modellers arrive at these houses to mould the images as their ancestors have done for generations. Their work complete, the dressers take over. In the Pathuriaghata Mallik family, the ladies of the house themselves dye the sarees and decorate them with *zari* (gold brocade). In other homes, the *malakar* cuts intricate designs on *shola*, white cork or pith. Coloured foil is also used: it is known as *daker saj*, as the foil used for decoration (*saj*) was at first imported through the *dak* or post.

On Shashthi, the sixth day of the moon, the clay image of Durga is brought to life by the recitation of *mantras*. Married women renew their vows to Shiva at the foot of a *bel* or wood-apple tree and fast for the welfare of their children. Come Mahasaptami, the seventh day, and hundreds of *nabapatrikas* or nine chosen plants, bound in the shape of a female form and embodying nine powers of the mother goddess, are carried to the river for ablution: an offshoot of a pre-Aryan agricultural ritual. The adoptive branch of the Deb family reverted to vegetable sacrifice on this day after the sacrificial goat escaped its tether and ran for protection to the head of the house, Raja Radhakanta Deb. Many Vaishnav homes have similar stories to tell.

Sweets are distributed on Mahashtami, the most propitious day of the Puja. The Deb household distributes king-sized laddus. In the Mallik family, *khaja* and *gaja* are prepared.

The *lagna* (set time) of the most auspicious Sandhi Puja approaches, at the moment of conjunction (*sandhi)* when Mahashtami gives way to Mahanabami and the joy of victory. Drums beat, cymbals clash and conch shells blow. The air is thick with incense, obscuring even the Devi's face.

Bijaya Dashami, the tenth and last day, brings the pang of parting. Durga is drummed a grand but tearful farewell with repeated requests to return next year. From the 'great houses', Durga is carried in the procession to the river on the shoulders of liveried porters or the men of the family itself. The community pujas postpone the farewell as long as possible and give Durga a rousing send-off. Miniature pandals atop lorries, lit by portable generators and accompanied by floats – pageant follows pageant through the streets to the Strand. Some old families, like the Debs, release a *nilkantha* or roller bird, sacred to Shiva, towards Kailash to tell the god of his wife's imminent return to her husband's home.

At the river, the goddess and her children are rowed midstream between two boats lashed together; to cries of 'Jai Ma Durga', the boats separate and the Puja is over for the year. A second roller bird flies back to Shobhabazar to tell the family of the Devi's safe departure.

[…] the family spirit of Durga Puja has descended on the many households in the multi-storeyed buildings which are rapidly changing both the skyline and the life-style of the city. Many of these now hold their own Durga Puja, run by a committee of residents. Community lunch on the Puja days restores the spirit of the joint family without its problems, while variety shows in the evening bring out the hidden talents of the residents. Yet the rituals are followed meticulously: the same priest, drummer and decorator usually appear year after year, in the tradition of the old pujas. And the deepest sanctity of Durga Puja is preserved at the Ramkrishna Mission, Bharat Sevashram Sangha and other monasteries and religious societies.

Calcutta is transformed during this unique festival. Religious fervour and merry-making mingle remarkably. Durga Puja has now become an integrated celebration absorbing all castes and creeds. The whole city takes a holiday. From the colonnaded *thakur dalans* of Shobhabazar, Natun Bazar and Thanthania, Durga Puja has moved outdoors: first to small club-houses and later, as community affairs, to temporary pandals.

An important puja, which still survives, was first organized by the Simla Byayam Samiti, a nationalist group at Simla (Shimulia) Street in 1926. Here in 1939, Subhashchandra Basu unveiled a 21-foot Durga created by Nitai Pal. Since then the pandals have proliferated and now number over two thousand.

Many of the family pujas are still supported by *debottar* foundations or religious trusts. With the advent of the Sarbajanin Puja, the onus of funding came to rest with the immediate community. The local toughs or *mastans*, as the self-appointed protectors of their areas, took the task of collection upon themselves. In their enthusiasm, they often turned militant in demanding subscriptions. This phenomenon was specially prevalent just after World War II. It has not disappeared, but contributions are usually voluntary and feature as an item in the Puja budget of most homes.

Durga herself has kept up with changing times and fashions. She often bears a clear resemblance to some leading film star, and popular hits are played for her in the pandals. In the 1960s, the Devi often laid aside her clay form to be ingeniously recreated in sea shells, *shola* or pith, thermocole, matchsticks and nails. She and her family also broke out of the conventional *chalchitra* or single backdrop uniting the group. At Bagbazar one year, a diorama of icons floated in the clouds while Durga sat on Mount Kailas.

At Maddox Square, however, the goddess is still dressed in traditional *daker saj*. There are no short cuts in the rituals here, and many senior citizens have a personal relationship with this public puja.

The image is often a secondary feature of the Sarbajanin Puja, commanding a small part of the budget allocation. Instead, competitions sponsored by commercial houses encourage taller pandals and elaborate illuminations. Durga returns each year to a novel abode. The construction of the pandals is a skilful craft. Coloured cloth, pleated, stretched and frilled, rises over bamboo frames in the city's parks and streets. In the 1950s, the *hogla* or reed roof gave way to tarpaulin and galvanized iron sheets. In 1989, the theme for the pandals was places of worship – of all denominations. Durga sojourned in temples and mosques, gurdwaras and churches and Buddhist *stupas*. At Harish Mukherji Road, however, Durga comes every year to a permanent *pukka* building. On Tarachand Datta Street a decade ago, the residents of Rambagan Bustee created the celestial world of Omkar Dham in their hereditary craft of basketry work.

Calcutta's leading artists have taken it in turn to design the image of the Bakul Bagan Durgotsab. Among them are Nirad Majumdar, Rathin Maitra, Paritosh Sen, Shanu Lahiri and Meera Mukherji. Mostly, however, the *pratimas* are made in the 'celestial colony' at Kumartuli in the oldest part of Calcutta. Images are ordered in advance: there are only a few off-the-shelf sales. Today the clientele of Kumartuli extends to America, Europe and Africa, among the Indian communities living there. In 1989, images made out of *shola* pith by Amarnath Ghosh were flown to Sweden, Australia, Malaysia and Nigeria: weighing only some three kilograms, they were ideal as air freight.

Kumartuli's own Durga Puja dates back to 1933. The image-maker was Gopeshwar Pal. Whereas private pujas still depend on family connections in Bardhaman and Chandannagar for dressing and decorating the images, Sarbajanin Pujas get theirs fully attired and armed from Kumartuli. Hence Kumartuli is also a beehive of ancillary crafts.

Power cuts, a lasting complaint through the rest of the year, are banished during Durga's short stay. Cascades of multi-coloured bulbs tumble from buildings. The trees bear festoons of lights. The walkways leading to the pandals are adorned with sparkling animated displays in coloured lights.

The transport and police authorities gear themselves with amazing success to cope with the colossal crowds as the whole city pours out into the streets and thousands of visitors arrive by plane, train and bus. Trams, buses and the Metro operate round the clock, and vendors of all sorts do a roaring business. The daily newspapers publish street maps showing the most important pandals, and identity badges are issued to children in case they are lost.

Durga Puja grows in pomp and festivity – though in Calcutta, no longer in number – every year. The display has inevitably burgeoned faster than the devotion. But all told, the heritage of Calcutta's Greatest Show has been honourably preserved.

Section B HERE'S HISTORY OF SCIENCE

B1 Alfred Russel Wallace, The South Wales farmer

From A.R. Wallace (1905) 'The South Wales farmer: his modes of agriculture, domestic life, customs and characters' in *My Life: A Record of Events and Opinions*, London, Chapman & Hall, vol.1, pp.207–22, written in 1843.

The generality of mountain farms in Glamorganshire and most other parts of South Wales are small, though they may appear large when the number of acres only is considered, a large proportion being frequently rough mountain land. On the average they consist of from twenty to fifty acres of arable land in fields of from four to six, and rarely so much as ten acres; the same quantity of rough, boggy, bushy, rushy pasture, and perhaps as much, or twice as much, short-hay meadow, which term will be explained hereafter; and from fifty to five hundred acres of rough mountain pasture, on which sheep and cattle are turned to pick up their living as they can.

Their system of farming is as poor as the land they cultivate. In it we see all the results of carelessness, prejudice, and complete ignorance. We see the principle of doing as well as those who went before them, and no better, in full operation; the good old system which teaches us not to suppose ourselves capable of improving on the wisdom of our forefathers, and which has made the early polished nations of the East so inferior in every respect to us, whose reclamation from barbarism is ephemeral compared with their long period of almost stationary civilization. The Welshman, when you recommend any improvement in his operations, will tell you, like the Chinaman, that it is an 'old custom', and that what did for his forefathers is good enough for him. But let us see if the farmer is so bad as this mode of doing his business may be supposed to make him. In his farmyard we find the buildings with broken and gaping doors, and the floors of the roughest pitching. In one corner is a putrid pond, the overflowings of which empty themselves into the brook below. Into this all the drainings from the dungheaps in the upper part of the yard run, and thus, by evaporation in summer and the running into the brook in winter, full one-half of the small quantity of manure he can obtain (from his cattle spending the greater part of their time on the mountain and in wet bushy pastures) is lost.

The management of his arable land is dreadfully wasteful and injurious. Of green crops (except potatoes can be so called) he has not the slightest idea, and if he takes no more than three grain crops off the land in succession, he thinks he does very well; five being not uncommon. The first and principal crop is wheat, on which he bestows all the manure he can muster, with a good quantity of lime. He thus gets a pretty good crop. The next year he gets a crop of barley without any manure whatever, and after that a crop of oats, unmanured. He then leaves the field fallow till the others have been treated in the same manner, and then returns to serve it thus cruelly again; first, however, getting his potato crop before his wheat. Some, after the third crop (oats), manure the land as well as they can, and sow barley with clover, which they mow and feed off the second year, and then let it remain as pasture for some time; others, again, have three crops of oats in succession after the wheat and barley, and thus render the land utterly useless for many years.

In this manner the best crops of wheat they can get with abundance of manure, on land above the average quality, is about twenty bushels per acre – ten bushels is, however, more general, and sometimes only seven or eight are obtained.

The rough pastures on which the cattle get their living and waste their manure a great part of the time consist chiefly of various species of rushes and sedges, a few coarse grasses, and gorse and fern on the drier parts. They are frequently, too, covered with brambles, dwarf willows, and alders.

The 'short-hay meadows', as they are called, are a class of lands entirely unknown in most parts of England; I shall, therefore, endeavour to describe them.

They consist of large undulating tracts of lands on the lower slopes of the mountains, covered during autumn, winter, and spring with a very short brownish yellow wet turf. In May, June, and July the various plants forming this turf spring up, and at the end of summer are mown, and form 'short-hay'; and well it deserves the name, for it is frequently almost impossible to take it up with a hayfork, in which case it is raked up and gathered by armfuls into the carts. The produce varies from two to six hundredweight per acre; four may be about the average, or five acres of land to produce a ton of hay. During the rest of the year it is almost good for nothing. It is astonishing how such stuff can be worth the labour of mowing and making into hay. An English farmer would certainly not do it, but the poor Welshman has no choice; he must either cut his short-hay or have no food for his cattle in the winter; so he sets to, and sweeps away with his scythe a breadth which would astonish an English mower.

The soil which produces these meadows is a poor yellow clay resting on the rock; on the surface of the clay is a stratum of peaty vegetable matter, sometimes of considerable thickness though more generally only a few inches, which collects and retains the moisture in a most remarkable manner, so that though the ground should have a very steep slope the water seems to saturate and cling to it like a sponge, so much so that after a considerable period of dry weather, when, from the burnt appearance of the surface, you would imagine it to be perfectly free from moisture, if you venture to kneel or lie down upon it you will almost instantly be wetted to the skin.

The plants which compose these barren slopes are a few grasses, among which are the sweet vernal grass (*Anthoxanthum odoratum*) and the crested hair grass (*Kœleria cristata*), several Cyperaceæ – species of carex or sedge which form a large proportion, and the feathery cotton grass (*Eriophorum vaginatum*). The toad-rush (*Funcus bufonius*) is frequently very plentiful, and many other plants of the same kind. Several rare or interesting British plants are here found often in great profusion. The Lancashire asphodel (*Narthecium ossifragum*) often covers acres with its delicate yellow and red blossoms. The spotted orchis (*O. maculata*) is almost universally present. The butterwort (*Pinguicula vulgaris*) is also found here, and the beautiful little pimpernel (*Anagallis tenella*). The louseworts (*Pendicularis sylvatica* and *P. palustris*), the melancholy thistle (*Cincus heterophyllus*), and the beautiful blue milkwort (*Polygala vulgaris*), and many others, are generally exceedingly plentiful, and afford much gratification to the botanist and lover of nature.

The number of sheep kept on these farms is about one to each acre of mountain, where they live the greater part of the year, being only brought down to the pastures in the winter, and again turned on the mountain with their lambs in the spring. One hundred acres of pasture and 'short-hay meadow' will support from thirty to forty cattle, ten or a dozen calves and oxen being sold each year.

The farmers are almost invariably yearly tenants, consequently little improvement is made even in parts which could be much bettered by draining. The landlord likes to buy more land with his spare capital (if he has any) rather than improve these miserable farms, and the tenant is too poor to lay out money, or if he has it will not risk his being obliged to leave the farm or pay higher rent in return for his permanently improving another person's land.

The hedges and gates are seldom in sufficiently good repair to keep out cattle, and can hardly be made to keep out mountain sheep, who set them completely at defiance, nothing less than a six-foot stone wall, and not always that, serving to confine them. The farmer consequently spends a good deal of his time in driving them out of his young clover (when he has any) or his wheat. He is also constantly engaged in disputes, and not unfrequently litigation, with his neighbours, on account of the mutual trespasses of their stock.

The Welshman is by no means sharp-sighted when his cattle are enjoying themselves in a neighbour's field, especially when the master is from home, otherwise the fear of the 'pound' will make him withdraw them after a short time.

On almost every farm water is very plentiful, often far too much so, and it is sometimes run over a meadow, but in such a manner as to lose one half of the advantage which might be derived from it. The farmer is contented with merely cutting two or three gaps in the watercourse at the top, from which the water flows over the field as it best can, scarcely wetting some parts and making complete pools in others.

Weeding he considers quite an unnecessary refinement, fit only for those who have plenty of money to waste upon their fancies – except now and then, when the weeds have acquired an alarming preponderance over the crop, he perhaps sets feebly to work to extract the more prominent after they have arrived at maturity and the mischief is done. His potatoes are overrun with persicarias, docks, and spurges; his wheat and barley with corn cockle, corn scabious, and knapweed, and his pastures with thistles, elecampine, etc., all in the greatest abundance. If you ask him why he leaves his land in such a disgraceful state, and try to impress upon him how much better crops he would have if he cleared it, he will tell you that he does not think they do much harm, and that if he cleaned them this year, there would be as many as ever next year, and, above all, that he can't afford it, asking you where he is to get money to pay people for doing it.

The poultry, geese, ducks, and fowls are little attended to, being left to pick up their living as well as they can. Geese are fattened by being turned into the corn stubble, the others are generally killed from the yard. The fowls, having no proper places to lay in, are not very profitable with regard to eggs, which have to be hunted for and discovered in all sorts of places. This applies more particularly to Glamorganshire, which is in a great measure supplied with eggs and poultry from Carmarthenshire, or 'Sir Gaer' (pronounced there *gar*), as it is called in Welsh, where they manage them much better.

If there happens to be in the neighbourhood any one who farms on the improved English system, has a proper course of crops, with turnips, etc., folds his sheep, and manages things in a tidy manner, it is impossible to make the Welshman believe that such a way of going on pays; he will persist that the man is losing money by it all the time, and that he only keeps it on because he is ashamed to confess the failure of his new method. Even should the person go on for many years, to all appearance prosperously and in everybody else's eyes be making money by his farm, still the Welshman will declare that he has some other source from which he draws to purchase his dear-bought farming amusement, and that the time will come when he will be obliged to give it up; and though you tell him that the greater part of the land in England is farmed in that manner, and ask him whether he thinks they can all be foolish enough to go on losing money year after year, he is still incredulous, says that he knows 'the nature of farming', and that such work as that can never pay. While the ignorance which causes this incredulity exists, it is evidently a difficult task to improve him.

Domestic life, customs, etc.

The house is a tiled, white-washed edifice, in the crevices of which wall
rue, common spleenwort, and yarrow manage generally to vegetate,
notwithstanding their (at the very least) annual coat of lime. It consists on
the ground floor of a rather large and very dark room, which serves as
kitchen and dining-room for the family, and a rather better one used as a
parlour on high days or when visitors call; this latter frequently serves as
the bedroom of the master and mistress. The kitchen, which is the theatre
of the Welsh farmer's domestic life, has either a clay floor or one of very
uneven stone paving, and the ceiling is in many cases composed of
merely the floor boards of the room above, through the chinks of which
everything going on aloft can be very conveniently heard and much
seen. The single window is a small and low one, and this is rendered
almost useless by the dirtiness of the glass, some window drapery, a
Bible, hymn book and some old newspapers on the sill, and sickly-
looking geranium or myrtle, which seems a miracle of vital tenacity in
that dark and smoky atmosphere. On one side may be discerned an oak
sideboard brilliantly polished, on the upper part of which are rows of
willow pattern plates and dishes, in one corner an open cupboard filled
with common gaudily-coloured china, and in the other a tall clock with a
handsome oak case. Suspended from the ceiling is a serious impediment
to upright walking in the shape of a bacon rack, on which is, perhaps, a
small supply of that article and some dried beef, also some dried herbs in
paper, a large collection of walking sticks, and an old gun. In the
chimney opening a coal fire in an iron grate takes the place of the open
hearth and smoky peat of Radnorshire and other parts. A long substantial
oak table, extending along the room under the window, an old armchair
or two, a form or bench and two or three stools, complete the furniture
of the apartment. From the rack before mentioned is generally suspended
a piece of rennet for making cheese, and over the mantelpiece is
probably a toasting-fork, one brass and two tin candlesticks, and a milk
strainer with a hole in the bottom of it; on the dresser, too, will be
perceived a brush and comb which serve for the use of the whole family,
and which you may apply to your own head (if you feel so inclined)
without any fear of giving offence.

Upstairs the furniture is simple enough: two or three plain beds in each
room with straw mattresses and home-made blankets, sheets being
entirely unknown or despised; a huge oak chest full of oatmeal, dried
beef, etc., with perhaps a chest of drawers to contain the wardrobe; a
small looking-glass which distorts the gazer's face into a mockery of
humanity; and a plentiful supply of fleas, are all worth noticing. Though
the pigs are not introduced into the family quite so familiarly as in
Ireland, the fowls seem to take their place. It is nothing uncommon for
them to penetrate even upstairs; for we were once ourselves much
puzzled to account for the singular phenomenon of finding an egg upon
the bed, which happened twice or we might have thought it put there by

accident. It was subsequently explained to us that some persons thought it lucky for the fowls to lay there: the abundance of fleas was no longer a mystery. The bed in the parlour before mentioned serves, besides its ostensible use, as a secret cupboard, where delicacies may be secured from the junior members of the family. I have been informed by an acquaintance whose veracity I can rely on (and indeed I should otherwise find no difficulty in believing it) that one day, being asked to take some bread and cheese in a respectable farmhouse, the wheat bread (a luxury) was procured from some mysterious part of the bed, either between the blankets or under the mattress, which my informant could not exactly ascertain. The only assistant in the labours of the farm, besides the sons and daughters, is generally a female servant, whose duties are multifarious and laborious, including driving the horses while ploughing and in haytime, and much other out-of-door work.

If you enter the house in the morning, you will probably see a huge brass pan on the fire filled with curdled milk for making cheese. Into this the mistress dips her red and not particularly clean arm up to the elbow, stirring it round most vigorously. Meals seem to be prepared solely for the men, as you seldom see the women sit down to table with them. They will either wait till the others have done or take their dinner on their laps by the fire. The breakfast consists of hasty-pudding or oatmeal porridge, or cheese with thin oatmeal cakes or barley bread, which are plentifully supplied at all meals, and a basin of milk for each person; for dinner there is perhaps the same, with the addition of a huge dish of potatoes, which they frequently break into their basin of milk or eat with their cheese; and for supper, often milk with flummery or 'siccan' (pronounced *shiccan*). As this is a peculiar and favourite Welsh dish, I will describe its composition. The oat bran with some of the meal left in it is soaked for several days in water till the acetous fermentation commences; it is then strained off, producing a thin, starchy liquid. When wanted for use this is boiled, and soon becomes nearly of the consistence and texture of blancmange, of a fine light brown colour and a peculiar acid taste which, though at first disagreeable to most persons, becomes quite pleasant with use. This is a dish in high repute with all real Welshmen. Each person is provided with a basin of new milk, cold, and a spoon, and a large dish of hot flummery is set on the table, each person helping himself to as much as he likes (and that is often a great deal), putting it in his basin of milk; and it is, I have no doubt, very wholesome and nourishing food. I must mention that the women, both in the morning and evening (and frequently at dinner too), treat themselves to a cup of tea, which is as universal a necessary among the fair sex here as in other parts of the kingdom. They prefer it, too, without milk, which they say takes away the taste, and as it is generally made very weak, that may be the case. [...]

When a birth takes place in a family all the neighbours and relations call within a few days to inquire after the health of the mother and child, and take a cup of tea or bread and cheese, and every one brings some present, either a pound of sugar, quarter pound of tea, or a shilling or more in money, as they think best. This is expected to be returned when the givers are in a similar situation.

The 'bidding', which is a somewhat similar custom at a marriage, is not quite so general, though it is still much used in Carmarthenshire. When a young couple are married they send notice to all their friends, that 'on a day named they intend to have a "bidding", at which they request their company, with any donation they may think proper, which will be punctually returned when they are called upon on a similar occasion.' At such biddings £20 or £30 are frequently collected, and sometimes much more, and as from various causes they are not called upon to return more than one-half, they get half the sum clear and a loan without interest of the other half to commence life with.

The national dress or costume of the men (if ever they had any) is not now in use; that of the women, however, is still very peculiar. [...] One of the most striking parts of the women's dress is the black beaver hat, which is almost universally worn and is both picturesque and becoming. It is made with a very high crown, narrowing towards the top, and a broad, perfectly flat brim, thus differing entirely from any man's hat. They frequently give thirty shillings for one of these hats, and make them last the greater part of their lives. The body dress consists of what they call a bedgown, or *betcown*, as it is pronounced, which is a dress made quite plain, entirely open in front (like a gentleman's dressing gown), with sleeves a little short of the elbow. A necessary accompaniment to this is an apron, which ties it up round the waist. The bedgown is invariably formed of what they call flannel, which is a stuff formed by a mixture of wool, cotton, and sometimes a little silk. It is often striped black or dark blue, or brown and white, with alternate broad and narrow stripes, or red and black, but more frequently a plaid of several colours, the red and black being wool, the white or blue cotton, and often a narrow yellow stripe of silk, made in plaid patterns of every variety of size and colour. The apron is almost always black-and-white plaid, the only variety being in the form and size of the pattern, and has a pretty effect by relieving the gay colours of the other part of the dress. They in general wear no stays, and this, with the constant habit of carrying burdens on the head, produces almost invariably an upright carriage and good figure, though rather inclined to the corpulency of Dutch beauties. On their necks they usually wear a gay silk kerchief or flannel shawl, a neat white cap under the hat; laced boots and black worsted stockings complete their attire. In Carmarthenshire a jacket with sleeves is frequently worn by the women, in other respects their dress does not much differ from what I have described.

The women and girls carry (as before mentioned) great loads upon their heads, fifty or sixty pounds weight, and often much more. Large pitchers (like Grecian urns) of water or milk are often carried for long distances on uneven roads, with both hands full at the same time. They may be often seen turning round their heads to speak to an acquaintance and tripping along with the greatest unconcern, but never upsetting the pitcher. The women are almost invariably stout and healthy looking, notwithstanding their hard work and poor living. These circumstances, however, make them look much older than they really are. The girls are often exceedingly pretty when about fifteen to twenty, but after that, hard work and exposure make their features coarse, so that a girl of five-and-twenty would often be taken for nearer forty.

All, but more especially the young ones, ride most fearlessly, and at fairs they may be seen by dozens racing like steeple-chasers.

Many of these farmers are freeholders, cultivating their own land and living on the produce; but they are generally little, if any, better off than the tenants, leaving the land in the same manner, thus showing that it is not altogether want of leases and good landlords that makes them so, but the complete ignorance in which they pass their lives.

All that I have hitherto said refers solely to the poorer class, known as hill farmers. In the valleys and near the town where the land is better, there are frequently better educated farmers, who assimilate more to the English in their agricultural operations, mode of living, and dress.

In all the mining districts, too, there is another class – the colliers and furnacemen, smiths, etc., who are as different from the farmers in everything as one set of men can be from another. [...] The wages which these men get – in good times £2 or £3 per week – prevents them, with moderate care, from being ever in great distress. They likewise always live well, which the poor farmer does not, and though many of them have a bit of land and all a potato ground, the turnpike grievances, poor-rates, and tithes do not affect them as compared with the farmers, to whom they are a grievous burden, making the scanty living with which they are contented hard to be obtained.

The rents, too, continue the same as when their produce sold for much more and the above-mentioned taxes were not near so heavy. The consequence is that the poor farmer works from morning to night after his own fashion, lives in a manner which the poorest English labourer would grumble at, and as his reward, perhaps, has his goods and stock sold by his landlord to pay the exorbitant rent, averaging 8s. or 10s. per acre for such land as I have described.

Language, character, etc.

The Welsh farmer is a veritable Welshman. He can speak English but very imperfectly, and has an abhorrence of all Saxon manners and innovations. He is frequently unable to read or write, but can sometimes con over his Welsh Bible, and make out an unintelligible bill; and if in addition he can read a little English and knows the four first rules of arithmetic, he may be considered a well-educated man. The women almost invariably neither read nor write, and can scarcely ever understand two words of English. They fully make up for this, however, by a double share of volubility and animation in the use of their own language, and their shrill clear voices are indications of good health, and are not unpleasant. The choleric disposition usually ascribed to the Welsh is, I think, not quite correct. Words do not often lead to blows, as they take a joke or a satirical expression very good humouredly, and return it very readily. Fighting is much more rarely resorted to than in England, and it is, perhaps, the energy and excitement with which they discuss even common topics of conversation that has given rise to the misconception. They have a ready and peculiar wit, something akin to the Irish, but more frequently expressed so distantly and allegorically as to be unintelligible to one who does not understand their modes of thought and peculiarities of idioms, which latter no less than the former they retain even when they converse in English. They are very proud of their language, on the beauty and expression of which they will sometimes dilate with much animation, concluding with a triumphant assertion that theirs *is* a language, while the English is none, but merely a way of speaking.

The language, though at times guttural, is, when well spoken, both melodious and impressive. There are many changes in the first letters of words, for the sake of euphony, depending on what happens to precede them; *m* and *b*, for instance, are often changed into *f* (pronounced *v*), as *melin* or *felin*, a mill; *mel* or *fel*, honey. The gender is often changed in the same manner, as *bach* (masculine), *fach* (feminine), small; *mawr* (m.), *fawr* (f.), great. The modes of making the plural is to an Englishman rather *singular,* a syllable being taken off instead of being added, as is usually the case with us, as *plentyn*, a child; *plent*, children: *mochyn*, a pig; *moch*, pigs. But in other cases a syllable or letter is added.

Their preachers or public speakers have much influence over them. During a discourse there is the most breathless attention, and at the pauses a universal thrill of approbation. Allegory is their chief speciality, and seems to give the hearers the greatest pleasure, and the language appears well fitted for giving it its full effect.

As might be expected from their ignorance, they are exceedingly superstitious, which is rather increased than diminished in those who are able to read by their confining their studies almost wholly to the Bible. The forms their superstitions take are in general much the same as in Scotland, Ireland, and other remote parts of the kingdom. Witches and wizards and white witches, as they are called, are firmly believed in, and their powers much dreaded. There is a witch within a mile of where I am now writing who, according to report, has performed many wonders. One man who had offended her she witched so that he could not rise from his bed for several years, but he was at last cured by inviting the witch to tea and making friends with her. Another case was of a man driving his pig to market when the witch passed by. The pig instantly refused to move, sat up on its hind legs against the hedge in such a manner as no pig was ever seen to do before, and, as it could not be persuaded to walk, was carried home, where it soon died. [...]

But the most characteristic and general superstition of this part of the country is the 'corpse candle'. This is seen in various shapes and heard in various sounds; the normal form, from which it takes its name, being, however, a lighted candle, which is supposed to foretell death, by going from the house in which the person dies along the road where the coffin will be carried to the place of burial. It is only a few of the most hardy and best educated who dare to call in question the reality of this fearful omen, and the evidence in support of it is of such a startling and voluminous character, that did we not remember the trials and burnings and tortures for witchcraft and demonianism, and all the other forms of superstition in England but a few years ago, it would almost overpower our common sense. [...]

Besides these and numberless other instances of almost universal belief in supernatural agency, their superstition as well as their ignorance is further shown by their ascribing to our most harmless reptiles powers of inflicting deadly injury. The toad, newt, lizard, and snake are, they imagine, virulently poisonous, and they look on with horror, and will hardly trust their eyes, should they see them handled with impunity. The barking of dogs at night, hooting of owls, or any unusual noise, dreams, etc., etc., are here, as in many parts of England, regarded as dark omens of our future destiny, mysterious warnings sent to draw aside the veil of futurity and reveal to us, though obscurely, impending danger, disease or death.

Reckoned by the usual standards on these subjects, the religion of the lower orders of Welshmen may be said to be high in the scale, while their morality is decidedly low. This may appear a contradiction to some persons, but those who are at all acquainted with mankind well know that, however luxuriantly religion in its outward forms and influence on the tongue may flourish in an uncultivated soil, it is by no means necessarily accompanied by an equal growth of morality. The former, like the flower of the field, springs spontaneously, or with but little care; the latter, like the useful grain, only by laborious cultivation and the careful eradication of useless or noxious weeds.

If the number of chapels and prayer-meetings, the constant attendance on them, and the fervour of the congregation can be accounted as signs of religion, it is here. Besides the regular services on the Sabbath and on other days, prayer meetings are held early in the morning and late at night in different cottages by turns, where the uneducated agriculturist or collier breathes forth an extemporary prayer. The Established Church is very rarely well attended. There is not enough of an exciting character or of originality in the service to allure them, and the preacher is too frequently an Englishman who speaks the native tongue, but as a foreigner.

Their preachers, while they should teach their congregation moral duties, boldly decry their vices, and inculcate the commandments and the duty of doing to others as we would they should do unto us, here, as is too frequently the case throughout the kingdom, dwell almost entirely on the mystical doctrine of the atonement – a doctrine certainly not intelligible to persons in a state of complete ignorance, and which, by teaching them that they are not to rely on their own good deeds, has the effect of entirely breaking away the connection between their religion and the duties of their everyday life, and of causing them to imagine that the animal excitement which makes them groan and shriek and leap like madmen in the place of worship, is the true religion which will conduce to their happiness here, and lead them to heavenly joys in a world to come.

Among the youth of both sexes, however, the chapel and prayer meeting is considered more in the light of a 'trysting' place than as a place of worship, and this is one reason of the full attendance, especially at the evening services. And as the meetings are necessarily in a thinly populated country, often distant, the journey, generally performed on horseback, affords opportunities for converse not to be neglected.

Thus it will not be wondered at, even by those who affirm the connection between religion and morality, that the latter is, as I said before, at a very low ebb. Cheating of all kinds, when it can be done without being found out, and all the lesser crimes are plentiful enough. The notoriety which Welsh juries and Welsh witnesses have obtained (not unjustly) shows how little they scruple to break their word or their oath. Having to give their evidence through the medium of an interpreter gives them an advantage in court, as the counsel's voice and manner have not so much effect upon them. They are, many of them, very good witnesses as far as sticking firmly to the story they have been instructed in goes, and returning the witticisms of the learned counsel so as often to afford much mirth. To an honest jury a Welsh case is often very puzzling, on account of its being hardly possible to get at a single fact but what is sworn against by an equal number of witnesses on the opposite side; but to a Welsh jury, who have generally decided on their verdict before the trial commences, it does not present any serious difficulty.

The morals and manners of the females, as might be expected from entire ignorance, are very loose, and perhaps in the majority of cases a child is born before the marriage takes place.

But let us not hide the poor Welshman's virtues while we expose his faults. Many of the latter arise from his desire to defend his fellow countrymen from what he considers unfair or unjust persecution, and many others from what he cannot himself prevent – his ignorance. He is hospitable even to the Saxon. His fire, a jug of milk, and bread and cheese being always at your service. He works hard and lives poorly. He bears misfortune and injury long before he complains. The late Rebecca disturbances, however, show that he may be roused, and his ignorance of other effectual measures should be his excuse for the illegal and forcible means he took to obtain redress – means which, moreover, have been justified by success. It is to be hoped that he will not have again to resort to such outrages as the only way to compel his rulers to do him justice.

A broader system of education is much needed in the Principality. Almost all the schools, it is true, teach the English language, but the child finds the difficulty of acquiring even the first rudiments of education much increased by his being taught them in an unfamiliar tongue of which he has perhaps only picked up a few common-place expressions. In arithmetic, the new language presents a greater difficulty, the method of enumerating being different from their own; in fact, many Welsh children who have been to school cannot answer a simple question in arithmetic till they have first translated it into Welsh. Unless, therefore, they happen to be thrown among English people or are more than usually well instructed, they get on but little with anything more than speaking English, which those who have been to school generally do very well. Whatever else they have learnt is soon lost for want of practice. It would be very useful to translate some of the more useful elementary works in the different branches of knowledge into Welsh, and sell them as cheaply as possible. The few little Welsh books to be had (and they are very few) are eagerly purchased and read with great pleasure, showing that if the means of acquiring knowledge are offered him, the Welshman will not refuse them.

I will now conclude this brief account of the inhabitants of so interesting a part of our island, a part which will well repay the trouble of a visit, as much for its lovely vales, noble mountains, and foaming cascades, as for the old customs and still older language of the inhabitants of the little white-washed cottages which enliven its sunny vales and barren mountain slopes.

B2   Alfred Russel Wallace, Among the Uaupés

From A.R. Wallace (1889, 2nd edn) *A Narrative of Travels on the Amazon and Rio Negro*, London, Ward, Lock, pp.189–95, 330, 335–6, 342, 360–61, first published 1853.

I do not remember a single circumstance in my travels so striking and new, or that so well fulfilled all previous expectations, as my first view of the real uncivilised inhabitants of the river Uaupés. [...]

On the 7th [of June 1851] we entered a narrow winding channel, branching from the north bank of the river, and in about an hour reached a 'malocca', or native Indian lodge, the first we had encountered. It was a large, substantial building, near a hundred feet long, by about forty wide and thirty high, very strongly constructed of round, smooth, barked timbers, and thatched with the fan-shaped leaves of the Caraná palm. [...]

On entering this house, I was delighted to find myself at length in the presence of the true denizens of the forest. An old and a young man and two women were the only occupiers, the rest being out on their various pursuits. The women were absolutely naked; but on the entrance of the 'brancos' they slipped on a petticoat, with which in these lower parts of the river they are generally provided but never use except on such occasions. Their hair was but moderately long, and they were without any ornament but strongly knitted garters, tightly laced immediately below the knee.

It was the men, however, who presented the most novel appearance, as different from all the half-civilised races among whom I had been so long living, as they could be if I had been suddenly transported to another quarter of the globe. Their hair was carefully parted in the middle, combed behind the ears, and tied behind in a long tail reaching a yard down the back. The hair of this tail was firmly bound with a long cord formed of monkeys' hair, very soft and pliable. On the top of the head was stuck a comb, ingeniously constructed of palm-wood and grass, and ornamented with little tufts of toucans' rump feathers at each end; and the ears were pierced, and a small piece of straw stuck in the hole; altogether giving a most feminine appearance to the face, increased by the total absence of beard or whiskers, and by the hair of the eyebrows being almost entirely plucked out. A small strip of 'tururí' (the inner bark of a tree) passed between the legs, and secured to a string round the waist, with a pair of knitted garters, constituted their simple dress. [...]

The Uaupés are generally rather tall, five feet nine or ten inches being not an uncommon height, and they are very stout and well formed. Their hair is jet-black and straight, only turning grey with extreme old age. [...] The colour of the skin is a light, uniform, glossy reddish-brown. [...] Paint, with these people, seems to be looked upon as a sufficient clothing; they are never without it on some part of their bodies, but it is at their festivals that they exhibit all their art in thus decorating their persons: the colours they use are red, yellow, and black, and they dispose them generally in regular patterns. [...]

We passed the night in the malocca, surrounded by the naked Indians hanging round their fires, which sent a fitful light up into the dark smoke-filled roof. A torrent of rain poured without, and I could not help admiring the degree of sociality and comfort in numerous families thus living together in patriarchal harmony. [...]

In the afternoon [of the 8th] we reached another village. [...] The inhabitants had gone to a neighbouring village, where there was caxirí and dancing. [...] The next day we reached Ananárapicóma, or 'Pine-apple Point', the village where the dance was taking place. [...] On entering the great malocca a most extraordinary and novel scene presented itself. Some two hundred men, women, and children were scattered about the house. [...] The wild and strange appearance of these handsome, naked, painted Indians, with their curious ornaments and weapons, the stamp and song and rattle which accompanies the dance, the hum of conversation in a strange language, the music of fifes and flutes and other instruments of reed, bone, and turtles' shells, the large calabashes of caxirí constantly carried about, and the great smoke-blackened gloomy house, produced an effect to which no description can do justice, and of which the sight of half-a-dozen Indians going through their dances for show, gives but a very faint idea.

I stayed looking on a considerable time, highly delighted at such an opportunity of seeing these interesting people in their most characteristic festivals. I was myself a great object of admiration, principally on account of my spectacles, which they saw for the first time and could not at all understand. A hundred bright pairs of eyes were continually directed on me from all sides, and I was doubtless the great subject of conversation. An old man brought me three ripe pine-apples, for which I gave him half-a-dozen small hooks, and he was very well contented. [...]

The main feature in the personal character of the Indians of this part of South America, is a degree of diffidence, bashfulness, or coldness, which affects all their actions. It is this that produces their quiet deliberation, their circuitous way of introducing a subject they have come to speak about, talking half an hour on different topics before mentioning it: owing to this feeling, they will run away if displeased rather than complain, and will never refuse to undertake what is asked them, even when they are unable or do not intend to perform it.

It is the same peculiarity which causes the men never to exhibit any feeling on meeting after a separation; though they have, and show, a great affection for their children, whom they never part with; nor can they be induced to do so, even for a short time. They scarcely ever quarrel among themselves, work hard, and submit willingly to authority. They are ingenious and skilful workmen, and readily adopt any customs of civilised life that may be introduced among them; and they seem capable of being formed, by education and good government, into a peaceable and civilised community.

This change, however, will, perhaps, never take place: they are exposed to the influence of the refuse of Brazilian society, and will probably, before many years, be reduced to the condition of the other half-civilised Indians of the country, who seem to have lost the good qualities of savage life, and gained only the vices of civilisation.

B3 Charles Darwin, Among the Fuegians

From C. Darwin (1839) *Journal of Researches into the Geology and Natural History of the Various Countries Visited by H.M.S. 'Beagle' under the Command of Captain FitzRoy, R.N., from 1832 to 1836*, London, Colburn, pp.227–9, 234–7.

In the morning [of 18 December 1832] the Captain sent a party to communicate with the Fuegians. When we came within hail, one of the four natives who were present advanced to receive us, and began to shout most vehemently, wishing to direct us where to land. When we were on shore the party looked rather alarmed, but continued talking and making gestures with great rapidity. It was without exception the most curious and interesting spectacle I had ever beheld. I could not have believed how wide was the difference, between savage and civilized man. It is greater than between a wild and domesticated animal, in as much as in man there is a greater power of improvement. The chief spokesman was old, and appeared to be the head of the family; the three others were powerful young men, about six feet high. The women and children had been sent away. [...] Their only garment consists of a mantle made of guanaco skin, with the wool outside; this they wear just thrown over their shoulders, as often leaving their persons exposed as covered. Their skin is of a dirty coppery red colour.

The old man had a fillet of white feathers tied round his head, which partly confined his black, coarse, and entangled hair. His face was crossed by two broad transverse bars; one painted bright red reached from ear to ear, and included the upper lip; the other, white like chalk, extended parallel and above the first, so that even his eyelids were thus coloured. Some of the other men were ornamented by streaks of black powder, made of charcoal. The party altogether closely resembled the devils which come on the stage in such plays as Der Freischutz.

Their very attitudes were abject, and the expression of their countenances distrustful, surprised, and startled. After we had presented them with some scarlet cloth, which they immediately tied round their necks, they became good friends. This was shown by the old man patting our breasts, and making a chuckling kind of noise, as people do when feeding chickens. I walked with the old man, and this demonstration of friendship was repeated several times; it was concluded by three hard slaps, which were given me on the breast and back at the same time. He then bared his bosom for me to return the compliment, which being done, he seemed highly pleased. The language of these people, according to our notions, scarcely deserves to be called articulate. Captain Cook has compared it to a man clearing his throat, but certainly no European ever cleared his throat with so many hoarse, guttural, and clicking sounds.

They are excellent mimics: as often as we coughed or yawned, or made any odd motion, they immediately imitated us. Some of our party began to squint and look awry; but one of the young Fuegians (whose whole face was painted black, excepting a white band across his eyes) succeeded in making far more hideous grimaces. They could repeat with perfect correctness, each word in any sentence we addressed them, and they remembered such words for some time. Yet we Europeans all know how difficult it is to distinguish apart the sounds in a foreign language. [...] All savages appear to possess, to an uncommon degree, this power of mimicry. [...]

At a subsequent period the Beagle anchored for a couple of days under Wollaston Island. [...] While going on shore we pulled alongside a canoe with six Fuegians. These were the most abject and miserable creatures I any where beheld [... They] were quite naked, and even one full-grown woman was absolutely so. It was raining heavily, and the fresh water, together with the spray, trickled down her body. In another harbour not far distant, a woman, who was suckling a recently-born child, came one day alongside the vessel, and remained there whilst the sleet fell and thawed on her naked bosom, and on the skin of her naked child. These poor wretches were stunted in their growth, their hideous faces bedaubed with white paint, their skins filthy and greasy, their hair entangled, their voices discordant, their gestures violent and without dignity. Viewing such men, one can hardly make oneself believe they are fellow-creatures, and inhabitants of the same world. It is a common subject of conjecture what pleasure in life some of the less gifted animals can enjoy: how much more reasonably the same question may be asked with respect to these barbarians. At night, five or six human beings, naked and scarcely protected from the wind and rain of this tempestuous climate, sleep on the wet ground coiled up like animals. When it is low water, they must rise to pick shell-fish from the rocks; and the women, winter and summer, either dive to collect sea eggs, or sit patiently in their canoes, and, with a baited hair-line, jerk out small fish. If a seal is killed, or the floating carcass of a putrid whale discovered, it is a feast: such miserable food is assisted by a few tasteless berries and fungi. Nor are they exempt from famine, and, as a consequence, cannibalism accompanied by parricide.

The tribes have no government or head, yet each is surrounded by other hostile ones, speaking different dialects; and the cause of their warfare would appear to be the means of subsistence. [... In] search of food they are compelled to wander from spot to spot, and so steep is the coast, that they can only move about in their wretched canoes. They cannot know the feeling of having a home, and still less that of domestic affection; unless indeed the treatment of a master to a laborious slave can be considered as such. How little can the higher powers of the mind be brought into play! What is there for imagination to picture, for reason to compare, for judgment to decide upon? to knock a limpet from the rock does not even require cunning, that lowest power of the mind. Their skill in some respects may be compared to the instinct of animals; for it is not improved by experience: the canoe, their most ingenious work, poor as it is, has remained the same, for the last two hundred and fifty years. [...]

There is no reason to believe that the Fuegians decrease in number; therefore we must suppose that they enjoy a sufficient share of happiness (of whatever kind it may be) to render life worth having. Nature by making habit omnipotent, and its effects hereditary, has fitted the Fuegian to the climate and the productions of his country.

B4 Alfred Russel Wallace, A new kind of baby

From A.R. Wallace (1856) 'A new kind of baby', *Chambers's Journal,* 3rd ser., vol.6, pp.325–7.

Not a newly-born infant but a really new baby, or, to speak as a naturalist, a new *species* of baby. How this strange phenomenon came into my possession, I shall presently relate: I now wish to give the public, and particularly the better-half of it, some account of the baby itself, its appearance and habits. I know not the little innocent's age: it may have been a few days, or a few weeks, or even months old when I first obtained it. The only guide to its age is, that it had not a tooth in its head. Two days afterwards, however, it cut its two lower teeth, and it was exactly a month more before the two corresponding upper teeth began to appear. From these dates, no doubt its age may be speculated on by those learned in such matters; but, as I am a bachelor and am not a doctor, I have not myself the most remote conception. It must always be remembered, too, that as this is a new baby, it is not to be supposed that it cuts its teeth at the same time, and in the same manner, as common babies.

For the same reason, its size can be no proof of age – I have a suspicion, however, that it is a baby of the smallest size, being not quite a foot and a half long; but then, as it has very short legs, its body is larger in proportion, and its arms are as much too long as its legs are too short. In colour, it is a dirty brown – something of the colour one may imagine to be produced by a mixture of all the races existing upon the earth, which makes me think it must be a descendant of some very primitive people. Its hands and feet, and mouth and eyes, are, however, much paler, and very much like those of any other baby; but its greatest peculiarity is its long red hair, remarkably long for so young an infant, which has a propensity to stand out on end like that of an electrified doll, making the little creature look always frightened, which I am sure it is not, as it is a sweet-tempered baby, and very seldom cries but when it wants to be cleaned or fed.

I hardly know how to describe the personal appearance of the infant prodigy, so as to give a proper idea of its numerous peculiarities, without making it appear less pleasing and pretty than it really is; but the attempt must be made. The general appearance of its head is very much the same as that of other infants, except the red hair, which is certainly a rare phenomenon. Its face, however, is remarkable for a very large mouth and a very small nose, rather more depressed than in the little children of the Earthmen tribe now exhibiting in London. Its arms, as before mentioned, are very large; as are also its fingers, which, however, in other respects, present nothing peculiar. Its little short legs have a strange facility of motion; they are either held aloft in the air, or bent back against the sides of the body, or its toes are put into its mouth for want of something else to suck; but I believe other infants besides this do the same thing. Its feet, however, are most remarkable in having very long toes, and a little thumb to them instead of a great toe. The skin of its neck, breast and stomach is quite smooth; but strange to say, all its back and the outside of its arms and legs are covered with long soft red hair. 'Why', exclaims the reader, 'the creature must be a monkey!' But I beg leave entirely to repudiate the suggestion. The baby in question has no sign of a tail and if you could see its expressive countenance while slowly eating its soft rice, you would scorn the insinuation as much as I do.

Another peculiarity which this interesting infant possesses, is an appearance of extreme old age. To look at it, you can hardly believe that it is only just cutting its teeth, and is quite incapable of going alone, or of eating anything but what is put into its mouth by other people. The little wrinkles about its mouth and eyes give it an air of precocious wisdom, and the workings of its countenance express so many feelings and passions, as seem quite incompatible with a state of helpless infancy. Still more extraordinary is its possession alike of strength and weakness to an unparalleled degree. It cannot turn itself over on the ground; it is incapable of moving an inch; and yet the most active sailor could not hold on to a rope with so much tenacity, and for so long a time. It will sometimes hang so for an hour together, and seem quite contented; and I generally give it some exercise of this sort once a day to keep it in health. Its little, long fingers are bent at the ends, and even its nails turn inwards, as if formed expressly for hanging on to something, which it is always wanting to do. It sleeps with its hands tight clutched, or sometimes grasping its own hair. There is nothing, in fact, it likes to catch hold of so much as hair. It has a very passion for hair; and if, while feeding it, I inadvertently approach too close, it seizes the opportunity, grasps hold of my whiskers as if it would tear them out by the roots; and when, after some difficulty, and many twinges, I have made my escape, it generally sets up a scream, which can only be stopped by immediately administering a mouthful of rice.

Another thing that would lead one to think it must have come of decent parents, is its love of being clean. If I hear a scream at any time other than eating-time, I am sure the poor creature is dirty, and wants to be washed. And how it enjoys its washing, and being rubbed dry, and having its hair brushed! It never screams or kicks, as do many naughty children under the wholesome operation, but lies perfectly still, however long it may take, and seems rather sorry when it is over.

In my bachelor establishment, I was, of course, put to some shifts to provide for such an unexpected visitor. I contrived a pap-bottle with a wide-mouthed phial, till I found the baby would eat out of a spoon. A small box did duty for a cradle; but as I was obliged to be out a good deal in the day, and the nights were rather chilly, I purchased a little monkey, to be a companion to my abnormal infant, and to keep it warm at night. It might not have been quite proper, but necessity has no law, and I am glad to say the baby was much pleased with little Jacko, and they became excellent friends. The baby, however, was a little exacting, and would try to keep Jacko always with it, seizing hold of his hair and grasping his tail; and when all was of no avail, and the monkey, by desperate efforts, succeeded in escaping, screaming violently with rage. Still, however, they got on very well together; and after the baby had been fed, Jacko would always come and sit upon its stomach, and pick off any little bits of rice that were left about its mouth, or even put in his hand and pull out whatever baby had not quite swallowed.

But alas! milk was not to be procured, and a diet of rice and water was not sufficiently nourishing for so small an infant. It pined away, and suffered from a complication of diseases – from diarrhoea or dropsy. I once gave it a little castor-oil, after which it recovered for a time; but a relapse again occurred, and, after lingering some weeks, death terminated its sufferings.

I had indulged hopes of sending this infant prodigy to England, where it might have rivalled in popularity the ape-like Aztecs, and the public would have been enabled to judge the accuracy of my statements. Such hopes, however, being now entirely frustrated, and it being highly probable that neither I nor any one else will ever look upon its like again, I shall simply narrate the circumstances of its discovery, and leave every one to form his own opinion.

I was walking in search of game in one of those vast primeval forests which clothe so large a portion of the tropics; no human habitation or sign of culture was near; parasitical plants swarmed upon the trees, and twisted climbers hung in festoons from their loftiest branches, or, trailing on the ground, helped, with prickly canes, to form impenetrable barriers. All was sombre and silent. No birds fluttered on the branches, and but rarely an insect's wing glittered in a stray gleam of sunshine. Suddenly I heard a rustling in the topmost branches of a lofty tree. I gazed upward, and for some time could not discover its cause; but after moving right and left, so as to see in succession every part of the tree, I discovered a large red animal walking along a branch, in a semi-erect posture. Without losing a moment, I fired a ball, which apparently only served to make the creature move more rapidly. It passed along till the branch became so slender as to bend beneath its weight, when its long arms enabled it to seize the adjacent bough of another tree. This with great strength it pulled towards it, till it had hold of a portion sufficiently thick to bear its weight, when it swung itself across with surprising agility, and continued its journey to the opposite branches, where it succeeded in passing on to a third tree in the same manner. I now fired again, and with decisive effect, for in a sudden attempt to escape more rapidly, it lost its hold, and fell with a crash to the earth. I of course imagined that it was dead; but what was my surprise, before I could reach it, to see it rise from the ground, and grasping with its large hands a small tree close to it, begin to ascend again with great rapidity. It had reached a considerable height before I could fire again, when it again fell to the ground, this time mortally wounded, and soon breathed its last. It was then that I discovered, close to where it had first fallen, the singular infant whose eventful history I have here recorded, lying half buried in a sand-hole, to which my attention was drawn by a half-stifled little scream. Some water being near, I washed the mud out of its mouth and eyes, and discovered a marvellously baby-like and innocent-looking little creature, apparently quite unhurt by its fall, and which clung to me with a most amazing tenacity. I had killed the mother, so I determined, if possible, to save her offspring; with what success has been already seen.

Some natives of the country brought the dead body to the place where I was living. It was three feet six inches high, and its outstretched arms were six feet across. The natives called it a 'mias', but the Malays say it is an 'orang-outang', which means 'man of the forest'.

B5 Alfred Russel Wallace, Natural selection

From A.R. Wallace (1905) *My Life: A Record of Events and Opinions*, London, Chapman & Hall, vol.1, pp.360, 361–3.

[A] It was while waiting at Ternate in order to get ready for my next journey, and to decide where I should go, that the idea [...] occurred to me. [...] At the time in question I was suffering from a sharp attack of intermittent fever, and every day during the cold and succeeding hot fits had to lie down for several hours, during which time I had nothing to do but to think over any subjects then particularly interesting me.

[B] One day something brought to my recollection Malthus's 'Principles of Population', which I had read about twelve years before. I thought of his clear exposition of 'the positive checks to increase' – disease, accidents, war, and famine – which keep down the population of savage races to so much lower an average than that of more civilized peoples.

[C] It then occurred to me that these causes or their equivalents are continually acting in the case of animals also; and as animals usually breed much more rapidly than does mankind, the destruction every year from these causes must be enormous in order to keep down the numbers of each species, since they evidently do not increase regularly from year to year, as otherwise the world would long ago have been densely crowded with those that breed most quickly. Vaguely thinking over the enormous and constant destruction which this implied, it occurred to me to ask the question, Why do some die and some live? And the answer was clearly, that on the whole the best fitted live. From the effects of disease the most healthy escaped; from enemies, the strongest, the swiftest, or the most cunning; from famine, the best hunters or those with the best digestion; and so on.

[D] Then it suddenly flashed upon me that this self-acting process would necessarily *improve the race*, because in every generation the inferior would inevitably be killed off and the superior would remain – that is, *the fittest would survive.*

[E] Then at once I seemed to see the whole effect of this, that when changes of land and sea, or of climate, or of food-supply, or of enemies occurred – and we know that such changes have always been taking place – and considering the amount of individual variation that my experience as a collector had shown me to exist, then it followed that all the changes necessary for the adaptation of the species to the changing conditions would be brought about; and as great changes in the environment are always slow, there would be ample time for the change to be effected by the survival of the best fitted in every generation. In this way every part of an animal's organization could be modified exactly as required, and in the very process of this modification the unmodified would die out, and thus the *definite* characters [...] of each new species would be explained.

[F] The more I thought over it the more I became convinced that I had at length found the long-sought-for law of nature that solved the problem of the origin of species. [...] I waited anxiously for the termination of my fit so that I might at once make notes for a paper on the subject. The same evening I did this pretty fully, and on the two succeeding evenings wrote it out carefully in order to send it to Darwin by the next post, which would leave in a day or two.

B6 Alfred Russel Wallace, The Malay–Papuan boundary

From A.R. Wallace (1877, 6th edn) *The Malay Archipelago: The Land of the Orang-utan and the Bird of Paradise; A Narrative of Travel with Studies of Man and Nature*, London, Macmillan, pp.311, 313–14, 316–17, first published 1869.

Soon after my first arrival in Ternate I went to the island of Gilolo, accompanied by two sons of Mr Duivenboden, and by a young Chinaman, a brother of my landlord, who lent us the boat and crew. These latter were all slaves, mostly Papuans. [...] My first stay was at Dodinga, situated at the head of a deep bay exactly opposite Ternate, and a short distance up a little stream which penetrates a few miles inland. The village is a small one, and is completely shut in by low hills.

As soon as I arrived, I applied to the head man of the village for a house to live in, but all were occupied, and there was much difficulty in finding one. In the meantime I unloaded my baggage on the beach and made some tea, and afterwards discovered a small hut which the owner was willing to vacate if I would pay him five guilders for a month's rent. [...]

On the top of a bank, of about a hundred feet ascent from the water, stands the very small but substantial fort erected by the Portuguese. Its battlements and turrets have long since been overthrown by earthquakes, by which its massive structure has also been rent; but it cannot well be thrown down, being a solid mass of stonework, forming a platform about ten feet high, and perhaps forty feet square. It is approached by narrow steps under an archway, and is now surmounted by a row of thatched hovels, in which live the small garrison, consisting of a Dutch corporal and four Javanese soldiers, the sole representative of the Netherlands Government in the island. The village is occupied entirely by Ternate men. The true indigenes of Gilolo, 'Alfuros' as they are here called, live on the eastern coast, or in the interior of the northern peninsula. The distance across the isthmus at this place is only two miles, and there is a good path, along which rice and sago are brought from the eastern villages. The whole isthmus is very rugged, though not high, being a succession of little abrupt hills and valleys, with angular masses of limestone rock everywhere projecting, and often almost blocking up the pathway. Most of it is virgin forest, very luxuriant and picturesque, and at this time having abundance of large scarlet Ixoras in flower, which made it exceptionally gay. I got some very nice insects here, though, owing to illness most of the time, my collection was a small one; and my boy Ali shot me a pair of one of the most beautiful birds of the East, Pitta gigas, a large ground-thrush. [...]

[I]n the interior, there is a large population of indigenes, numbers of whom came daily into the village, bringing their produce for sale, while others were engaged as labourers by the Chinese and Ternate traders.

A careful examination convinced me that these people are radically distinct from all the Malay races. Their stature and their features, as well as their dispositions and habits, are almost the same as those of the Papuans. [...] Of course there has been intermixture, and there occur occasionally individuals which it is difficult to classify; but in most cases the large, somewhat aquiline nose, with elongated apex, the tall stature, the waved hair, the bearded face, and hair body, as well as the less reserved manner and louder voice, unmistakeably proclaim the Papuan type. Here then I had discovered the exact boundary line between the Malay and Papuan races, and at a spot where no other writer had expected it.

B7 Alfred Russel Wallace, The origin of human races

From A.R. Wallace (1864) 'The origin of human races and the antiquity of man deduced from the theory of "natural selection"', *Journal of the Anthropological Society of London*, vol.2, clxvii–clxx.

If the views I have here endeavoured to sustain have any foundation, they give us a new argument for placing man apart, as not only the head and culminating point of the grand series of organic nature, but as in some degree a new and distinct order of being. From those infinitely remote ages, when the first rudiments of organic life appeared upon the earth, every plant, and every animal has been subject to one great law of physical change. As the earth has gone though its grand cycles of geological, climatal and organic progress, every form of life has been subject to its irresistible action, and has been continually, but imperceptibly moulded into such new shapes as would preserve their harmony with the ever changing universe. No living thing could escape this law of its being; none could remain unchanged and live, amid the universal change around it.

At length, however, there came into existence a being in whom that subtle force we term *mind*, became of greater importance than his mere bodily structure. Though with a naked and unprotected body, *this* gave him clothing against the varying inclemencies of the seasons. Though unable to compete with the deer in swiftness, or with the wild bull in strength, *this* gave him weapons with which to capture or overcome both. Though less capable than most other animals of living on the herbs and the fruits that unaided nature supplies, this wonderful faculty taught him to govern and direct nature to his own benefit, and make her produce food for him when and where he pleased. From the moment when the first skin was used as a covering, when the first rude spear was formed to assist in the chase, the first seed sown or shoot planted, a grand revolution was effected in nature, a revolution which in all the previous ages of the earth's history had had no parallel, for a being had arisen who was no longer necessarily subject to change with the changing universe – a being who was in some degree superior to nature, inasmuch, as he knew how to control and regulate her action, and could keep himself in harmony with her, not by a change in body, but by an advance of mind.

Here, then, we see the true grandeur and dignity of man. On this view of his special attributes, we may admit that even those who claim for him a position as an order, a class, or a sub-kingdom by himself, have some reason on their side. He is, indeed, a being apart, since he is not influenced by the great laws which irresistibly modify all other organic beings. Nay more; this victory which he has gained for himself gives him a directing influence over other existences. Man has not only escaped 'natural selection' himself, but he actually is able to take away some of that power from nature which, before his appearance, she universally exercised. We can anticipate the time when the earth will produce only cultivated plants and domestic animals; when man's selection shall have supplanted 'natural selection', and when the ocean will be the only domain in which that power can be exerted, which for countless cycles of ages ruled supreme over all the earth.

Briefly to recapitulate the argument; – in two distinct ways has man escaped the influence of those laws which have produced unceasing change in the animal world. By his superior intellect he is enabled to provide himself with clothing and weapons, and by cultivating the soil to obtain a constant supply of congenial food. This renders it unnecessary for his body, like those of the lower animals, to be modified in accordance with changing conditions – to gain a warmer natural covering, to acquire more powerful teeth or claws, or to become adapted to obtain and digest new kinds of food, as circumstances may require. By his superior sympathetic and moral feelings, he becomes fitted for the social state; he ceases to plunder the weak and helpless of his tribe; he shares the game which he has caught with less active or less fortunate hunters, or exchanges it for weapons which even the sick or the deformed can fashion; he saves the sick and wounded from death; and thus the power which leads to the rigid destruction of all animals who cannot in every respect help themselves, is prevented from acting on him.

This power is 'natural selection'; and, as by no other means can it be shewn that individual variations can ever become accumulated and rendered permanent so as to form well-marked races, it follows that the differences we now behold in mankind must have been produced before he became possessed of a human intellect or human sympathies. This view also renders possible, or even requires, the existence of man at a comparatively remote geological epoch. For, during the long periods in which other animals have been undergoing modification in their whole structure to such an amount as to constitute distinct genera and families, man's *body* will have remained generically, or even specifically, the same, while his *head* and *brain* alone will have undergone modification equal to theirs. We can thus understand how it is that, judging from the head and brain, Professor Owen places man in a distinct sub-class of mammalia, while, as regards the rest of his body, there is the closest anatomical resemblance to that of the anthropoid apes, 'every tooth, every bond, strictly homologous – which makes the determination of the difference between *Homo* and *Pithecus* the anatomist's difficulty'. The present theory fully recognises and accounts for these facts; and we may perhaps claim as corroborative of its truth, that it neither requires us to depreciate the intellectual chasm which separates man from the apes, nor refuses full recognition of the striking resemblances to them which exist in other parts of its structure.

In concluding this brief sketch of a great subject, I would point out its bearing upon the future of the human race. If my conclusions are just, it must inevitably follow that the higher – the more intellectual and moral – must displace the lower and more degraded races; and the power of 'natural selection', still acting on his mental organisation, must ever lead to the more perfect adaptation of man's higher faculties to the conditions of surrounding nature, and to the exigencies of the social state. While his external form will probably ever remain unchanged, except in the development of that perfect beauty which results from a healthy and well organised body, refined and ennobled by the highest intellectual faculties and sympathetic emotions, his mental constitution may continue to advance and improve till the world is again inhabited by a single homogeneous race, no individual of which will be inferior to the noblest specimens of existing humanity.* Each one will then work out his own happiness in relation to that of his fellows; perfect freedom of action will be maintained, since the well balanced moral faculties will never permit any one to transgress on the equal freedom of others; restrictive laws will not be wanted, for each man will be guided by the best of laws; a thorough appreciation of the rights, and a perfect sympathy with the feelings, of all about him; compulsory government will have died away as unnecessary (for every man will know how to govern himself), and will be replaced by voluntary associations for all beneficial public purposes; the passions and animal propensities will be restrained within those limits which most conduce to happiness; and mankind will have at length discovered that it was only required of them to develop the capacities of their higher nature, in order to convert this earth, which had so long been the theatre of their unbridled passions, and the scene of unimaginable misery, into as bright a paradise as ever haunted the dreams of seer or poet.

*In the 1870 reprint of his paper Wallace replaced the rest of the paragraph with the following new one:

Our progress towards such a result is very slow, but it still seems to be a progress. We are just now living at an abnormal period of the world's history, owing to the marvellous developments and vast practical results of science having been given to societies too low morally and intellectually to know how to make the best use of them, and to whom they have consequently been curses as well as blessings. Among civilised nations at the present day it does not seem possible for natural selection to act in any way, so as to secure the permanent advancement of morality and intelligence; for it is indisputably the mediocre, if not the low, both as regards morality and intelligence, who succeed best in life and multiply fastest. Yet there is undoubtedly an advance – on the whole a steady and a permanent one – both in the influence on public opinion of a high morality, and in the general desire for intellectual elevation; and as I cannot impute this in any way to 'survival of the fittest', I am forced to conclude that it is due to the inherent progressive power of those glorious qualities which raise us so immeasurably above our fellow animals, and at the same time afford us the surest proof that there are other and higher existences than ourselves, from whom these qualities may have been derived, and towards whom we may be ever tending.

(From A.R. Wallace (1870) 'The development of human races under the law of natural selection', in *Natural Selection and Tropical Nature: Essays on Descriptive and Theoretical Biology,* London, Macmillan, 1891, p.185)

B8   Alfred Russel Wallace, Notes of a séance with Miss Nicholl, 1866

From A.R. Wallace (1867) *Spiritual Magazine,* new ser., vol.2, pp.51–2.

On Friday morning, December 14th [1866], my sister, Mrs S., had a message purporting to be from her deceased brother William, to this effect: 'Go into the dark at Alfred's this evening, and I will shew that I am with you.' On arriving in the evening with Mrs [sic] N. my sister told me of this message. When our other friends, four in number, had arrived, we sat down as usual, but instead of having raps on the table as on previous occasions, the room and table shook violently; and finding we had no manifestations, I mentioned the message that had been received, and we all adjourned into the next room, and the doors and windows being shut, sat round the table, (which we had previously cleared of books, etc.) holding each other's hands. Raps soon began, and we were told to withdraw from the table. This we did, but thinking it better to see how we were placed before beginning the *séance*, I rose up to turn on the gas, which was down to a blue point, when just as my hand was reaching it the medium who was close to me cried out and started, saying that something cold and wet was thrown in her face. This caused her to tremble violently, and I took her hand to calm her, and it struck me this was done to prevent me lighting the gas. We then sat still, and in a few moments several of the party said faintly that something was appearing on the table. The medium saw a hand, others what seemed flowers. These became more distinct, and some one put his hand on the table and said, 'There *are* flowers here.' Obtaining a light, we were all thunderstruck to see the table half covered with fern leaves, all fresh, cold, and damp, as if they had that moment been brought out of the night air. They were ordinary winter flowers which are cultivated in hot houses, for table decoration, the stems apparently cut off as if for a bouquet. They consisted of fifteen chrysanthemums, six variegated anemones, four tulips, five orange-berried solanums, six ferns of two sorts, one *Auricula sinensis* with nine flowers, thirty-seven stalks in all. All present had been engaged for some time in investigating spiritualism, and had no motive for deceiving the others, even if that were possible, which all agreed it was not. If flowers had been brought in and concealed by any of the party (who had all been in the warm room at least an hour) they could not possibly have retained their perfect freshness, coldness, and dewy moisture they possessed when we first discovered them. I may mention that the door of the back drawing room (where this happened) into the passage was locked inside, and that the only entrance was by the folding doors into the lighted sitting room, and that the flowers appeared unaccompanied by the slightest sound, while all present were gazing intently at the table, just rendered visible by a very faint diffused light entering through the blinds. As a testimony that all present are firmly convinced that the flowers were not on the table when we sat down, and were not placed there by any of those present, I am authorised to give the names and addresses of the whole party:– Miss Nicholl, 76½, Westbourne Grove, W.; Mrs Sims, 76½, Westbourne Grove, W.; Mr H.T. Humphreys, 1, Clifford's Inn, E.C.; Dr Wilmshurst, 22, Priory Road, Kilburn, W.; Mr T. Marshman, 11, Gloucester Crescent, N.W.; Mrs Marshman, 11, Gloucester Crescent, N.W.; A.R. Wallace, 9, St Mark's Crescent, N.W.

B9 Alfred Russel Wallace, Notes of a séance with Miss Nicholl, 1867

From A.R. Wallace (1867) 'Notes of a séance with Miss Nicholl at the house of Mr A.S. — 15th May', *Spiritual Magazine*, new ser., vol.2, pp.254–5.

There were present at this séance the party that sit together weekly, with the addition of a friend who accompanied me. The room was made dark, and we joined hands round the table, when we had a number of interesting phenomena, such as a hand bell rung under the table and then brought up and carried in the air round the circle, touching several of the party and ringing loudly. Several notes were also struck loudly on the piano, and a book was twice brought from the piano and placed on the table with a blow. But by far the most remarkable phenomenon of the evening, and that which I wish in particular to place on record, was the following.

My friend, Mr Smith, who was a perfect stranger to all the rest of the party, sat next the medium and held both her hands, when her chair was drawn away from under her and she was left standing. About a minute afterwards I heard a slight sound, about as much as would be caused by placing a wine glass on the table, accompanied by a movement of the glass chandelier overhead and an exclamation from Miss Nicholl. I saw something dark close in front of me, and putting out my hand felt a chair and a lady's dress, and on procuring a light Miss N. was found seated upon the top of the table with her head just touching the chandelier. The table at which we sat was an ordinary round one, with a centre pillar and tripod feet. Miss Nicholl is tall, stout and very heavy; there were ten persons sitting round the table as closely as possible. Mr Smith, who held Miss N.'s hands, declared that she simply slid away from him, and the next instant was found seated on her chair in the middle of the table, near which there was no other unoccupied chair; she was seated under the glass chandelier, where there was just room for her head, and yet this had been effected instantaneously and noiselessly! If any sceptics read the *Spiritual Magazine*, I beg of them to offer some explanation of this phenomenon. I pledge my word for the reality of the facts, and I maintain, that it implies the manifestation of some strange and preterhuman power. Let those who believe it to be a trick, devote themselves to practise it, and when they are able to succeed in repeating the experiment, *under exactly the same conditions*, I will allow that some far more conclusive proof of the reality of these manifestations is required.

This remarkable phenomenon has now occurred to Miss Nicholl some half dozen times, in different houses in London, and there must be at least twenty persons, of the highest respectability, who can testify to the facts. I call upon them to come forward and confirm my statement with their names and any further particulars they may have noticed, since this is a test experiment perhaps even more conclusive than the flotation of Mr. Home.

B10 Alfred Russel Wallace, Human selection

From A.R. Wallace (1890) 'Human selection', *Fortnightly Review*, vol.48, pp.330–31, 335–6, 337.

It is my firm conviction [...] that, when we have cleansed the Augean stable of our existing social organization, and have made such arrangements that *all* shall contribute their share of either physical or mental labour, and that all workers shall reap the *full* reward of their work, the future of the race will be ensured by those laws of human development that have led to the slow but continuous advance in the higher qualities of human nature. When men and women are alike free to follow their best impulses; when idleness and vicious or useless luxury on the one hand, oppressive labour and starvation on the other, are alike unknown; when all receive the best and most thorough education that the state of civilisation and knowledge at the time will admit; when the standard of public opinion is set by the wisest and the best, and that standard is systematically inculcated on the young; then we shall find that a system of selection will come spontaneously into action which will steadily tend to eliminate the lower and more degraded types of man, and thus continuously raise the average standard of the race. [...] This improvement I believe will certainly be effected through the agency of female choice in marriage. Let us, therefore, consider how this would probably act.

It will be generally admitted that, although many women now remain unmarried from necessity rather than from choice, there are always a considerable number who feel no strong inclination to marriage, and who accept husbands to secure a subsistence or a home of their own rather than from personal affection or sexual emotion. In a society in which women were all pecuniarily independent, were all fully occupied with public duties and intellectual or social enjoyments, and had nothing to gain by marriage as regards material well-being, we may be sure that the number of the unmarried from choice would largely increase. It would probably come to be considered a degradation for any woman to marry a man she could not both love and esteem, and this feeling would supply ample reasons for either abstaining from marriage altogether or delaying it till a worthy and sympathetic husband was encountered. In man, on the other hand, the passion of love is more general, and usually stronger; and as in such a society as is here postulated there would be no way of gratifying this passion but by marriage, almost every woman would receive offers, and thus a powerful selective agency would rest with the female sex. Under the system of education and of public opinion here suggested there can be no doubt how this selection would be exercised. The idle and the selfish would be almost universally rejected. The diseased or the weak in intellect would also usually remain unmarried: while those who exhibited any tendency to insanity or to hereditary disease, or who possessed any congenital deformity would in hardly any case find partners, because it would be considered an offence against society to be the means of perpetuating such diseases or imperfections. [...] This weeding-out system has been the method of natural selection, by which the animal and vegetable worlds have been improved and developed. The survival of the fittest is really the extinction of the unfit. In nature this occurs perpetually on an enormous scale, because, owing to the rapid increase of most organisms, the unfit which are yearly destroyed form a large proportion of those that are born. Under our hitherto imperfect civilisation this wholesome process has been checked as regards mankind; but the check has been the result of the development of the higher attributes of our nature. Humanity – the essentially *human* emotion – has caused us to save the lives of the weak and suffering, of the maimed or imperfect in mind or body. This has to some extent been antagonistic to physical and even intellectual race-improvement; but it has improved us morally by the continuous development of the characteristic and crowning grace of our human, as distinguished from our animal, nature.

In the society of the future this defect will be remedied, not by any diminution of our humanity, but by encouraging the activity of a still higher human characteristic – admiration of all that is beautiful and kindly and self-sacrificing, repugnance to all that is selfish, base, or cruel. When we allow ourselves to be guided by reason, justice, and public spirit in our dealings with our fellow-men, and determine to abolish poverty by recognising the equal rights of all the citizens of our common land to an equal share of the wealth which all combine to produce, – when we have thus solved the lesser problem of a rational social organisation adapted to secure the equal well-being of all, then we may safely leave the far greater and deeper problem of the improvement of the race to the cultivated minds and pure instincts of the Women of the Future.

Section C STUDYING *PYGMALION*

C1 Ovid, *Pygmalion in Love with a Statue*

From *Ovid's Metamorphoses in Latin and English*, bk X, fable IX, vol.I, facsimile of the 1732 edition printed in Amsterdam. Reprinted in *The Renaissance and the Gods: A Comprehensive Collection of Renaissance Mythographies, Iconologies and Iconograhies, with a Selection of Works from The Enlightenment,* New York and London, Garland Publishing Inc., 1976, p.340–42.

The argument

Pygmalion a famous Statuary, provoked by the dissolute Lives of the Propoetides, throws off all Fondness of the Sex, and resolves on a perpetual Celibacy. He afterwards falls in Love with a Statue he had made. Venus, at his Request, animates it; he marries his newly inspired Mistress, and has a Son by her, who built the City of Paphos, which bears the Name of its Founder.

> *Pygmalion* loathing their lascivious Life,
> Abhorr'd all Womankind, but most a Wife:
> So single chose to live, and shunn'd to wed,
> Well pleas'd to want a Consort of his Bed.
> Yet fearing Idleness, the Nurse of Ill,
> In Sculpture exercis'd his happy Skill;
> And carv'd in Iv'ry such a Maid, so fair,
> As Nature could not with his Art compare,
> Were she to work; but in her own Defence
> Must take her Pattern here, and copy hence.
> Pleas'd with his Idol, he commends, admires,
> Adores; and last, the Thing ador'd, desires.
> A very Virgin in her Face was seen,
> And had she mov'd, a living Maid had been:
> One wou'd have thought she cou'd have stirr'd, but Strove
> With Modesty, and was asham'd to move.
> Art hid with Art, so well perform'd the Cheat,
> It caught the Carver with his own Deceit:
> He knows, 'tis Madness, yet he must adore,
> And still the more he knows it, loves the more:
> The Flesh, or what so seems, he touches oft,
> Which feels so smooth, that he believes it soft.
> Fir'd with this Thought, at once he strain'd the Breast,
> And on the Lips a burning Kiss impress'd.
> 'Tis true, the harden'd Breast resists the Gripe,
> And the cold Lips return a Kiss unripe:
> But when, retiring back, he look'd again,
> To think it Iv'ry, was a Thought too mean:
> So wou'd believe she kiss'd, and courting more,
> Again embrac'd her naked Body o'er;

And straining hard the Statue, was afraid
His Hands had made a Dint, and hurt his Maid:
Explor'd her Limb by Limb, and fear'd to find
So rude a Gripe had left a livid Mark behind:
With Flatt'ry now he seeks her Mind to move,
And now with Gifts, (the pow'rful Bribes of Love:)
He furnishes her Closet first; and fills
The crowded Shelves with Rarities of Shells;
Adds Orient Pearls, which from the Conchs he drew,
And all the sparkling Stones of various Hue:
And Parrots, imitating Human Tongue,
And Singing-birds in Silver Cages hung;
And ev'ry fragrant Flow'r, and od'rous Green
Were sorted well, with Lumps of Amber laid between;
Rich fashionable Robes her Person deck,
Pendants her Ears, and Pearls adorn her Neck:
Her taper'd Fingers too with Rings are grac'd,
And an embroider'd Zone surrounds her slender Waste.
Thus like a Queen array'd, so richly dress'd,
Beauteous she shew'd, but naked shew'd the best.
Then, from the Floor, he rais'd a Royal Bed,
With Cov'rings of *Sidonian* Purple spread:
The solemn Rites perform'd, he calls her Bride,
With Blandishments invites her to his Side;
And as she were with vital Sense possess'd,
Her Head did on a plumy Pillow rest.

The Feast of *Venus* came, a solemn Day,
To which the *Cypriots* due Devotion pay;
With gilded Horns the Milk-white Heifers led,
Slaughter'd before the sacred Altars, bled:

Pygmalion off'ring, first, approach'd the Shrine,
And then with Pray'rs implor'd the Pow'rs Divine;
'Almighty Gods, if all we Mortals want,
'If all we can require, be yours to grant;
'Make this fair Statue mine, he wou'd have said,
'But chang'd his Words for Shame; and only pray'd,
'Give me the Likeness of my Iv'ry Maid.

The Golden Goddess, present at the Pray'r,
Well knew he meant th' inanimated Fair,
And gave the Sign of granting his Desire;
For thrice in chearful Flames ascends the Fire.
The Youth, returning to his Mistress, hies,
And impudent in Hope, with ardent Eyes,
And beating Breast, by the dear Statue lies.
He kisses her white Lips, renews the Bliss,
And looks, and thinks they redden at the Kiss;
He thought them warm before: Nor longer stays,
But next his Hand on her hard Bosom lays:

Hard as it was, beginning to relent,
It seem'd, the Breast beneath his Fingers bent;
He felt again, his Fingers made a Print,
'Twas Flesh, but Flesh so firm, it rose against the Dint:
The pleasing Task he fails not to renew;
Soft, and more soft at ev'ry Touch it grew;
Like pliant Wax, when chafing Hands reduce
The former Mass to Form, and frame for Use.
He would believe, but yet is still in Pain
And tries his Argument of Sense again,
Presses the Pulse, and feels the leaping Vein.
Convinc'd, o'erjoy'd, his studied Thanks, and Praise,
To her, who made the Miracle, he pays:
The Lips to Lips he join'd; now freed from Fear,
He found the Savour of the Kiss sincere:
At this the waken'd Image op'd her Eyes,
And view'd at once the Light, and Lover with Surprize.
The Goddess present at the Match she made,
So bless'd the Bed, such Fruitfulness convey'd,
That e're ten Months had sharpen'd either Horn,
To crown their Bliss, a lovely Boy was born;
Paphos his Name, who, grown to Manhood, wall'd
The City *Paphos*, from the Founder call'd.

C2 Lisë Pedersen, 'Shakespeare's *The Taming of the Shrew* vs. Shaw's *Pygmalion*: male chauvinism vs. women's lib?'

From R. Weintraub (ed.) (1977) *Fabian Feminist: Bernard Shaw and Woman*, Pennsylvania State University Press, pp.77–85.

Shaw's comparisons of himself to Shakespeare and his frequent, explicit and often extravagant criticisms of Shakespeare are so prominent a part of his critical writings as to be familiar to everyone who knows anything at all about Shaw. Nevertheless, critics have for the most part failed to notice that these same criticisms are often indirectly expressed in Shaw's plays through his handling of characters and situations similar to characters and situations handled in quite different ways by Shakespeare. To be sure, implicit criticisms of *Julius Caesar* and *Antony and Cleopatra* occurring in *Caesar and Cleopatra* have been widely noted and commented upon; indeed, they could hardly have been overlooked since Shaw himself points them out and discusses them under the heading 'Better than Shakespeare?' in the preface to his play. In a number of other cases, however, Shaw deals with fictitious characters who, though bearing different names and occurring in different ages, are nevertheless in themselves or in their situations so similar to characters and situations depicted by Shakespeare that it is difficult to believe that Shaw's depiction was not, whether consciously or unconsciously so, suggested by Shakespeare's. In these cases the similarities of depiction establish the relationship between the two plays but the differences in treatment illustrate one or more of the major criticisms which Shaw has elsewhere made of Shakespeare.

Basic to all Shaw's criticisms of Shakespeare is Shaw's belief that the purpose of drama is 'to force the public to reconsider its morals' and that Shakespeare, except in the three 'problem' comedies and possibly in *Hamlet*, makes no attempt to fulfill this purpose. Quite the contrary, in most of his plays he is content to dramatize a conventional, 'reach-me-down,' or 'readymade' morality instead of working out an original morality as Shaw believed any writer of the 'first order in literature' must do. Two plays which illustrate this fundamental difference in the approach of the two playwrights to a similar situation are *The Taming of the Shrew* and *Pygmalion*. Indeed, Shaw's working out of the central situation of the two plays is so diametrically opposed to that of Shakespeare that *Pygmalion* seems deliberately designed to challenge and contradict Shakespeare's handling of this central situation.

The similarities in the two plays are readily apparent. In both plays a man accepts the task of transforming a woman from one kind of person to another, radically different kind. In both plays the man who undertakes this task is an overbearing bully. Petruchio consistently plays the role of a bully in his relationship with Kate, and it is, indeed, the means by which he transforms her from a quarrelsome shrew to a sweet-tempered and obedient wife. Not only does he frustrate her every wish, but he subjects her to mental anguish in the humiliation brought upon her by his attire and behavior at their wedding and to physical abuse in causing her horse to dump her into the mud, in preventing her from sleeping night after night, and in keeping food from her with the declared intention of starving her into submission.

Though Higgins does not resort to physical abuse of Eliza, except for a moment in the last act when he completely loses control of himself as a result of her taunts, he nevertheless does bully Eliza in every other way, ordering her about in a very brusque manner without the slightest concern for her feelings and uttering threats of physical violence which in the early stages of their acquaintance she takes quite seriously. In the act 2 interview in his flat, when Eliza has first come to inquire about taking elocution lessons from Higgins, his treatment of her is extremely rude and abusive. He orders her '*peremptorily*' to sit down, and when she does not do so immediately he repeats the order, '*thundering*' it at her. When she interrupts his speculations about the price she has offered for the lessons, he barks out, 'Hold your tongue,' and when as a consequence of those speculations and of his rudeness, she begins to cry, he threatens, 'Somebody is going to touch you, with a broomstick, if you dont stop snivelling.' Immediately upon deciding to undertake the challenge to transform her into a duchess, Higgins begins to issue orders to Mrs. Pearce about giving Eliza a bath, disinfecting her, and burning all her clothes, without consulting Eliza at all, just as though she had nothing to say in the matter, and as Eliza begins to protest he tells Mrs. Pearce, 'If she gives you any trouble, wallop her.' Pickering's objection to Higgins's rudeness – 'Does it occur to you, Higgins, that the girl has some feelings?' – elicits the quite serious reply from Higgins, 'Oh no, I dont think so. Not any feelings that we need bother about.' Subsequently Higgins adds that Pickering ought to realize from his military experience that there is no use trying to explain matters to Eliza, who is too ignorant to understand any such explanation, and that therefore the proper treatment of her is simply to 'Give her her orders: thats enough for her.' Furthermore, in act 5 Higgins calls Eliza, among other things, one of the 'squashed cabbage leaves of Covent Garden' and a 'damned impudent slut,' and instead of inviting her to come back to Wimpole Street he orders her to do so: 'Get up and come home; and dont be a fool.' Thus he demonstrates that his bullying treatment of her has not changed in the course of the play, though she has in that time changed into an entirely different person from what she was at the beginning of the play.

Petruchio and Higgins are alike, then, in being bullies, though they are different in that Higgins does not resort to physical abuse and in that the motivation behind their bullying tactics is different. Petruchio has deliberately adopted such tactics in order to 'tame' Kate in the same way that he would tame a falcon, as he reveals in a soliloquy:

> Thus have I politicly begun my reign,
> And 'tis my hope to end successfully.
> My falcon now is sharp and passing empty,
> And till she stoop, she must not be full gorged,
> For then she never looks upon her lure.
> Another way I have to man my haggard,
> To make her come and know her keeper's call,
> That is, to watch her, as we watch these kites
> That bate, and beat, and will not be obedient.

On the other hand, Higgins's bullying treatment of Eliza is merely his natural way of behaving toward people and is not a special behavior adopted in connection with the task of transforming Eliza. On the contrary, as he insists to her, his behavior toward all people is the same:

> The great secret, Eliza, is not having bad manners or good manners or any other particular sort of manners, but having the same manner for all human souls.

A number of similarities in the development of the basic plot by the two dramatists are easily discernible. In each case a test is set up to determine the success of the transformation of the woman in question: in Shakespeare's play the test compares Kate's response to an order of her husband's with the responses of Bianca and the Widow to similar orders of their husbands, and in Shaw's play the test involves passing Eliza off as a duchess at an ambassador's garden party. In each case there is a wager on the outcome of the test. And in each case the transformation of the woman succeeds beyond anyone's expectations and she passes the test with ease. [...]

In examining the differences between Shakespeare's and Shaw's handling of the basic plot of *The Taming of the Shrew* and *Pygmalion*, it is instructive to keep in mind the principal criticisms which Shaw made of *The Taming of the Shrew*. In June 1888, he wrote the *Pall Mall Gazette* a letter signed with a woman's name, Horatia Ribbonson, asking 'all men and women who respect one another' to boycott *The Taming of the Shrew*; describing Shakespeare's Petruchio as a 'coarse, thick-skinned money hunter, who sets to work to tame his wife exactly as brutal people tame animals or children – that is, by breaking their spirit by domineering cruelty'; and complaining that Katherine's 'degrading speech' to Bianca and the Widow to the effect that 'thy husband is thy lord, thy life, thy keeper, / Thy head, thy sovereign' might have been acceptable to 'an audience of bullies' in 'an age when woman was a mere chattel,' but should be intolerable to a modern audience. Nine years later Shaw said virtually the same thing in a *Saturday Review* article. Though he praised the realism of the early acts of the play, particularly in the depiction of Petruchio's selfishness and brutality, he complained that Shakespeare was unable to maintain this realism throughout the play and that the last scene is so 'disgusting to modern sensibility' that 'no man with any decency of feeling can sit it out in the company of a woman without being extremely ashamed of the lord-of-creation moral implied in the wager and the speech put into the woman's own mouth.'

The attitudes toward woman – and toward man, for that matter – implicit in these criticisms are reflected in the differences between Shaw's working out of the *Pygmalion* plot and Shakespeare's working out of the plot of *The Taming of the Shrew*. These differences are principally in the methods by which the woman is transformed and in the final attitudes of the man and the woman toward each other.

At first glance it may seem that a comparison of the methods used to transform the women cannot be valid since the qualities requiring transformation were not of the same kind in both cases, Kate's case involving a change of such psychological qualities as temper and temperament and Eliza's involving changes in qualities which seem much more superficial – speech, dress and awareness of the rules of etiquette. It should be noted, however, that although Eliza was not shrewish at the beginning of her play, she was completely lacking in self-control, very quick to take offense, and very bad-tempered in her reaction to offenses, real or imagined, so that a mere change in speech, dress and superficial manners could not have transformed her into a lady. Like Kate, she too had to learn self-control and consideration for others. Once she has successfully made all the changes necessary to transform her into a woman who can pass for a duchess, Eliza herself recognizes that the acquiring of self-restraint was by far the most important of these changes. She speaks slightingly of Higgins's accomplishment in teaching her to speak correctly, maintaining that 'it was just like learning to dance in the fashionable way: there was nothing more than that in it,' and tells Pickering that her 'real education' came from him because he provided her with the example of self-restraint and consideration for others:

> You see it was so very difficult for me with the example of Professor Higgins always before me. I was brought up to be just like him, unable to control myself, and using bad language on the slightest provocation. And I should never have known that ladies and gentlemen didnt behave like that if you hadnt been there.

This speech expresses a direct repudiation of the method by which Shakespeare allows Petruchio to 'tame' Kate, because it asserts that the example of bad-tempered, uncontrolled behavior can only bring about behavior of the same kind in the learner, not a change to sweet-tempered reasonableness such as Kate exhibits. Furthermore, as Eliza continues her indirect attack on Higgins's methods through her praise of Pickering's treatment of her, she insists to Pickering that the real beginning of her transformation came with 'your calling me Miss Doolittle that day when I first came to Wimpole Street. That was the beginning of self-respect for me.' This statement is a criticism of Higgins, who calls her 'Eliza' from the first – that is, when he is not calling her 'this baggage,' 'presumptuous insect' or the like – but it also recalls the fact that Petruchio, on first meeting Kate, calls her 'Kate,' though, except for her sister, her family and acquaintances all call her by the more formal 'Katherina' or 'Katherine'. In addition, Kate herself rebukes Petruchio for calling her 'Kate,' asserting that 'they call me Katherine that do talk of me,' whereupon he replies with a speech in which he uses the name 'Kate' eleven times in six lines:

> You lie, in faith, for you are called plain Kate,
> And bonny Kate, and sometimes Kate the Curst;
> But Kate, the prettiest Kate in Christendom,
> Kate of Kate-Hall, my superdainty Kate,
> For dainties are all Kates – and therefore, Kate,
> Take this of me, Kate of my consolation:

This perverse insistence on using the familiar, informal name which she has asked him not to use is paralleled by Higgins's reply to Eliza's request that he call her 'Miss Doolittle': 'I'll see you damned first.' Thus, again, Eliza's criticism of Higgins's method of dealing with her is also a criticism of Petruchio's method of dealing with Kate.

Moreover, a repudiation of physical abuse as a means of dominating a woman's spirit is implied by the fact that in *Pygmalion* physical abuse plays no part in transforming Eliza, but instead appears in the play solely as the feeble, ineffectual and unintentional response of Higgins to Eliza's freeing of herself from his domination. When Eliza, realizing that Higgins will never treat her as she wants to be treated and therefore searching desperately for some means by which she can free herself from dependence on him, hits on the idea of becoming an assistant to a teacher of phonetics whom Higgins considers a quack, Higgins lays hands on her to strike her, and is deterred from doing so only by her triumphant nonresistance. Milton Crane construes this loss of self-control on Higgins's part as an indication that 'his confusion is complete' and therefore 'Galatea has subdued Pygmalion.' Thus, instead of being the means to domination, as it is in *The Taming of the Shrew*, in *Pygmalion* the resort to physical abuse is an admission of defeat, a reaction of frustrated rage to the failure to dominate.

In addition to these differences in the method by which the transformation of the woman is achieved, the other major differences in the working out of the plot by the two playwrights are in the final attitudes of the teacher and the learner to one another. Kate's final attitude to Petruchio is shown not only by her instant obedience to him, but also by the speech which Shaw criticized as 'degrading,' a speech in which she says that in a marriage the husband is the 'lord,' 'king,' 'governor,' 'life,' 'keeper,' 'head,' and 'sovereign' of the wife and that the wife owes her husband 'such duty as the subject owes the prince,' and in which she consequently urges her sisters-in-law to follow her example by placing their hands below their husbands' feet as a token of their willingness to obey their husbands. Eliza's final attitude to Higgins is the direct opposite of Kate's to Petruchio. She exults in having achieved her freedom from his domination:

> Aha! Thats done you, Henry Higgins, it has. Now I dont care that [*snapping her fingers*] for your bullying and your big talk. ... Oh, when I think of myself crawling under your feet and being trampled on and called names, when all the time I had only to lift up my finger to be as good as you, I could just kick myself.

The reference to her former 'crawling' under his feet and 'being trampled on' even seems to be a verbal echo of Kate's reference to placing her hand below her husband's foot as a token of her submission to him. Certainly, here, at the conclusion of *Pygmalion*, there is a deliberate repudiation of the idea of male domination of the female which underlies the theme of *The Taming of the Shrew*.

Furthermore, that this repudiation is not simply Eliza's view, but is the view set forth by the play, is suggested by the fact that Higgins shares it. Though he has a habit of expecting that Eliza – and everyone else, for that matter – should automatically fall in with his plans because in his view his plans naturally offer the most proper and sensible course of action open to everyone, Higgins has never consciously desired to make Eliza subservient to him, whereas Petruchio has, of course, expressly declared that the whole purpose of his strange and violent behavior is to make Kate subservient to him. Indeed, Higgins brands the conventionally expected acts of subservience on the part of women toward men as 'Commercialism,' attempts to buy affection. He tells Eliza:

I dont and wont trade in affection. You call me a brute because you couldnt buy a claim on me by fetching my slippers and finding my spectacles. You were a fool: I think a woman fetching a man's slippers is a disgusting sight: did I ever fetch your slippers? I think a good deal more of you for throwing them in my face. No use slaving for me and then saying you want to be cared for: who cares for a slave? If you come back, come back for the sake of good fellowship ... and if you dare to set up your little dog's tricks of fetching and carrying slippers against my creation of a Duchess Eliza, I'll slam the door in your silly face.

And after Eliza has declared her independence of Higgins, he says:

You damned impudent slut, you! But it's better than snivelling; better than fetching slippers and finding spectacles, isnt it? ... By George, Eliza, I said I'd make a woman of you; and I have. I like you like this.

At the conclusion of *Pygmalion*, then, both Eliza and Higgins reject the concept of male dominance over women, a concept which is not only supported but actually exalted by the conclusion of *The Taming of the Shrew*.

In supporting this concept in *The Taming of the Shrew* Shakespeare was, of course, supporting the conventional morality of his own day, and in rejecting this concept in *Pygmalion* Shaw was rejecting the conventional morality of his own day and substituting for it an original view of morality. Thus Shaw clearly used his play not only to repudiate the male chauvinism of his day and Shakespeare's and to support women's liberation, a cause for which he was an early pioneer, but also to dramatize a criticism which was fundamental to all Shaw's complaints about Shakespeare and which Shaw had often expressed in very explicit terms in his critical writings – that Shakespeare failed to create and espouse an original morality in opposition to the conventional morality of his time.

Section D *MEDEA*

D1 Reviews of a modern theatre performance of *Medea* at the Lyric, Hammersmith, 1986

From *The Guardian*, 1 June 1986, *Today*, 4 June 1986, *The Observer*, 8 June 1986.

The Guardian, 1 June 1986

Mary McMurray succumbs to the present directorial craze for reviving Euripides' Medea with a production rather lost in a contemporary no man's land. It is high on sound and decoration, but never governed or goaded by the kind of pathological fury which would explain Medea's murder of her two children and the poisoning of the woman Jason has chosen to succeed her.

It is true that the production begins with one huge dividend – the Indian actress Madhur Jaffrey, ideally suited to play the 'Asian' outcast in Greece, but Miss Jaffrey, adorned in black with scarlet linings, large weighty ear rings and a fixed expression of angry disdain, turns out to be all adagio and a smouldering – a rocket which refuses to go off, though she sparks beautifully.

Jane Martin's set, a white and ochre facade of a windowless Greek temple, is initially the rendezvous for a troop of tourists, who gather with their cameras and their amplified transistors, until the light fades and at a blank window there appears an ancient shawled figure, as if the myths and memories of other centuries were indelibly inscribed upon contemporary times. But this rivetting scene is like a single illumination.

For Richard Blackford's eerie, repetitive music, in the tones of Philip Glass, introduces us to a slightly banal Greece – the chorus reduced to a thoroughly modern Lynn Farleigh, the Nurse smart in modern white. As if to suggest the way in which the play belongs both to now and to a distant past Miss McMurray arrays the two monarchs in modern suits and a bizarrely uniform jewellery, large rings on gloved hands, gold baubles at the chest. And the music, whether woodwind and piano or great crashing blasts of sound to mark the act of infanticide becomes an accompanying melodramatic accessory.

The effect of these devices is not very powerful, even though Miss Jaffrey exudes a kind of pained desolation. She always looks daggers but fails to plunge the knife. Hers is a performance which I fancy would function better on film, since physically speaking there is too much leisure, poise and relaxation about her playing. Her face tells a different, tragic story, and when Julian Glover seems almost to become dizzy and disorientated with grief one catches an idea of potential squandered: the tutor in track suit and a scarlet hued Messenger, squatting to tell of catastrophe, are redolent of a theatre of camp and gesture rather than one of classical potency.

The translation by Philip Vellacott, who has produced several of the Penguin classic texts, seems a further obstacle. Mr Vellacott's translation, which has been followed with blind faithfulness, adopts graceless, antiquated idiom, which sinks to bathos, strange syntactic order and an awkwardness which inhibits a brave cast. And Miss Jaffrey, last seen with a head-dress of serpents, exultant and mad, is finally breathtaking.

Today, 4 June 1986

Greek tragedy is very old and can be very boring. It is stuffed with myths you may not know and Gods you certainly won't worship. The characters can seem remote, the language over-blown, and the most exciting action always happens off stage.

But occasionally a production comes along which will remove 2,500 years of cobwebs and make the plays live again. Euripides' *Medea*, at London's Lyric Hammersmith Theatre, is one of them.

It is not without excesses and won't be to everyone's taste. But for vigour of acting, design and direction, it deserves high praise.

Medea is the story of a woman who gives up everything for love, and then has the love thrown back at her. But rather than contact her solicitors, Medea finds another way of getting back at the man who has spurned her. She murders their two sons. 'Why?' he asks. 'To break your heart,' she replies. Her behaviour is extraordinary but, in Madhur Jaffrey's performance, never unbelievable.

The only real disappointment is Philip Vellacott's translation. Plodding and clichéd, it is as poetic as a letter from the DHSS. 'Life has been cruel to me!' comments Medea, moments before she butchers her children. It hardly sums up her anguish.

The production's final miracle is that, despite such banalities, it is still a thrilling theatrical experience.

The Observer, 8 June 1986

I have saved the worst till last. I had thought that nothing this year could be worse than Jan Fabre's 'The Power of Theatrical Madness' at the Albert Hall, but Medea at the Lyric Hammersmith rivals even the mind-numbing qualities of Belgian performance art. For a production to be as fascinatingly bad as this one it needs to be ambitious, which Mary McMurray's certainly is, and preferably to approach the blackest tragedy with unintentionally comic effects.

I heard a murmered sigh behind me of 'Oh dear' as the lights went up on a tourist beach in modern Greece, full of laughing young tourists carrying noisy radios, laughing and flirting as a black-shawled figure appears ominously in a window above. There is nothing intrinsically wrong with this, although it suggests more than it delivers, nor does the use of elements of pop-culture style necessarily spell disaster for Euripides – but this production is an object for any director tempted by flashy and irrelevant effects.

The production has aimed at a breezy contemporary relevance, so the royal tutor wanders on wearing a sweat band and jogging clothes; Creon comes on like Michael Jackson in dark glasses and one black glove; Jason as an ageing juvenile delinquent with metal-studded arm band. Madhur Jaffrey's Medea creates an interesting stir on first entrance because she appears to be Chinese, although the pig tail and highcoat are in fact the all-purpose dress of a barbarian princess.

In other circumstances, in a much quieter and more sensitive production, Jaffrey could have made an interesting Medea. Here, asked for stridency she sounds merely petulant, droning with a constant sob in her voice and a manner that sounds oddly conversational: when she says 'I will make Jason's whole house a shambles' it sounds as if she's planning to muss it up a little.

In the end the chief villain was the amplification. In recognition of the fact that all the great and bloody events will take place off-stage, McMurray has arranged for us to hear it through huge loudspeakers at the side, off the stage. It would take an actress of god-like talent to transcend a production where the audience is deafened with the off-stage sounds of murder: 'Mama no! Aghhh! Glug, glug … choke.' The audience rippled slightly in embarrassment, and as the lights went up had the white and confused look of people who don't quite know what to say.

D2 Ruth Hazel, 'Monsters and stars: *Medea* in a modern context'

From *CA News*, December 1994, No. 11, pp.2–3. The Classical Association may be contacted at PO Box 38, Alresford, Hants, SO24 02Q.

Early this year, in the first of her Reith lectures (*Managing Monsters*), Marina Warner considered some modern re-creations of mythical female monsters. She suggested that in contrast to pre-feminist butts of misogyny (women as seductive, rapacious, devious man-hunters), the late twentieth-century 'monstrous women' are, typically, those who deny the need for men in their lives, who reject motherhood, or, conversely, elect to be lone parents.

Euripides' Medea combines elements of both kinds of 'female monster': she has a history, outside the play, of murderous deviousness; she is a predator, imagistically described as a ferocious wild animal which, by implication, has its claws in Jason, and will not let go without drawing blood. Yet the Chorus – with a kind of horrified awe – remarks what she is doing for women generally; she is right to protest and resent Jason's political marriage, and his consequent rejection of her. Both in standing for her rights as wife and woman, and in the 'heroic' scale of her protest, she will force the rivers of convention and normality to run uphill. For her audience, as for her Choric observers, manifestations of Medea's 'otherness' such as her foreign exile status, her sorcery, her sexual possessiveness, all pale into relative insignificance beside the supreme expression of her difference from human (female) normalcy – the murder of her sons. Yet, in performance, her explanation of her reasons for this monstrous behaviour should charismatically engage our sympathy, even while the deed itself repulses it. As a villainess, Medea should have heroic stature and star quality.

Not surprisingly, modern actresses have found the role attractive. Pasolini's 1970 film version starred Maria Callas giving a 'virtual mime performance' (Tony Rayns, *Time Out Film Guide 1989*), and, in 1978, Jules Dassin's *A Dream of Passion* (which Paul Taylor in the *Time Out Film Guide* described as 'nightmare of pretension) juxtaposed Melina Mercouri as an actress playing Medea with Ellen Burstyn as a triple infanticide religious fanatic. The play is regularly revived in live theatre (the last issue of *CA News* carried a review of Shoestring Theatre's touring production) and the most recent 'star vehicle' production was Jonathan Kent's for the Almeida, with Diana Rigg in the title role. A BBC2 programme (7/7/94) followed this production from its close at the London Haymarket to its opening on Broadway on 7/4/94; a transfer seen as a considerable gamble. How would Broadway respond to an ancient Greek tragedy, played without interval, with some sung sections, but no songs, a Chorus, but no chorus-line, and only one really well-known, and English, actor? (Diana Rigg is no stranger to acting dangerously; quite apart from her run as Emma Peel in *The Avengers*, she appeared in one of the earliest nude scenes in late twentieth-century drama (in *Abelard and Heloise*), and had the chutzpah to include a review of her performance in that play – 'Diana Rigg is built like a brick mausoleum with insufficient flying buttresses' – in her anthology of terrible reviews, *No Turn Unstoned*, 1982.) In the event, *Medea* scored a notable success on Broadway, despite a disastrous malfunction of the set on the opening night. The production was hailed as a triumph by the *New York Times*, and Rigg as a 'mighty Medea ... full of blazing intelligence and elegant ferocity'.

Jonathan Kent's production does not make Medea a spectacular and fantastic monster. Her final flight, for example, is not by dragon-powered chariot, but suggested by wind machine and a cyclorama full of rolling clouds. Diana Rigg's Medea is elegant rather than exotic. One feels that the poison on Creusa's gifts is the product of advanced pharmacology rather than witchcraft. Medea's foreign or barbarian 'otherness' is not stressed, as it has been with success in past productions. In 1983, Barney Simon's production of Franz Grillparzer's *Medea* premiered at The Space Theatre in Cape Town before touring to the Edinburgh Traverse, and then The Riverside in London. With Yvonne Bryceland as a moving Medea, this version used the race/colour conflict to provide commentary on the Greek/barbarian division. In 1986, the Lyric, Hammersmith, production (directed by Mary McMurray) had Madhur Jaffrey as a 'passionate alien brushed aside as an exotic plaything' (David Nice, *Plays & Players*, August 1986), and in the 1991 Manchester Royal Exchange production (directed by Phyllida Lloyd), Claire Benedict was an immensely powerful black Medea, whose foreignness, as a voodoo sorceress, and sexual jealousy were strongly signalled. The M.R.E. production also capitalised on textual references to Medea's Sun ancestry, with circular design and Chorus movement.

Another way of approaching Medea's 'otherness' is to see the play in terms of gender opposition, as Tony Harrison did in his 1985 script for a projected New York Metropolitan Opera Company production, *Medea – A Sex-War Opera*. Jason (like Hippolytus – and, indeed, like Posthumus in Shakespeare's *Cymbeline*) expresses male fear of woman's dangerous passionate potential in a perverse wish that it could be possible to continue the human race (all-male, presumably) without involving women. Though Kent's *Medea* does not fully exploit this theme (which has implications for the playing of Aegeus – is he Medea's dupe, or a genuine friend? In this production one was not sure), it does succeed in showing Creon, Jason and Aegeus as cogs in as well as upholders of the patriarchal machine. All have to put political considerations first; all are vulnerable through their children (in Aegeus's case, his child-to-be). The three men are dressed in slightly 'broken-down' costumes of drab, thick material which contrast (as do the Greek villager black and greys of the three Chorus women) with Medea's colour-coded (red, white, white spattered with red) chic. This Medea has style, intelligence, strength of character; it does not matter so much that there is no great feel of past sexual chemistry between her and Jason, since her motivation comes less from rejected love than from a sense that she is being demoted, almost 'disappeared' by the man for whom she has given up family and home. A voluntary exile from her fatherland, rejected as wife and lover, the remaining role by which she is defined is as the mother of sons. Diana Rigg's Medea redefines herself by her terrible decision, even if that definition shows that to be a woman is to be able to take life as well as give it, to inflict pain as well as to give pleasure.

Whether Medea is irretrievably monstrous is just one of a number of issues in the play which have resonance and relevance for the late twentieth century. They are issues which may fruitfully be investigated in performance, not just in productions of 'straight translations', but through versions and re-creations of the play. In 1992, *Antigone* provided the stimulus for an exciting RSC performance project involving new writers and young people from around Britain. *Medea* would seem to offer great potential for a similar young theatre sortie into myth.

D3 Lysias 1.6–10

From J.P. Sabben-Clare and M.S. Warman (eds) (1978) *The Culture of Athens* LACTOR 12, Lact Publications, Text CA129, p.49.

Lysias (*c.*459–380 BCE) was a distinguished forensic orator, who wrote speeches for litigants in the Athenian courts. This extract is from a speech written for a man attempting to defend himself against a charge of killing his wife's seducer. Although it is not an objective source – the defendant obviously has a strong motive for presenting the facts in a particular way – it nevertheless throws some light on relations between the sexes in Classical Athens.

> When I decided to marry, gentlemen, and brought a wife into the house, I was generally disposed not to harass her or be too repressive about her doing what she wanted, and I looked after her as well as I could and was properly attentive: by the time my child was born, I already had trust in her and I put all my resources at her disposal, thinking this the truest expression of the close tie between us. At first, gentlemen, she was superb – a clever housekeeper, thrifty and exact in her stewardship. It was my mother's death that was the start of my troubles. When she was carried out to burial, my wife went with the cortege, was seen by the defendant and eventually seduced. He used to wait for her maid as she came to market and got messages through to her and brought about her downfall. In the first place I must explain that I have a small house on two floors, of equal size upstairs and downstairs, that is in the women's and the men's quarters. When our child was born, its mother suckled it, and so that she shouldn't risk coming down the stairs whenever she wanted to wash, I started to live upstairs and the women down below. This custom became established, so that my wife often went below to the child to sleep, so that she could give it the breast and stop it crying. This went on for a long time and I never suspected anything but was simple enough to suppose that my wife was the most chaste in town.

D4 Xenophon, Memorabilia 2.2.4–5

From John Ferguson and Kitty Chisholm (eds) (1978) *Political and Social Life in the Great Age of Athens*, London, Open University/Ward Lock Educational, p.147.

Xenophon (*c.*428–*c.*354 BCE) was a soldier and man of letters. His *Memorabilia*, while purporting to provide an account of the life and teachings of the philosopher Socrates, reflect an aristocratic ideal of relations between the sexes, as in this passage.

> Plainly we look for wives who will produce the best children for us, and marry them to raise a family. The husband supports the wife who is to share in the production of his family, and provides in advance whatever he thinks the expected children will find useful for life, on as generous a scale as possible. The wife conceives and bears her burden. She suffers pains and endangers her life; she gives away the food that sustains her. She goes through a period of labour, gives birth and brings up the child with care. She has had no blessing in advance. The baby does not know its helper, and cannot convey its needs. She has to guess what is good for it and will satisfy it, and tries to provide these to the full. She cares for the baby night and day laboriously for a long period, with no expectation of reward.

D5a Demosthenes 59.16 (Quotation of law)

From J.P. Sabben-Clare and M.S. Warman (eds) (1978) *The Culture of Athens*, LACTOR 12, Lact Publications, Text CA97, p.36.

Demosthenes (384–322 BCE) was the greatest Athenian orator of the fourth century. These extracts, like that of Lysias, come from forensic speeches composed for clients. The first, a quotation from a law, illuminates Athenian attitudes to the relationship between citizens (of either sex) and foreigners. The second expresses a commonly-held view about the proper relations between the sexes.

> If an alien man cohabits with a female citizen in any way whatsoever, anyone who wishes and has the right shall indict him before the Thesmothetae. If he is convicted, he and his property shall be sold, and one third given to the successful prosecutor. The same procedure shall be followed if an alien woman lives with a male citizen; if she is convicted, he shall be fined 1000 dr.

D5b Demosthenes 59.122

From J.P. Sabben-Clare and M.S. Warman (eds) (1978) *The Culture of Athens*, LACTOR 12, Lact Publications, Text CA92, p.34.

> Living together means producing children, enrolling sons among clansmen and demesmen and giving away daughters as one's own to husbands. Courtesans we have for pleasure and concubines to satisfy our daily bodily needs, but wives to produce true-born children and to be trustworthy guardians of the household.

D6 Aristophanes, *Frogs*

From K. Mcleish (trans.) (1993) *Aristophanes, Plays: Two*, Methuen, pp.302–4, 347–9, 366–8.

Aristophanes (*c.*457–385 BCE), a comic poet, composed his *Frogs* for the Lenaia (late winter) festival of 405 BCE, shortly after Euripides' death. The play won first prize. In it the god Dionysus (the god who presided over dramatic performance), goes to the Underworld to bring back Euripides and finds that he has to be the judge in a literary contest between Aeschylus and Euripides for the throne of poetry in Hades; he ends up by bringing back Aeschylus as the dramatist most likely to give good guidance to the state. In (i), Dionysus encounters the god Herakles at the entrance to the Underworld and explains his quest. In (ii) and (iii) the two dramatists compete by defending their respective styles and subject-matter.

(i)

DIONYSUS.

The point is, I was sitting on deck,
Reading Euripides' *Andromeda*,
When I felt a sudden prick. Of desire.

HERAKLES.

How big?

DIONYSUS.

This big.

HERAKLES.

For a woman?

DIONYSUS.

No.

HERAKLES

A boy, then?

DIONYSUS

No.

HERAKLES.

A man?

DIONYSUS.

Don't be daft.

HERAKLES.

Not ... Kleisthenes?

DIONYSUS.

This isn't a joke. It's serious.
It's eating me away. I just can't cope.

HERAKLES.

There, there. What are the symptoms?

DIONYSUS.

How can I explain?   60
Make it simple ...? Use words you'll understand ...?
Have you ever craved, really craved, pea soup?

HERAKLES.

A million times. Pea soup!

DIONYSUS.

Is that quite clear? Shall I try again?

HERAKLES.

No, no. Pea soup's quite clear. If you see what I mean

DIONYSUS.

Well, that's the kind of craving that's eating me.
For Euripides.

HERAKLES.

But he's a corpse.

DIONYSUS.

I *know* that.
I'm going to see him, and no one's going to stop me.

HERAKLES.

But he's ... Down There. In the Underworld.

DIONYSUS.

I *know*.
I'll go as low as I have to. Lower   70

HERAKLES.

But *why?*

DIONYSUS.

I need a classy poet, fast.
Where are the snows of yesteryear? Not here.

HERAKLES.

You're joking. There's Iophon.

DIONYSUS.

Oh, really?
You're really recommending Iophon?
Some yesteryear. Some snow.

HERAKLES.

What about his Daddy?
Sophocles? If you must bring someone back.
Bring Sophocles. Who needs Euripides?

(lines 54–75)

(ii)

AESCHYLUS.

All right, what are *your* tragedies about?

EURIPIDES.

Not horse-cocks or goat-leopards. I leave those to you.
I don't get *my* inspiration from a Persian carpet.
When you handed me Tragedy, she was in bad, bad way:
Bloated with adverbs, plumped-up with particles,   940
So stuffed with syllables she could hardly move.
I put her on a diet right away. Pure logic,
A pinch of prosody, carefully-selected metaphors,
Non-fattening similes, a touch of this, a touch of that –

AESCHYLUS.

– and more than a touch of Kephisophon.

EURIPIDES.

I didn't start in the middle, or babble on.
The first person onstage told the audience
Exactly what to expect.

AESCHYLUS.

They knew before they came.

EURIPIDES.

In *my* plays, no one stands about doing nothing.
Everyone gets a say: wife, daughter-in-law,
Slaves, even old Granny in the corner.

AESCHYLUS.

Ridiculous.   950

EURIPIDES.

Democracy in action.

DIONYSUS.

Oh, don't let's start on politics.

EURIPIDES.

I taught *them* –

He gestures at the audience.

– how to argue.

AESCHYLUS.

You should have been mashed to mincemeat.

EURIPIDES.

I taught them to *use* language.
Arrange words *neatly:*
Careful examination, logical argument,
Look at everything twice, no stone unturned –

AESCHYLUS.

He's *proud* of it!

EURIPIDES.

I kept to ordinary matters in my plays,
Things everyone knows, we all understand.
My audience could follow every word.   960
I didn't baffle them with Kyknoses and Memnons,
All horsebrasses and hippomanic crests.
You want to know what we're like? Look at our admirers.
His are Phormisios, Megainetos the Maniac,
By-the-lord-Harry merchants, Tear-em-limb-from-limb;
Mine are lean and spry: Theramenes, Kleitophon –

DIONYSUS.

Theramenes? Lean and spry?
I think you mean Mean and sly,
Rolls into trouble,
Quick change of policy,

Quick turn of the coat,
And rolls right out again.   970

EURIPIDES.

Question everything, I taught them.
First principle in drama,
First rule in life:
Don't let anything go by.
'Why's that?
What's going on?

How? When?
Where did that come from?'
Beg pardon?
Whose idea was that?

DIONYSUS.

I know exactly what you mean.   980
They're all at it now.
Come home, call the slaves,
Start shouting and yelling.
'Who moved that jug?
Who scoffed that sardine?
How? When?
Once all they did was sit

On a stool   990
Like *this*, and drool.

(lines 936–91)

(iii)

DIONYSUS.

No more singing. Please.

AESCHYLUS.

I quite agree.
There's only one real way to settle this.
We'll weigh the lines. It's time for the scales.

DIONYSUS.

The scales! The scales!
We'll weigh those tragedies like lumps of cheese.

The scales are set up.

CHORUS.

It's amazing. It's hard to believe   1370
What these supermen have up their sleeve.
Each one devises
A million surprises
For the other one soon to receive.

It's a good job we're here, and can view
It ourselves. For if any of you
Had outlined it,
Defined it,
We'd never have thought it was true.

DIONYSUS.

Right. Stand by your weighing pans.

AESCHYLUS.

There.

EURIPIDES.

There.

DIONYSUS.

Take hold and say a line each.
And don't let go till I say 'Cuckoo'. Right?   1380

AESCHYLUS.

Right.

EURIPIDES.

Right.

DIONYSUS.

Ready, steady, speak.

EURIPIDES.

O why did it have to sail, the good ship Argo?

AESCHYLUS.

O river Spercheios, where cattle drink ...

DIONYSUS.

Cuckoo. Let go. Ah. His is lower.

EURIPIDES.

Why?

DIONYSUS.

He put in a river, like a wool-merchant
Wetting his fleeces to make them heavier.
You put in a fast, light sailing-ship.

(lines 1365–84)

D7 Aristophanes, *Women at the Thesmophoria* (Festival Time)

From K. Mcleish (trans.) (1993) *Aristophanes, Plays: Two*, Methuen, pp.242, 254–8.

Aristophanes composed the *Women at the Thesmophoria* in 411 BCE. In this play, the women at the festival of the Thesmophoria, an exclusively women's festival in honour of Demeter, goddess of corn and crops, plan to get rid of Euripides. An elderly kinsman of his, Mnesilochos, attempts to defend him disguised as a woman, unsuccessfully as it turns out. The second piece here is a mock trial of Euripides for giving women a bad reputation with their husbands.

(i)

EURIPIDES.

That's it. That's what it's all about.
They're holding a meeting today, the women,
To decide whether I must live or die.

MNESILOCHOS.

Die? Why?

EURIPIDES.

They say my tragedies make fools of them.

MNESILOCHOS.

Well, so they do. You're done for, mate, unless –
Have you something in mind? Some clever plan?

EURIPIDES.

I'm going to ask Agathon, the paladin of poetry,
To go to the festival.

MNESILOCHOS.

What for?

EURIPIDES.

He can stand up, among all those women,   90
And plead my case.

MNESILOCHOS.

As himself, or in disguise?

EURIPIDES.

In disguise. In a dress. What else?

MNESILOCHOS.

Brilliant! I knew you were planning something.
When it comes to sneakiness, we take the cake.

(lines 81–95)

(ii)

HERALDESS.

O gods, Olympians, Pythians, Delians,
All others, hear our prayers.

Whoever here today
Slanders our city ...
Slanders our womenfolk ...
Favours the Persians ...
Favours Euripides ...
Plots against women ...
Works for dictatorship ...
Prattles and gossips ...
Finds a young man for you,   340
Then runs to master ...
Garbles your messages ...
Offers you the Moon, the stars, the Sun,
Then finds someone younger for fun ...

Rents a handsome and well-hung young stud
When she's past it, exhausted and dud ...
Takes your money then won't give you pleasure –
Oh, and wine-sellers giving short measure –
Bad luck to them all! Tears! Misery! Gloom!
Catastrophe! Disaster! Doom!
Send *us* good luck, we pray,   350
At our festival today.

CHORUS.

O gods above,
Praise moderation;
Praise all who love
This nation.
In your all-powerful way
Keep our secrets today;
If anyone blabs,
Keep tabs.
What possible reason
Could there be for such treason?   360
If you find a defector,
Please don't protect her;
A pain, a perversion,
Far worse than a Persian.
Betraying her gender –
Please don't defend her.

Lord Zeus, hear our prayer,
Spread word to the heavenly powers:
Be fair.
Be ours.   370

HERALDESS.

Attention please. MINUTES OF PREVIOUS MEETING.

(CHAIR: TIMOKLEIA. SECRETARY: LYSILLA.
SPEAKER: SOSTRATE.) MOTION: THAT
TOMORROW MORNING –
That's today, now, since the meeting was
yesterday –
AS SOON AS A QUORUM HAS GATHERED
FOR THE FESTIVAL –
We thought more people would be able to make it
If we chose today – DISCUSSION BE
COMMENCED

ABOUT JUST PUNISHMENT FOR EURIPIDES,
ALREADY CONDEMNED FOR INSULTING
WOMEN. NEM. CON.

Does anyone want to add anything?

MIKKA.

Yes. Me.

HERALDESS.

Put on the garland. Speak.   380

MIKKA.

Ladies. Listen. Ahem.

CHORUS.

Just hear how she clears her throat.
She's done this sort of thing before.

MIKKA.

I'm not trying to show off or anything.
But I *had* to say something. The point is,
I've had enough, I've really had enough
Of that man's mud-slinging. Euripides.
He just can't leave us alone. Who does he think he is?

You remember his mother: that greengrocer in the market.
Anyway, what *hasn't* he accused us of?
Every play of his, in every theatre everywhere,   390
Makes us out to be walking mysteries, shiftless,
Obsessed with sex, drink, lies and gossip,
Beyond saving, a plague to all ... *man*kind.
So when they come home from the theatre, our husbands,
They give us *very* funny looks, start turning out
All the cupboards and drawers to find our fancy-men.
Thanks to him, spilling the beans to our 'better halves',
We can't do *anything* we did in the good old days.
Draw the curtains late one morning, and it's
'Who's that you've hidden behind the arras?'   400
Put yourself on a diet, and it's
'Yon wife of mine hath a lean and hungry look – who for?'

Lose *one* little handkerchief, he's up the wall.
And what if he can't give you a baby?
You *have* to get one somewhere –
And how can you, the way he's watching you?

D'you remember how easy it used to be
To find a rich old man to marry? Not any more.   410
An old man weds a tyrant, not a wife –
Euripides. Put them off wedding-bells forever.
It's all that bigmouth's fault – like those bolts and bars
They put on women's quarters nowadays,
And those huge fanged hounds they breed
To scare the boyfriends away. And that's not all.
Once we were mistresses in our own kitchens:
It was up to us what corn, oil, wine we used.
Not any more. Who keeps the keys these days?   420
His Nibs – great fancy things with triple teeth.
Once, all you needed to get into the pantry
Was a ha'penny ring. Break the seal, open up,
Take what you want, reseal, hey presto.
Now, thanks to our playwright friend,
They've all got seals like spider's webs.

'Leave nothing to chance', he says.
And so do I. He's condemned himself. He's dead.
Shall we poison him, or find some other way? –
That's all there is to decide. Thank you, thank you...
There's a lot more I *could* say,
But I'll leave it in writing with the clerk.

(lines 331–432)

D8a James Morwood, extract from *Medea*

From J. Morwood (trans.) (1997) *Euripides: Medea, Hippolytus, Electra, Helen,* Oxford, World's Classics. This and the passages which follow translate lines 250–66 of the Greek text of *Medea*

I would rather stand three times in the battle line than bear one child.

However, the same reasoning does not apply to you and to me. You have this city, your father's house, a fulfilled life and the company of your friends, while I, a desolate woman without a city, shamefully injured by my husband who carried me as plunder from a foreign land, have no haven from this disaster, no mother, no brother, no relative at all. So I shall ask you to grant me this favour and no more. If I can find some means, some scheme to take a just revenge for these evils on my husband and the man who gave his daughter to him and that daughter whom he married, I ask you to keep silence. In all other respects a woman is full of fear and proves a coward at the sight of iron in the fight, but when she is wronged in her marriage bed, no creature has a mind more murderous.

D8b David Stuttard, extract from *Medea*

From the version performed by the Actors of Dionysus, 1996, p.5.

I'd rather stand my ground three times in a battle, in the shield-line than endure the agonies of child-birth once.

But the situation's not the same for you and me. You have your city here, your fathers' homes. You have life's luxuries, companionship and friends. But I have no-one. *I* have no city and my husband treats me shamefully. He took me from my home as plunder to a strange land and in the face of all my cruel disaster now I can't weigh anchor and sail safe home to my mother or my brother or my family.

And so I would ask this one thing of you: if I can find some way, some scheme by which I might exact some justice on my husband in return for all the wrongs he's done to me – keep quiet. For in all else, a woman is consumed by fear, no mettle when it comes to facing force or steel. But when she has been slighted in her marriage and her sex, there is no force more murderous.

D8c David Wiles, extract from *Medea*

From the version performed at the Gate Theatre, 1986, p.7.

I'd rather go into battle three times
Than once go into labour.

But we're not in the same situation, you and me.
This is your city, you originate here.
You enjoy yourselves and have a social life.
I'm on my own, rootless, victimized by
my husband, because I'm his foreign conquest.
There is no mother, no brother, no relative
who can shelter me from the storm.
That's why I have a request to make.
Suppose I came up with a plan
To make my husband pay for his wrongdoing,
And his bride and her father,
Then stay silent. A Woman is usually timid,
She cannot cope with the sight of cold steel.
But when she faces sexual humiliation,
No one is capable of greater savagery.

D8d Augusta Webster, *The Medea of Euripides*

From A. Webster (1868) *The Medea of Euripides: literally translated into English verse*, Macmillan & Co., pp.20–21.

[...] for I would liefer thrice
Bear brunt of arms than once bring forth a child.
Ah well! the like words fit not thee and me:
For thee there is a country, and for thee
A father's home, for thee are life's delights
And the familiar intercourse of friends;
But I, alone, calling no city mine,
Am outraged by a spouse, I led a prey
From a far land, who have no mother more,
Nor brother, nor a kinsman of my blood,
Where to seek harbour in the evil day.
Therefore this much I fain would gain of you,
That, if I find a way and a device
To recompense my husband for these wrongs,
And her he wed and him who gave his daughter,
Ye will keep counsel. For in other things
Is a woman full of fears and most ill-fit
For battles and to look upon the sword;
But come there treason to her bridal bed
There is no other mind more thirsts for blood.

D9 Margaret Williamson, 'A woman's place in Euripides' *Medea*'

From A. Powell (ed.) (1990) *Euripides, Women and Sexuality*, London, Routledge, pp.16–31.

1   The main stimulus for this treatment of the *Medea* was a distinction which has recently been gaining currency in the study of the Athens of the fifth century BC– namely that between public and private spheres. The recent growth of interest in this dichotomy has many sources, among them the concern of structuralist anthropology with the social categories constructed by different cultures. Another more specific one is the discussion within modern feminism of the long-standing association of women with the private sphere[1] – an association which was challenged by the 'private is political' slogan of the early 1970s.

2   Fifth-century Athens was clearly a crucial period in the construction of the idea of the private, and tragedy is an important source for our understanding of it. Two writers who have recently dealt with the public–private split in a way which opens up many possibilities for the interpretation of the plays are Sally Humphreys and John Gould. In the opening chapters of *The Family, Women and Death*[2] Humphreys

sketches the way in which the private world of the *oikos* and the public one of the *polis* became more sharply differentiated, and she points to tragedy as one index of the conflicts caused by this polarization. The distinction is invoked from a different angle by Gould in his essay on dramatic character, and again in considering our evidence about the position of women in classical Athens.[3] These two writers concur in relating the prominence of female characters in tragedy to the primary association of women with the *oikos*, in contrast to the public, male world of the *polis*. Thus, in Humphreys' view, the peculiarly active and larger-than-life women in tragedy 'belong to a discourse on the relation between public and private life rather than to a discourse on the relations between the sexes'.[4]

3   The Greek stage was, of course, rich in semantic possibilities when it came to exploring this relationship. Most of the action in a play takes place in an open, public space, the *orchestra*, which is partially surrounded by the audience; this space is also defined as public by the presence in it of the chorus for most of the play. Behind the *orchestra*, however, is the *skene*, the stage-building, and behind that a more remote space which the audience normally cannot see. In this and many other plays this unseen space represents the interior of a house: it is, in a phrase adapted by Gould from Wilamowitz, an 'offstage indoors',[5] and the tragedy takes place at the intersection between inside and outside, private and public. When Medea, in this play, emerges with the words 'I have come out of the house' (ἐξῆλθον δόμων, 214), her statement can be read symbolically as well as literally, as a movement from the private sphere of the house into the public one – normally associated with men – of the city.[6] An important corollary of this transition is the corresponding change in the language she uses. From within the house we hear her expressing extremes of rage, misery, and hatred in lyrical anapaests; as soon as she steps outside it her language becomes controlled, abstract, intellectualizing and indistinguishable from that of any of the male characters she confronts in the early scenes of the play – including Jason. It is the gap – never to be bridged – between these two modes which chiefly concerns me, and I shall suggest that it is intimately linked with the violence which the play portrays.

4   In what follows I shall do three things. First I want to consider some of the manifestations and implications of Medea's transition into the public sphere. Then I shall look at some of the registers in which she speaks in the early scenes of the play, and the language which she shares with the male characters; and finally I shall consider what the play seems to be implying about that language.

5   To dwell a little longer on the spatial semantics of the play: comparison with some of the plays which preceded this one suggests how problematic the relationship between public and private spaces will be here. In both Aeschylus' *Oresteia* and Sophocles' *Antigone* (both obvious comparisons because of the dominant female characters in them) the

sphere represented by the 'off-stage indoors' is the house of the ruling family, which is thus also the centre of the city: the spheres of *oikos* and *polis* are concentric. Despite disorder within both spheres (in the *Oresteia*) or conflict between them (in the *Antigone*), the possibility of a restoration of harmony is always there. In this play, however, the off-stage space has been displaced.[7] The centre of Corinth is not Medea's house but Creon's; Medea's house is in a kind of no-man's-land, and would be so even without Jason's desertion. The other thing which gives her household its problematic quality is the fact that she is barbarian, so that the space from which she emerges is not only inner, but also outer and alien. This troubling paradox makes the 'off-stage indoors' even more remote and inaccessible to the audience.[8]

6 In addition, of course, as the prologue makes clear, the *oikos* for Medea is fractured by betrayals, and has been so ever since her marriage to Jason. Even before telling us of Medea's present situation, the Nurse recounts her destruction of Pelias through his daughters (9); and shortly afterwards we hear that Medea has also betrayed her own father and home (31–2). It is these events, no less than Jason's desertion, which are responsible for her present plight: she has, unlike a divorced Athenian woman, no home to return to, and so she is precipitated perforce into the public domain.

7 This movement occurs, I think, on many levels, one of which is also indicated in the prologue. The Nurse tells us that Medea's marriage to Jason was guaranteed by ὅρκοι – oaths – and δεξιαί – pledges; it is these, and the gods who witnessed them, which the betrayed Medea invokes (21). The significance of this is two-fold. First, oaths did not normally form part of either the betrothal or the actual giving-away stages of a marriage ceremony;[9] they are usually associated with public life and especially, as Humphreys points out, with entry into it.[10] Second, any contract involved in a marriage would normally be between the husband and the wife's father or guardian. Medea, however, represents Jason's oaths and pledges as having been given to herself. In contracting a marriage on this basis she has already translated herself into the role of a male citizen, operating in the public sphere as Jason's equal.

8 There is a similar bias in her celebrated speech to the Corinthian chorus about their common lot as women. Medea's account of the giving of dowries contains a subtle distortion: she again represents the woman as an active partner in the transaction when she says that women must 'buy a husband for an extravagant sum' (χρημάτων ὑπερβολῇ πόσιν πρίασθαι, 232–3). In fact, once again, it would be a woman's father who engaged in the transaction, not the woman herself; and her dowry, rather than being exchanged for a husband, would both accompany her and, if she was divorced, return with her. Medea is here representing all women as practitioners of exchange, just as she herself contracted her own marriage; rather than, in Levi-Strauss's phrase, the exchange of women, she talks here of exchange by women.[11]

9 In the speech in which she first attempts to dissuade Creon from banishing her (292ff.), the extent to which she speaks like a male citizen is again remarkable. To his order to leave she replies with a sententious speech about the dangers of having a reputation for *sophia*. No *man* (ἀνήρ), she says, with any sense would have his children brought up to be very clever (σοφοί): because the ignorant will not understand you if you are clever, whereas those with aspirations will be made envious by your pre-eminence. She goes on to apply this to her own situation; but up to the point at which she makes explicit reference to herself, her words describe a community of male citizens and are scarcely applicable to the situation of a woman – much less of a foreigner in fifth-century Athens.[12]

10 The most remarkable manifestation of her entry into the public sphere is, however, her transaction with Aegeus. She and Aegeus meet as equals, and form a contract based on exchange; and in Medea's case what she both offers and receives is a version of what a woman would give and receive in marriage. She offers Aegeus fertility – the power to beget children; he gives her in return, not the safety of an *oikos*, but that of the Athenian *polis*. The equivalence between this exchange and the contract of marriage is confirmed by the account Medea later gives of it to Jason: she tells him that she is going to 'live with Aegeus' (Αἰγεῖ συνοικήσουσα, 1385). This relationship too, like Medea's with Jason, is sealed by oaths, and the transaction can be seen as completing the translation from private to public of the marriage bond which her relationship with Jason had already initiated.

11 Medea's move out of the house, then, is paralleled by other moves into the sphere and the discourse of male citizens, and its most remarkable effect is this version of the marriage relationship. Instead of a relationship based on an absolute and irrevocable difference of status, and a change in status which is usually also permanent, marriage has become a contract based on exchange and reciprocity between equals.

12 One of the reasons why this transmutation is interesting is that these two types of relationship are themselves the subject of discussion within the play, and Medea is an active participant in the discussion. They are particularly at issue in the scenes between her and Creon, and then between her and Jason. The degree to which, in these scenes, Medea commands the same range of arguments and analyses as her interlocutors is another indication of her transition into the world which they inhabit. However, the manner in which these arguments are wielded casts considerable doubt on their validity; and in addition, the very fact that Medea's exit from the house has involved the kind of transmutation and distortion which I have mentioned puts in doubt any claim she may have had to speak for the *oikos*. We would expect her, as a woman, to be closely associated with the sphere from which, symbolically, she emerged at line 214; but the early scenes of the play suggest that her emergence has fatally weakened her association with the *oikos* – and also that it is

irreversible. This is of crucial importance when – as in her debate with Jason – the topic at issue is the relationship which is at the heart of the *oikos* – marriage.

13 It is possible to sketch in the early scenes with Creon and Jason a spectrum of types of relationship. At one extreme are close blood-relationships – primarily those between parents and children – which are asymmetrical, fixed and irrevocable, and based on an absolute distinction of status between the people involved. At the other are relationships involving exchange between equals, which are fluid and subject to alteration. The first extreme is characteristic of relationships within the private sphere, and the second of relationships between male citizens in the public sphere of the *polis*.[13] Between these two poles are other kinds of relationship, most notably that between suppliant and supplicated, and that of ξενία (guest-friendship), which are based on differentiation and inequality in status but involve a change in status, effected by ritual and witnessed by the gods.

14 The scene between Medea and Creon alludes to the full range of these types of relationship, and juxtaposes them so sharply as to emphasize their discontinuity and set them against, as much as alongside, each other. Medea's attempt to persuade Creon to allow her to stay opens with the account of the dangers of being considered clever to which I have already referred. She continues with another highly abstract argument against his fear of her, this time framed in judicial terms. Creon has not, she says, wronged her in marrying his daughter to whomever he chose, and therefore should expect no retribution from her (307–10). This is an argument about the relationship between two equals whose exchange with each other is defined in terms of an abstract concept of justice. It is also partial in that it takes no account of personal feeling, and indeed runs counter to her inclusion of Creon in the category of enemies earlier in the scene (278); and he rejects it as mere words (321).

15 The next tactic which Medea employs is more successful. She becomes a suppliant, adopting a posture in which she has a tangible, and not merely theoretical, claim on Creon. The suggestion made by Gould about this episode seems to me right: that she begins by beseeching Creon only verbally, but becomes effective at the point when she adopts the physical posture of a suppliant and clings to him (335, 339, and later 370).[14] She has thus moved to what I have defined as the middle ground, and appealed to a relationship based on a sharp differentiation in status whose obligations are guaranteed by ritual. The success initiated by this move is consolidated by an appeal to Creon as being, like Jason, a father (344–5). She does not, obviously, appeal to an actual blood-relationship between Creon and her own children, but to Creon's feeling within a parallel relationship; and in so doing she has now moved to the other end of the spectrum.

16 Medea employs, then, in her persuasive assault on Creon three approaches which are sharply differentiated in every possible way. The first begins with a generalization which is elaborated at length before being applied to her own situation, and which entirely excludes personal feeling. The second, her supplication, is stichomythic; the third, which is based on personal feeling alone, is made in a speech of eight heavily alliterative lines. The discontinuity which is thus formally highlighted reflects particularly harshly, I think, on the abstract and judicial language of the first appeal. Besides being, in itself, an improbably sententious response to a sudden personal disaster, it is also the least successful of her ploys. All three approaches, however, are overshadowed by a mode of persuasion – Medea's supplicatory pose – which, if Gould is right, is effective by means of gesture rather than of words, and which thus casts doubt on the efficacy of any of Medea's arguments if taken alone.

17 The linguistic discontinuities which are thrown into relief in this scene do not end here. Medea's rationalistic arguments to Creon, and her adoption of the perspective of a male citizen in 292ff., can only heighten our sense of the gulf separating this from the voice we first heard from within the house. As if to widen this gulf Euripides now, on Creon's departure, gives to the chorus a lament which echoes the first cry we heard from Medea:

> δύστανε γύναι,
> φεῦ φεῦ, μελέα τῶν σῶν ἀχέων
>
> *(357–8)*

'Oh unhappy woman, alas, wretched in your pain', they sing, echoing Medea's

> ἰώ,
> δύστανος ἐγὼ μελέα τε πόνων

'Oh, unhappy that I am, wretched in my troubles' at 96. The mode of Medea's earlier expression of suffering is, it seems, no longer available to her, but only to the chorus: their evocation of it here, set beside the abstract and rhetorical way in which she is now using language, points to what has been lost in her exit from the house. The suffering she expressed from within the house is now issuing, in characteristic Euripidean sequence, in action outside it; but the sense of dislocation which this linguistic gap produces already – before we know what Medea's plans are – casts a shadow over that action. It is becoming clear that her emergence from the house involved both distortion and loss, and the eventual outcome of her plans is marked in advance by that distortion too.

18 The *agon* between Medea and Jason begins with another verbal echo hardly less significant than that of the chorus. Jason's first speech opens with a line which differs by only two words from that with which Medea began her attempt to sway Creon: compare her

> οὐ νῦν με πρῶτον, ἀλλὰ πολλάκις, Κρέον ...

'This is not the first time, Creon; [I have] often [had the same experience] ...' at 292 with his first words in this scene:

οὐ νῦν κατεῖδον πρῶτον ἀλλά πολλάκις ...

(446)

'This is not the first time: I have often seen ...' The association not only marks him as what he will indeed turn out to be – the arch-rationalizer and theoretician of the play – but also locates the debate, for Medea and Jason equally, at that level of persuasive rhetoric which emerged from the Creon scene as least successful.[15] In this scene what is at issue between Medea and Jason is principally the nature of their relationship. In this context, more than any other, we might expect Medea to associate herself with the relationships most characteristic of the *oikos*, and particularly with blood-relationships. However, the range which she commanded in the Creon scene, as well as the parallel already allusively suggested between her and Jason, should warn us that this will not be so; and indeed the case turns out to be more complex.

19   Both she and Jason have a range of ways of conceptualizing their relationship. Each at some point refers to it as one of exchange. Medea cites the fact that she saved him, and details the way in which she did so; it was, she says, after receiving this treatment from her that he betrayed her (488–9). We recall the Nurse in the prologue quoting Medea's cry to the gods to witness what kind of recompense – οἴας ἀμοιβῆς (23) – she has received from Jason: there the vocabulary of exchange was quite clear. Jason in turn invokes the same concept when he tells her that she has received more than she gave in saving him (534–5), and proceeds to list the benefits to her.

20   At the other extreme, Medea invokes blood-relationships when, after listing her benefits to Jason, she charges him with contracting a new marriage even though children have been born, saying that if he were childless his desire for a new marriage would be pardonable (490–1). The existence of children, according to her, creates a bond between husband and wife which, though it is not a blood-relationship, derives an inalienable quality from the relation of each to their children.

21   In this scene too, then, there are appeals made to ways of thinking about relationships which are fundamentally different; and once again the effect of their juxtaposition is to put them all in question. Although Medea invokes blood-relationships, she has no stable association with this as a way of thinking about marriage: she is equally capable of regarding exchange between equals as the basis of her link with Jason. In this scene even more than the previous one, each protagonist uses language to assault the other, and the scene abounds in allusions to language as instrument and even as weapon.[16] Here, however, the relationship which is at issue is of central importance to the continuation of the *oikos*; and the fact that Medea's and Jason's heterogeneous and colliding arguments have no purchase on it is the more damaging for this reason.

22 It is not, however, from either of the two extremes which I have mentioned that the motive force of Medea's revenge – which takes the action forward from this point – comes. The argument which she consistently offers, from now until her famous monologue at 1021ff., is that Jason's crime was to harm his *philoi*. This is the first charge she makes against him in the *agon* (470), and the chorus seem to confirm her definition of their relationship as one of *philia* in the two-line interjection (520–1) in which they say that anger is particularly implacable when it is between *philoi*. It was also stressed in the prologue that Jason had offended against the principle of doing good to one's friends and harm to one's enemies (84).

23 But the speech in which Medea pleads this principle before Jason also shows how problematic is its application here. Although a relationship of *philia* can arise in other ways, the sphere in which it can normally be assumed is with regard to relatives: the range of an individual's *philoi* would begin with his kin and spread outwards.[17] But in Medea's case Euripides makes it very clear that this central point does not exist. In her catalogue of benefits to Jason (476ff.), it is explicitly mentioned that saving Jason involved, twice over, the destruction of the bond between parent and child – first when she betrayed her own father, and again when she destroyed Pelias and his *oikos* by means of his daughters. She reiterates her account of both these crimes later in the speech, again stressing the damage to the two *oikoi* which was involved, and this time she makes it clear that she too, like Jason, has inverted the treatment due to friends and enemies:

τοῖς μὲν οἴκοθεν φίλοις
ἐχθρὰ καθέστηχ', οὓς δέ μ' οὐκ ἐχρῆν κακῶς
δρᾶν, σοὶ χάριν φέρουσα πολεμίους ἔχω.

(506–8)

'To my friends [*philoi*] at home I have become hateful; and in helping you I have made enemies of others I had no cause to harm'. When she speaks to Jason, then, of the duty to do good to one's *philoi*, her words are – almost literally – hollow. The relationship which she claims Jason has violated was itself based on a similar violation. She cannot, therefore, invoke the kind of relationship in which the claims of *philia* are clearest; the only place where she can take her stand is in an area where the relations involved are more fluid and ambiguous. Besides referring to close kinship the word can also cover less permanent associations between male citizens, including members of the same drinking group and those who, somewhat as Jason aspires to do, have formed a tie with another *genos* through marriage.[18] Logically, in view of her own actions, Medea can only be defending this much less clear-cut and less stable category of *philia*: the central area, and the one with which we would expect her, as a woman, to be associated, is absent.

24 This makes it all the more remarkable that the spur to action which she constantly places before herself and the chorus is the duty to do good to one's *philoi* and harm to one's enemies. In her monologue at the end of the Creon scene she refers twice to her enemies (374, 383), and she takes up the same theme again after her exchange with Aegeus. There she not only refers to her enemies four times, but also ends with an explicit statement of the old heroic ethic: she wants, she says, to be thought 'hard on her enemies and good to her friends' (βαρεῖαν ἐχθροῖς καὶ φίλοισιν εὐμενῆ, 809) because it is this kind of behaviour that wins renown.

25 Both these speeches, as Bernard Knox and others have pointed out, are framed in the language and style of a Sophoclean hero.[19] Medea's implacable anger against her enemies, and her definition of them as such, are equally uncompromising. Both the grief which she expressed earlier from inside the house and the range of arguments she deployed against Jason are absent from these two speeches. Instead, Jason, Creon, and his daughter are all defined in absolute terms as enemies, and her revenge on them as a matter of heroic daring, expressed in such lines as

> ἔρπ' ἐς τὸ δεινόν· νῦν ἀγὼν εὐψυχίας
>
> *(403)*

'On to the terrible deed; this is the test of my spirit' and

> νῦν καλλίνικοι τῶν ἐμῶν ἐχθρῶν ...
> γενησόμεσθα
>
> *(765–6)*

'Now I shall win a glorious victory over my enemies'.

26 Medea thus adds another vocabulary, another kind of discourse, to those over which she has already shown such mastery. One reading of this new style is that it gives Medea heroic dignity, and adds weight to her as a spokesman for the rights of women.[20] But the shift to a heroic, Sophoclean, and once again masculine style has another function too: it heightens even further our sense of the gaps and dislocations not only between her voice from within the house and that with which she speaks after emerging into the open, but also within her public voice. Her heroic stance is paradoxical and contradictory not only in its central formulation but also in its consequences: the distinction on which it rests has already been subverted by Medea herself, and it leads yet again to the destruction of the most intimate bond of *philia*, that between parents and children. It reappears twice in her crucial and apparently wavering monologue, each time as an argument in favour of the children's death, and each time with an uncompromising reference to her enemies (1049–50, 1059–61).

27 When Medea subsequently goes inside to carry out the murder, she is both re-entering the *oikos* and entering it for the first time. The transmutations and distortions which we have seen to be involved in her exit at line 214 mean that – to use the terms with which I began – it is partly as a representative of the public, male sphere that she now crosses the threshold. She now shares with Creon and Jason a vocabulary which has been discredited as a means of understanding the relationship central to the *oikos*, and her heroic language is equally inappropriate to it. It is inevitable, therefore, that the consequence of her entry into the house should be wordless violence – the murder of the children who are the most stable measure of its central relationship.

28 The violence can, indeed, be traced further back than this. Medea's relationship to the *oikos* has always been marked by violence: her emergence at line 214 represented in spatial terms a movement which in fact began long before the action of the play, and which was initiated by destruction within her own *oikos* and then Pelias'. It is this destruction which is the condition of her presence on stage: violence to the *oikos* is both cause and consequence of her emergence into view at line 214. In marking that emergence so sharply by means of the linguistic and conceptual discontinuities and distortions which I have discussed, the play seems to me to be pointing, among other things, to the inadequacy of the language available for thinking about the *oikos*. The private, it suggests by analogy, cannot be spoken in the language of the public except on condition of its destruction; and Medea's status as representative of the private was compromised as soon as she emerged into public view.

29 I began by relating the two juxtaposed theatrical spaces in this play to the division between public and private; but it would be misleading to suggest that this is the only meaning which they have. Some of their other resonances are suggested by the work of Ruth Padel, who argues that women's possession of an inner space makes them particularly suited to the representation of inner experience in general: the inner space of the *oikos* would be an extension of the same metaphor.[21] This can be related to another opposition which is important in the play but which I have not mentioned – between *eros* and the rationality exemplified in its purest form by Jason (though also, of course, shared by Medea) – as well as between the languages of passion and of action. The discrepancies I have mentioned between different ways of defining relationships can be related to conflicts existing within public life as well as between public and private life; so that the *oikos* may stand both for itself and for a type of relationship within the public sphere.[22]

30 I would not want, however, to lose sight entirely of the fact that, whatever else it may represent, the *oikos* is the province of women, so that the linguistic inadequacies to which the play points are in part inadequacies in the representation of women. The opposition between male and female may be articulated with that between public and

private; but this does not mean that the former opposition need be completely displaced by the latter in the interpretation of the plays. This may seem like a move back towards a simplistic and over-literal kind of reading. I find support for it, though, in the ode which the chorus sing immediately after Medea's first monologue, and which is directly about the representation of women.

31   In this monologue (364–409) Medea has for the first time revealed a plan to kill Creon, his daughter, and (at this point) Jason, using the heroic language to which I have referred. This heroic mode is, however, undercut even here, most obviously at the end of the speech. After asserting her determination not to be her enemies' laughing-stock, Medea closes the speech by saying that women are, after all

> ἐς μὲν ἐσθλ' ἀμηχανώταται,
> κακῶν δὲ πάντων τέκτονες σοφώταται.
>
> *(408–9)*

'incapable of doing good, but the cleverest contrivers of all evil'. Immediately after this comes an ode in which the chorus seem, at first sight, to be singing the praises of women. They begin with a reference to general moral and religious disorder, which they appear, in the following line, to attribute to the faithlessness of, above all, men:

> ἀνδράσι μὲν δόλιαι βουλαί ...
>
> *(412)*

'It is men who make deceitful plans ...' They conclude the strophe by saying that women's reputation and honour will now be enhanced.

32   As a response to Medea's speech, this is strange; and the ode is in fact in a deeply paradoxical relationship with what went before it. It is Medea who has just exposed her 'deceitful plans', and whose mastery of strategy has been revealed in the exchange with Creon. In view of this, and of her own closing comment, the improvement in women's standing which the chorus are projecting seems a dubious honour: it is based on a judgement which Medea has shown to apply at least equally to herself, and at best it can only consist of women not being as bad as men.

33   The antistrophe builds on the paradoxical nature of this praise by pointing to the inadequacy of the terms being used, even by the chorus themselves – and they are, we remember, a chorus of women played by male actors and orchestrated by a male poet. Essentially the chorus say that the true history of women is as yet unspoken. If women had been granted the power of divine song, they could have countered that of men, and the story would be a different one:

> μακρὸς δ' αἰὼν ἔχει
> πολλὰ μὲν ἀμετέραν ἀνδρῶν τε μοῖραν εἰπεῖν
>
> *(429–30)*

'The passing of time has much to tell of our lot and of men's.'

34 Knox, writing about this ode, declares that it is unnecessary for the chorus to use the future tense in predicting a change of direction in legends about women; because, he says, 'Euripides' play itself is the change of direction'.[23] I should prefer to see this change as dependent on a more complex syntactical alteration. The appropriate mode both for this ode and for the play is that of an unfulfilled condition – in which one does not use the future, or even the present, tense. The possibility of true speech by and about women remains, like the domain from which Medea emerged, off-stage.

[1] See, for example, Michelle Rosaldo, 'A theoretical overview', in M.Z. Rosaldo and L. Lamphere (eds), *Women, Culture and Society* (Stanford, 1974) pp.17–42.

[2] S.C. Humphreys, *The Family, Women and Death* (London, 1983).

[3] J. Gould, 'Dramatic character and "human intelligibility" in Greek tragedy', *PCPhS* ns 24 (1978) pp.43–67, and 'Law, custom and myth: aspects of the social position of women in classical Athens', *JHS* 100 (1980) pp.38–59. There is also an interesting section on the private-public dichotomy in Helene Foley's essay 'The conception of women in Athenian drama', in H. Foley (ed.), *Reflections of Women in Antiquity* (New York, London, and Paris, 1981).

[4] Humphreys (n. 2), p.72.

[5] Gould, 'Dramatic character' (n. 3), p.64 n. 21.

[6] The importance of this moment is also stressed in a suggestive essay by K. Reckford, 'Medea's first exit', *TAPA* 99 (1968) pp.329–59.

[7] This point is made by A.P. Burnett, who refers to other 'centrifugal' plays – *Ajax, Hecuba, Trojan Women* – but points out that Medea's household is in an even more unstable position (A.P. Burnett, '*Medea* and the tragedy of revenge', *CPh* 68 (1973), pp.1–24). It was also nicely made in a recent adaptation by Barney Simon of *Medea* at the Riverside Studios, London, in which Medea's 'home' was a makeshift canvas tent.

[8] Vernant's discussions of the organization of space in ancient Greece are relevant here: see particularly 'Hestia-Hermes', in which he explores the paradoxes inherent in the position of a wife, who comes into the *oikos* from outside but is also at its centre (ch. 5 in J.-P. Vernant, *Myth and Thought among the Greeks*, London, 1983), and 'Space and political organisation in ancient Greece' (ch. 8 in the same volume).

[9] A brief account of both stages of a marriage is given in R. Flacelière, *Daily Life in Greece at the Time of Pericles* (London, 1965), pp.60–6.

[10] Humphreys (n. 2), p.1.

[11] Humphreys comments on this speech as a whole that it represents a man's view of 'what it would feel like ... to be the kind of wife Athenian men wanted' (73), and she regards this as symptomatic of the limitations of 'even the most strenuous attempt ... to see life from a woman's point of view' on the part of the dramatists. Sophocles, however, puts into the mouth of Procne, in his *Tereus*, a far more orthodox version of this transaction: 'When we are girls, our life in our father's house is sweetest. ... But when we come to years of discretion, we are thrust out and sold in marriage (διεμπολώμεθα) far away from our ancestral gods and from our parents ...' (Radt 583, tr. Jebb). This suggests that more is involved in Euripides' account than a simple failure of imagination.

[12] Line 300 – τῶν δ' αὖ δοκούντων εἰδέναι τι ποικίλον ('Those who have a reputation for subtlety') – bears some resemblance – perhaps fortuitous – to parts of the passage in

which Plato, fifty years later, represents Socrates as describing the dangers which arose from his reputation: see *Apology* 20d–23c, esp. 21b–22.

[13] This association is most clearly described by Michael Shaw, 'The female intruder: women in fifth-century drama', *CPh* 70 (1975), pp.255–66. On the different types of relationship in general, and contemporary thinking about them, see Reckford (n. 6), pp.340–2, Humphreys (n. 2), p.74 and *passim*, Vernant (n. 8), p.227 and *passim*.

[14] J. Gould, 'Hiketeia', *JHS* 93 (1973) pp.74–103, esp. 85–6.

[15] Another striking echo occurs at 1.583: compare Medea's description of Jason as οὐκ ἄγαν σοφός ('not so very clever') with her earlier εἰμὶ δ' οὐκ ἄγαν σοφή (305) ('I am not so very clever').

[16] See, for example, 523–5, 546, 585.

[17] 'The Greek is surrounded, as it were, by a series of concentric fortifications against the outside world ... the innermost fortress includes his nearest kin and friends, the outermost wall embraces all Hellenes': F.R. Earp, *The Way of the Greeks* (London, 1929), p.32. See also K.J. Dover, *Greek Popular Morality in the Time of Plato and Aristotle* (Oxford, 1974), esp. pp.273ff.

[18] W.R. Connor, *The New Politicians of Fifth Century Athens* (Princeton, NJ, 1971), esp. pp.30ff.

[19] B.M.W. Knox, 'The *Medea* of Euripides', *YCS* 25 (1977), pp.193–225.

[20] See esp. Knox (n. 19), p.211.

[21] R. Padel, 'Women: model for possession by Greek demons', in A. Cameron and A. Kuhrt (eds), *Images of Women in Antiquity* (London, 1983), pp.3–19.

[22] See the works cited in notes 13 and 18, and esp. Connor, p.53.

[23] Knox (n. 19), p.224. On the place of the idealizing odes in the play, see Reckford (n. 6), pp.342–6, and P. Pucci, *The Violence of Pity in Euripides' 'Medea'* (Ithaca, NY, and London, 1980), esp. pp.116ff. The influence of Pucci's reading of the play on my argument will be apparent.

D10 P.E. Easterling, 'The infanticide in Euripides' *Medea'*

From *Yale Classical Studies*, vol.25, 1977, pp.177–91, footnotes edited.

In many respects Euripides' *Medea* is not a problematic play. It is a singularly bold, clear-cut, assured piece of writing, the concentration and dramatic intensity of which are readily felt by reader or audience and command the respect even of those who find the subject matter repellent or who cavil at the Aegeus scene and the dragon chariot. But its starkness makes it deeply disturbing; and this unease is reflected in the critical literature on the play. The language, though consistently powerful, lacks the rich expansiveness of *Hippolytus* or *Bacchae*, almost never allowing us to range in imagination away from the immediate painful situation; it is typical that one of the most prominent of the recurring images is of Medea as a wild beast.[1] Then there is the striking absence of a cosmic frame of reference: we are given no sense of divine motivation or sanction or control. Medea is admittedly grand-daughter of the Sun, but the fact has no theological significance: its function is to symbolize her sense of her heroic identity and – at a different level – to motivate the final scene. The most uncompromising feature of all is Euripides' handling of the story, his design which makes the murder of the children the centrepiece of the play.

This horrific act is something from which we naturally recoil. 'No sane person', we say, 'would do such a thing', and indeed Euripides' many imitators have tended to present Medea's behaviour as that of a madwoman.[2] Or 'no civilized person would do it'; Sir Denys Page, for example, writes, 'The murder of children ... is mere brutality: if it moves us at all, it does so towards incredulity and horror. Such an act is outside our experience, we – and the fifth-century Athenian – know nothing of it'.[3] Doubts have been felt in particular about Medea's great speech at 1021ff. in which she wrestles with her conflicting feelings of injured pride and love for her children: is Euripides merely playing with our emotions through a rhetorical handling of the situation, exploiting the dramatic effectiveness of Medea's debate with herself rather than having an eye to what a person would really do in such circumstances?[4] Or conversely, is this conflict in Medea's soul the real high point of the drama, of more tragic importance than the violent act itself?[5] Or is it possible, as has recently been suggested, that we retain some sympathy with Medea right through to her final triumph, so that the final scene is the real climax of the play?[6] Clearly an important question to be faced by any critic who wishes to interpret *Medea* is whether Euripides is exploring the realities of human behaviour or creating only an illusion of reality out of a sequence of essentially melodramatic actions.

'Real life' in drama is not, of course, the same phenomenon as real life outside. Distortion or suppression of documentary fact and neglect – within certain limits – even of probability are part of the dramatist's stock-in-trade which we accept at the same time as believing in the truthfulness of his situations. Thus it is no fundamental failure on Euripides' part that he abandons probability in his treatment of the chorus. It is highly unlikely that these respectable ladies of Corinth would really have stood ineffectually by when Medea announced her intention to kill their king and princess and then her own children. In real life they would have taken steps to have Medea taken into custody, or at the very least would have gone to warn the royal family and Jason. But we accept their inactivity because these women are not at the centre of the play: they are peripheral figures whose role is not to do and suffer but to comment, sympathize, support or disapprove. The advantages of providing Medea with a sympathetic and understanding audience within the play far outweigh any loss of naturalism. A much graver breach is committed by Seneca, when he makes Medea after killing the children toss the corpses down to Jason.[7] The whole motivation of the mother who murders her children is unintelligible if she is willing to surrender their corpses to the husband whom she is punishing. Similarly, in Corneille's *Médée* there is no conviction at all in the scene where *Jason* thinks of killing the children to punish Medea.[8]

It is worth considering how Euripides manipulates the story in order to force us to take Medea seriously. The barbarian sorceress with a melodramatic criminal record who could so easily be a monster must become a tragic character, a paradigm, in some sense, of humanity. The Nurse's opening speech alludes briefly to that record: Medea is in exile for persuading the daughters of Pelias to kill their father, but there is no suggestion that she is shunned or feared by the Corinthians; the Nurse says she 'pleases' them (11f.) and the friendly words of the chorus (137, 178ff.) imply that she is an accepted, even a respected, figure. According to a scholiast on Pindar (*O.* 13, 74) Medea served the Corinthians by stopping a famine in their city; but Euripides makes no explicit mention of a story which on the face of it looks ideally suited to his purpose, for the good reason that it would introduce distracting complications into the scene with Creon. Unlike Seneca and Corneille, he clearly wanted to avoid giving the situation even the vaguest political dimension: there are to be no outside pressures on Creon, and he is to have no obligations to Medea for past services. So Euripides with fine sleight-of-hand contrives to imply that Medea's status at Corinth is one of some dignity, but without explaining why; later it becomes clear that she has a reputation as a wise woman, but the picture that is very lightly sketched in (for example in the scene with Aegeus) is as close to that of a respectable religious authority as to that of an outlandish witch.[9]

Medea as foreigner is another theme which is delicately handled by Euripides. At the most superficial level the fact that she is a barbarian from Colchis must have helped a Greek audience to accept both her past crimes and her expertise as a powerful sorceress, but we should be rash to conclude that it offered them an adequate explanation of the child murder. If Medea is to be seen as a distinctively oriental type ('because she was a foreigner she could kill her children'[10]) why does Euripides make her talk like a Greek, argue like a Greek, and to all appearances *feel* like a Greek? It is hard to believe, particularly in view of the astonishingly crass words he gives to Jason at 536ff., that Euripides was seriously imputing moral superiority to the Greeks, implying that only a foreigner could or would murder her own kin. On the contrary, he seems to exploit the theme of Medea's foreignness in order to emphasize her vulnerability and isolation and also to make a searching analysis of the nature of civilization and barbarism, a deep preoccupation of this play, to which we shall return.

Similarly, the record of Medea's past crimes is used – initially at any rate – more to arouse than to alienate the audience's sympathy. Euripides does not suppress the murder of Apsyrtus (166–7) or the killing of Pelias (9), though he is careful not to dwell on the grisly details of dismemberment and boiling. The subdued recall of these past horrors no doubt foreshadows the violence to come; but one of its main functions is to make clear that Medea has sacrificed literally everything for Jason, thus emphasizing his special ingratitude and her special defencelessness: she has not merely abandoned her family, she has betrayed them for Jason's sake. Nor does Euripides allow any character to raise the question of the legal relationship between Jason and Medea. None of them suggests[11] that Jason was perfectly entitled to abandon Medea without bad faith because as a foreigner she could not be his legitimate wife. Like other dramatists in other plays[12] Euripides permits himself a certain vagueness in legal matters, relying on the fact that the story is set in the heroic age, not in fifth-century Athens, however strongly the social comment may strike us as contemporary. This is one of those questions which in real life would be crucially important, but which it suits a dramatist to suppress. The essential situation is perfectly clear-cut: Jason and Medea are to be regarded as permanently pledged,[13] so that when Jason abandons Medea he *is* breaking faith (and even he does not deny it).

Euripides has taken pains, therefore, to present the situation in such a way that we are obliged to take Medea seriously. The structure of the first part of the play and the detail of these early scenes seem to be aimed at the same objective, the audience's full response to Medea as a tragic character.

The prologue from 46ff., the entry of the children, can fairly be described as a 'mirror scene', a tightly self-contained presentation in miniature of the course that the action is going to take. It has very little direct connection with the immediately following scene, beyond the fact that the chorus ask the Nurse to coax Medea out of the house and she does actually emerge at 214, the beginning of the first episode, its main function seems rather to be prophetic, like the short scene in *Hippolytus* where the old servant reproves Hippolytus for his neglect of Aphrodite (88–120). Here the Nurse three times expresses her fear for the children's safety at their mother's hands (90ff; 100ff.; 116ff.), having already glancingly introduced the theme in her opening speech: 'She hates the children and takes no pleasure in seeing them. I am afraid she may make some new [i.e. sinister] plan' (36f.). Medea's own curses reinforce this sense of foreboding: 'O cursed children of a hateful mother, may you perish with your father, and the whole house go to ruin!' (112ff.). And the children themselves appear, fresh from their games, to impress their significance on the audience. From the start, then , it is made clear that this is not just a quarrel between man and wife, but a family drama in which the future and even the safety of the children are at stake. Medea herself is presented in all the alarming violence of her passion, but framed by the sympathy of Nurse and chorus, and therefore to be seen by the audience as a victim, even if also as a potential criminal.

When Medea comes out to talk to the chorus all the wildness has gone and she develops her arguments with complete composure. The focus of the dramatic interest is now this commanding personality in a sequence of encounters, first with the chorus, then with three men who in different ways have power to affect her life. With the chorus she is at her most frank and open, winning their whole-hearted support with her account of the miseries of a woman's life. At this stage the audience, too, must readily give her their sympathy, but complications already begin to arise. How much, we may ask, of what she says to the chorus is special pleading, designed to make them promise to keep her secret? As always with Medea it is hard to be sure; and here we meet for the first time the subtle complexity of Euripides' character-portrayal. At least her description of the constraints on women is deeply convincing, but when she complains of her special lack of resource as a foreigner with 'no mother, no *brother*, no kinsman' to support her (257f.) we perhaps remember that it was she herself who caused her brother's death and betrayed her family. These words lead straight into her plea for collusion on the part of the chorus if she finds some way of punishing her husband: 'for woman is fearful and timid in other respects and a coward when it comes to looking on steel, but when her marriage is treated with contempt there is no bloodier purpose than hers' (263ff.). We are left in no doubt that this is a formidable woman; and, despite all that she has said in this scene about the limitations of the feminine role, it is clear that she herself is capable of overcoming them. When she makes her famous claim (250f.) that she would rather stand three times in the battle line than bear one child she wins our respect – she is talking, of course, about the emotional hazards of being a mother, not just about the physical pain and danger of childbearing – but even so, not many women would say what Medea says; these words may come back to our minds at the end of the scene with Creon.

With the king we see the full exposure of Medea's cleverness, her *sophia*. Creon is explicit that he is exiling her because he fears what her cleverness may devise to harm his family; Medea's response is a dazzling virtuoso display of the very quality he fears. First she argues that her cleverness could not possibly be used to harm *him*, next exerts extreme emotional pressure by appealing to his feelings as a father,[14] and finally makes a disarmingly modest request: just one day's grace, time for making the necessary arrangements for going into exile. But as soon as he has left and Medea has got her way there is a striking change of tone: now we see all the contempt of the clever person for the fool. 'Do you think I would have fawned on that man if I had not had some profit or plan in mind?' (368f.). Now in a highly professional way she discusses the possible modes of murder she might choose: shall it be fire, or sword, or poison, her speciality? This could easily be bloodcurdling for bloodcurdling's sake as in Seneca and Corneille, who both make much of her gruesome rites and incantations. In Euripides the effect is less gothic; indeed a main function of this detail seems to be to emphasize Medea's cleverness: in her own view of herself her magical skill is part of her heroic *arete*.

This speech at 364ff. (and particularly the last section from 392) illuminates a most important aspect of Euripides' Medea. She sees herself not just as a woman wronged, but as a great personage in the heroic mould of an Ajax or an Achilles: she owes it to herself and to her high pedigree to allow no enemy to triumph over her. The grand-daughter of Helios must face the test of courage: νῦν ἀγὼν εὐψυχίας, language that an Ajax or an Achilles might perfectly well use. In this context Medea standing in the battle line becomes fully intelligible. The scene ends on a less grandiose, more sinister, note: 'We are women, helpless when it comes to good deeds, but skilled practitioners of all kinds of evil' (408f.).[15] There is a clash here between Medea's self-image as a hero of the old style braving a great ordeal and her awareness of the destructiveness of thwarted female passion. We see very clearly that her cleverness is a potent force for evil as well as for good. The tragedy is that she does stand out above the limited or shabby people around her, does have a sharper moral awareness and far greater distinction and force of personality, yet the audience cannot help but shudder at the ruthlessness of her anger and passion for vengeance.

In her first scene with Jason, Medea is at her most sympathetic, because here we are allowed to see the full extent of the provocation she has been suffering. Jason is a status-seeker, embarrassed by his barbarian wife who refuses to go quietly, anxious to have her out of the way but insensitive enough to talk about exile being a hardship, crassly patronizing in his offer of material help. Medea's theme is simple: 'I saved you';[16] and she is right. All her past acts of betrayal were committed in the cause of Jason and her love for him; and now he is guilty of the greatest betrayal of all, the breaking of those dearly-bought oaths. The only extenuation would have been if their union had been childless: but they *have children* (παίδων γεγώτων at 490 carries the strongest possible emphasis). Jason's answer only confirms our sense of his outrageousness. He is sophistical in his argument that it was Cypris, not Medea, who saved him, ludicrously arrogant when he recalls the benefits he has conferred on his wife by bringing her to civilized Greece from her benighted barbarian home, patently self-deceptive[17] when he pretends that his only interest in the new marriage is the welfare of his existing family. Once more the importance of children is made very prominent, particularly at 565, when Jason implies that he needs a family more than Medea does. Medea's final taunt turns into a sinister threat which recalls the concluding lines of the two previous scenes: we are reminded that she is still planning revenge, though the encounter with Jason has done nothing to further the action in any practical sense and Medea still has no idea where she can go when she has punished her victims.

Then Aegeus arrives unexpectedly to answer her need. Aegeus is merely passing through Corinth on his way from the Delphic oracle to consult Pittheus, his old friend who is king of Troezen. The casualness of his arrival has been criticized from Aristotle[18] onwards, but as with Io's visit to the Caucasus in *Prometheus Bound* such casualness is readily acceptable to an audience provided that the scene itself is dramatically significant, and provided that it is seen to be part of a structural pattern. Here there is a clearly discernible design: three contrasting visits to Medea, of which the third offers a close parallel to the first.[19] Both the scene with Creon and the scene with Aegeus show Medea using her wits to get what she wants from a person in authority, but whereas Creon was all suspicion and misgivings Aegeus is full of honourable and rather naive trust. Medea is equal to either situation; and the most interesting link between the two scenes is in her choice of persuasive argument. With Creon it is his feelings as a parent she exploits, with Aegeus his longing to be a parent. Once more her cleverness succeeds: she now has a refuge in Athens, and she can afford to make a detailed plan of vengeance.

Her speech at 764ff. is the most remarkable in the play. It starts with her triumphant exultation and her plot for the murder of the princess and Creon, then leads without preparation into the terrible revelation that she intends to kill her children. Her own explanation makes the best starting point for a discussion of this speech. She sees the murder of her children as a means of *punishing her enemies.* The deed will be 'most unholy', but she will do it because her enemies' laughter is not to be tolerated. The penalty that is worse than death for her enemy Jason will be to have no children, neither Medea's nor any borne to him by the princess. And so 'let no one think me cowardly or weak, or peaceable, but of quite the opposite temper: dire to my enemies and kindly to my friends. For it is such people who live in the highest esteem.' This is the kind of language with which she exults in her success over Aegeus: 'now I shall win the victory over my enemies' (764–7), language that recalls the end of the scene with Creon with its image of the heroic Medea facing the 'test of courage'. These are all words that belong to the traditional code, in which the laughter of enemies is the ultimate disgrace and harming enemies and helping friends is the duty of a hero. But Medea's appropriation of the code seems hideously out of place in a situation where the enemy is her husband and the means of punishing him is to be an act of bloodthirsty treachery followed by the murder of her own children.

The essential relevance of the scene with Aegeus must be its stress on the value and importance of children. Euripides does not make clear exactly when Medea arrives at the details of her plan, and we cannot say that the encounter with Aegeus gives her the idea to kill the children; it is enough that after the scene with Aegeus she has the idea very fully worked out: this will be Jason's consummate punishment, to be robbed of his future. Her announcement comes as a surprise, but it is not factitious: the prologue's prophetic warnings and the prominence of the theme of parents and children in all three of Medea's encounters have effectively prepared the way.[20] This technique is perhaps subtler than the version preferred by Seneca, an episode in which Medea sees how much Jason loves his children and says 'Now I have him.' Euripides' Medea does not need to be shown evidence of Jason's fatherly love: she simply knows that even a man as selfish and coarse-grained as Jason, who for the moment is quite absorbed in his young bride and his new social status and content for his whole family to go into exile, can still be profoundly hurt by the loss of his children.

Even more than the scene with Aegeus it is the child murder itself that has caused the greatest critical unease. Perhaps this is because society so much abhors the murder of children that it refuses to regard it as anything but the rarest and most outrageous of deviations. Hence the attempt to explain Medea's act as something quite outside the experience of civilized people. In general we tend not to look on murder as such with the same disbelief; and it comes as a surprise to find from modern statistics that a large proportion of murder victims are in fact children – nearly one-third of the total in the United Kingdom between 1957 and 1968,[21] nearly half in Denmark in recent times[22] – and that the killers are predominantly their parents. Often the killing of children is accompanied by suicide on the part of the parents, but one parent may kill a child or children as a means of hurting the marriage partner. May it not be that in *Medea* we find Euripides exhibiting the same psychological sureness of touch as in his studies of Phaedra and Electra and Pentheus, or as in the scene where Cadmus brings Agave back to reality?[23]

Medea is trying to achieve the punishment of Jason; the death of the princess and Creon is not enough, because through her children Medea can still be hurt or insulted (by the 'laughter of her enemies'), if *they* are hurt or insulted. With them alive and in his care Jason can still look to the future through them. There is no question of Medea's admitting to a wish to punish the children: she calls them 'most beloved' (795) and her deed 'most unholy' (796): only in the prologue does she curse them and the Nurse say she 'hates the children' (presumably because they represent her vulnerability to Jason). Indeed she thinks she is being loyal to her dear ones and winning glory by her actions (809f.), heroic language which a psychologist would probably describe as an 'altruistic' and 'protective' rationalization of the child murder. It seems that very often the parents who kill their children convince themselves that the children would in their own interests be better dead.[24]

The scene of false reconciliation between Medea and Jason makes magnificent theatre; it also has a subtle importance in its relation to the rest of the play.[25] It emphasizes the link between the two stages of Medea's revenge by showing the children who are to be victims of the culminating deed innocently bearing the poisoned gifts which will make them the agents of the first murder, with Jason as their accomplice. From 894ff. the children are the focus of the action; and seeing them in Jason's embraces and hearing his confident words about their future, Medea twice breaks down, though each time she resourcefully contrives to explain her tears in a sense which furthers her deception of Jason. The episode has a complex function: it confirms our awareness of the children's importance to Jason and at the same time prepares for the moving passage (1029ff.) where Medea imagines the future that the children will never have. Moreover her self-mastery here, according to Steidle's persuasive analysis,[26] foreshadows the success of her resolve in the following scene. Certainly it must now seem clear to the audience, as it does to the chorus, that the children are bound to die: 'Now no longer have I any hope left for the children's lives, no longer. They go already to their deaths' (976ff.).

Now Medea learns that the first part of her plan has worked and the children have been allowed to stay in Corinth; she must say goodbye to them, ostensibly because she is going into exile, but we know that she confronts the essential issue. Time is short, and without the death of the children her revenge will not be complete; but can she face the deed? The speech at 1021ff. in which she expresses the struggle between her maternal love and her desire for revenge has been tirelessly discussed:[27] is it the tragic climax of the play, showing Medea caught in a conflict on the outcome of which we hang in suspense, or is the inevitability that she will kill her children strongly felt all through the speech, and the climax reached only in the final scene? Recent critics have been particularly concerned with the structural question and also with the apparent inconsistency of Medea's motivation. Within the space of a few lines she moves from the statement that she will take the children with her into exile (1058) to the assertion that there is no escape: they are certain to be killed in Corinth, and she must therefore do the deed (1059–64).

The detail of the speech suggests that despite a certain rhetorical formalism of manner Euripides keeps close to observed patterns of human behaviour. The reality of Medea's love for her children is evoked in her very precise recall of the hopes she used to cherish for their future and hers (1024–35) and in her response to the extraordinarily powerful appeal of their bright eyes and soft skin (1070–5). But the reality of her obsessive need to triumph over her enemies is also made inescapably clear (1049–55; 1059–60), the need to hurt Jason as deeply as anyone can ever be hurt, which has been fully explored earlier in the play, both in the betrayed wife's passion for vengeance and in the heroic self-image which makes Medea a far from ordinary but none the less convincing and tragic figure.

Euripides needs to make us believe in Medea's maternal feeling not because we are to think there is a real hope that she may change her mind for good, but in order to achieve the full depth of tragic seriousness. The deed she contemplates is so horrific that we cannot accept it unless we are given evidence that it has cost a profound struggle. Comparison with Seneca illustrates very well the difference between tragic and melodramatic treatment of the situation. Seneca's

Medea carries conviction only as a raving madwoman, whose moments of maternal feeling (938ff.) show none of the Euripidean Medea's precise awareness of what children mean to a mother. In any case, her softer emotions soon give way to visions of Furies accompanying the dismembered Apsyrtus, to whom Medea sacrifices one of the children, keeping the other to be killed in full view of Jason and the citizens. With her intended victim at her side she expresses a fleeting sense of remorse, but this is soon lost in the joy of gloating over Jason; of the child's presumed agony she seems (like Seneca) to be unaware:

> quid, misera, feci? misera? paeniteat licet,
> feci. uoluptas magna me inuitam subit,
> et ecce crescit. derat hoc unum mihi,
> spectator iste.

> [What, wretched woman, have I done? Wretched? Though I repent,
> I have done the deed. Great delight steals on me against my will,
> and behold, it increases. But this one thing I lacked,
> that man as spectator.]

> *(990–3)*

Euripides' master-stroke in this speech is Medea's announcement at 1059ff. that there is no going back: the poison must have done its work by now and the princess must already be dead. We can assume that the treacherous murder of the princess and Creon will in reality mean danger for the children from the outraged royal family, as Jason later confirms, (1303ff.). Medea's reaction, when she faces the fact that the murder must have happened, is to treat this danger as inescapable, although a moment earlier she has been speaking of taking the children away with her. She is filled, in fact, with a sudden sense that she is caught in the tide of events and has no longer any choice. This is the atmosphere of sudden urgency in which we are told that the murder of children is often committed: the parent becomes convinced of a threat to the children that clinches the feeling that they would be better dead.[28] Such an interpretation seems much more relevant to Medea's case than any of the others that have been put forward, of which the latest is that the children were too young to accompany their mother in a hasty escape.[29]

The sense of urgency is brought to a desperate climax in Medea's speech after the Messenger has told his story and urged her to fly. There is no word now of triumph over her enemies or of her own situation at all beyond her need to steel herself: her whole concentration is on the children. She must act 'as swiftly as possible', 'without delay'; since they are bound to be killed, she who loves them must be the one to do the deed, not some 'other more hostile hand' (1239ff.). The murder itself is represented by means of cries from the children and the chorus, but without any word from Medea; nowhere is there any hint of the gloating of Seneca's Medea as she raises the knife: 'perfruere lento scelere, ne propera, dolor' [enjoy a slow revenge, my grief, do not hasten] (1016).

The gloating (but never over the children) is to come in the stark final scene where Medea triumphs over Jason from the chariot, prophesying an evil death for him, refusing to let him even touch the children's bodies. The brute fact of Jason's loss moves us now; but it is Medea who speaks with prophetic authority. Clearly she has the role of the 'god from the machine' who so often in Euripides makes the final dispositions. This is one of the most alarming features of the play, the fact that there is no comparatively distant and objective divine figure to speak with the voice of authority, relating these events to real life through their link with some cult or institution and thereby restoring a sense of normality after the frightful extremes of the action. Medea makes a link between this story and a festival at Corinth (1381ff.); but she offers no relief whatever from the horror of the situation.

The powerful effect of this final scene depends on Euripides' use of the supernatural device of the dragon chariot, which transforms Medea's status from that of runaway criminal to something outside ordinary human experience. It was a bold dramatic experiment, but Euripides was justified in making it, granted that the effect could be adequately and not absurdly represented on the Greek stage. There has been criticism of the contrast between this very blatant use of the supernatural and the realistic tone of the rest of the action,[30] but some kind of miraculous device was needed if Euripides was to contrive a final confrontation between Jason and Medea in which Medea should at last have her triumph. The whole plot in fact rests on unrealistic data which we accept without qualm: for example, Medea's relationship to Helios (a frequently stressed motif which helps to prepare for the chariot) and the remarkable nature of her magical power. Yet throughout we are invited to take Medea seriously as a real human being, and even this final scene is perfectly consistent with the rest of the play in its handling of her motivation; it is only the spectacle of her in the chariot, high above Jason, taking with her the children's bodies that he may not touch, that makes her seem to have been transformed, in Murray's words, 'into a sort of living Curse ... Her wrongs and her hate fill the sky'.[31]

The sense that Euripides seems to be making out of all this is as comfortless as the conclusions to which he points in *Hippolytus* or *Bacchae*. What a vulnerable thing is civilization, when man's passions are so powerfully destructive. When he makes the insensitive Jason praise Greek society and values and when he gives the barbarian witch the ideals of a traditional Greek hero he is surely suggesting that there is no safe dividing line: civilized life is always most precariously poised, continually threatened from within.

One of the play's recurrent themes is that of song and the Muses: it comes in that curious passage at the end of the *parodos* where the Nurse meditatively wonders why poets have not devised songs to cure human miseries instead of accompanying their pleasures (190ff.); in the first *stasimon* when the chorus reflect how poetry has always represented the man's side of things (421ff.); most prominently in the great passage in praise of Athens after the departure of Aegeus (824ff.). Athens, city of the Muses, the ideal of civilized splendour, where *Sophia* and the Loves are in harmony: is this merely a fine compliment to an Athenian audience, or is it related more intimately to the deeper meaning of the play? All these passages draw attention to the ambivalence of human intelligence and creativity, which is potentially a source of beauty and harmony, but liable, too, to break out in destructive violence under the influence of passion. Medea in her *sophia* exemplifies this ambivalence: we see her great expertise and intellectual power turned, because of her betrayed love for Jason, to destructive – and self-destructive – ends. And her heroic sense of identity is used to bring out the tragic nature of what she does and suffers.

[1] 92; (103); 187ff.; 1342f.; 1358f.; 1407.

[2] Cf. W.H. Friedrich, 'Medeas Rache' in *Euripides*, ed. E.R. Schwinge (Darmstadt 1968), p.209.

[3] D.L. Page, *Euripides, Medea* (Oxford 1938), p.xiv.

[4] 'She has her struggle with her maternal feelings – a theatrical struggle rather than a psychologically convincing one'. H.D.F. Kitto, *Greek Tragedy*, 3rd ed. (London 1961), p.195.

[5] Cf. M. Pohlenz, *Die griechische Tragodie*, 2nd ed. (Göttingen 1954), vol. I, pp.255ff.

[6] So W. Steidle, *Studien zum Antiken Drama* (Munich 1968), p.165.

[7] If modern editors are right in so interpreting 'recipe iam natos parens' (*Medea* 1024).

[8] *Médée* V, v.

[9] Cf. D.J. Conacher, *Euripidean Drama* (Toronto 1967), pp.186–7, 190.

[10] Page (n. 3 above), p.xxi.

[11] Although at least one critic has done so (G. Murray, in the introduction to his translation (London 1910), pp.viif.).

[12] E.g. Sophocles on the edict in *Antigone*. Cf. D.A. Hester, *Mnemosyne* 24 (1971), 19–21.

[13] The theme of their oaths is given repeated stress: 21ff.; 160ff.; 168ff.; 208ff.; 438ff. (and the whole *stasimon*); 492ff.; 1392.

[14] E. Schlesinger, *Hermes* 94 (1966), 42, makes much of Creon's remark at 329 that his children are dearer to him than anything else in life. This is certainly important, in that it gives Medea her cue for exploiting Creon and keeps the theme of children in the foreground, but can we say that it actually gives her the idea of killing her children?

[15] The rhyme (ἀμηχανώταται ... σοφώταται) adds to the sonorousness of this ending.

[16] 476; 515: powerful use of ring-composition.

[17] The chorus are not deceived (578; 637ff.); and Jason's words to the princess (reported by the Messenger at 1150ff.) suggest that he was enjoying his role as royal bridegroom.

[18] *Poetics* 1461 b 21. At least Euripides has warned us to expect *someone* to arrive (390–4).

[19] Cf. D.W. Lucas, *The Greek Tragic Poets*, 2nd ed. (London 1959), p.197.

[20] Cf. D. Ebener, *Rheinisches Museum* 104 (1961), 224.

[21] Cf. E. Gibson and S. Klein, *Murder 1957 to 1968 = Home Office Research Studies 3* (London 1969). I am grateful to my colleague Mrs. A.M. Morris for a criminologist's view of the problem of child murder.

[22] Cf. T. Harder, *Acta Psychiatrica Scandinavica* 43 (1967), 197ff.

[23] Cf. G. Devereux, *J.H.S.* 90 (1970), 35ff. for a study of this scene.

[24] Harder n. 23 above, pp.235ff.

[25] Cf. A. Lesky, *Die tragische Dichtung der Hellenen*, 3rd ed. (Göttingen 1972), p.307; Steidle, *Studien*, pp.156f.

[26] See n. 25 above.

[27] Cf. A. Lesky (n. 26 above), pp.311f.

[28] Cf. Harder (n. 23 above), especially p.237, and L. Bender, *Journal of Nervous and Mental Disease* 80 (1934), 41.

[29] Steidle (n. 6 above), pp.159ff.

[30] R. Lattimore, for instance, regards the chariot as 'preposterous', merely a 'taxi to get from Corinth to Athens' (*The Poetry of Greek Tragedy* (Baltimore 1958), p.108).

[31] Murray (n. 11 above), pp.xif.

Section E EXPRESSION AND REPRESENTATION IN MUSIC

E1 Donald Macintyre, 'The inheritance'

From J.F. Campbell (trans.) (1994, new edn) *Popular Tales of the West Highlands*, Edinburgh, Birlinn Ltd, vol.1, pp.391–3, first published 1860–1 by Edmonston & Douglas, Edinburgh.

There was once a farmer, and he was well off. He had three sons. When he was on the bed of death he called them to him, and he said, 'My sons, I am going to leave you: let there be no disputing when I am gone. In a certain drawer, in a dresser in the inner chamber, you will find a sum of gold; divide it fairly and honestly amongst you, work the farm, and live together as you have done with me;' and shortly after the old man went away. The sons buried him; and when all was over, they went to the drawer, and when they drew it out there was nothing in it.

They stood for a while without speaking a word. Then the youngest spoke, and he said – 'There is no knowing if there ever was any money at all;' the second said – 'There was money surely, wherever it is now;' and the eldest said – 'Our father never told a lie. There was money certainly, though I cannot understand the matter.' 'Come,' said the eldest, 'let us go to such an old man; he was our father's friend; he knew him well; he was at school with him; and no man knew so much of his affairs. Let us go to consult him.'

So the brothers went to the house of the old man, and they told him all that had happened. 'Stay with me,' said the old man, 'and I will think over this matter. I cannot understand it; but, as you know, your father and I were very great with each other. When he had children I had sponsorship, and when I had children he had gostji. I know that your father never told a lie.' And he kept them there, and he gave them meat and drink for ten days.

Then he sent for the three young lads, and he made them sit down beside him, and he said –

'There was once a young lad, and he was poor; and he took love for the daughter of a rich neighbour, and she took love for him; but because he was so poor there could be no wedding. So at last they pledged themselves to each other, and the young man went away, and stayed in his own house. After a time there came another suitor, and because he was well off, the girl's father made her promise to marry him, and after a time they were married. But when the bridegroom came to her, he found her weeping and bewailing; and he said, "What ails thee?" The bride would say nothing for a long time; but at last she told him all about it, and how she was pledged to another man. "Dress thyself," said the man, "and follow me." So she dressed herself in the wedding clothes, and he took the horse, and put her behind him, and rode to the house of the other man, and when he got there, he struck in the door, and he called out, "Is there man within?" and when the other answered, he left the bride there within the door, and he said nothing, but he returned home. Then the man got up, and got a light, and who was there but the bride in her wedding dress.

"'What brought thee here?" said he. "Such a man," said the bride. "I was married to him today, and when I told him of the promise we had made, he brought me here himself and left me."

"'Sit thou there," said the man; "art thou not married?" So he took the horse, and he rode to the priest, and he brought him to the house, and before the priest he loosed the woman from the pledge she had given, and he gave her a line of writing that she was free, and he set her on the horse, and said, "Now return to thy husband."

'So the bride rode away in the darkness in her wedding dress. She had not gone far when she came to a thick wood where three robbers stopped and seized her. "Aha!" said one, "we have waited long, and we have got nothing, but now we have got the bride herself." "Oh," said she, "let me go: let me go to my husband; the man that I was pledged to has let me go. Here are ten pounds in gold – take them, and let me go on my journey." And so she begged and prayed for a long time, and told what had happened to her. At last one of the robbers, who was of a better nature than the rest, said, "Come, as the others have done this, I will take you home myself." "Take thou the money," said she. "I will not take a penny," said the robber; but the other two said, "Give us the money," and they took the ten pounds. The woman rode home, and the robber left her at her husband's door, and she went in, and showed him the line – the writing that the other had given her before the priest, and they were well pleased.'

'Now,' said the old man, 'which of all these do you think did best?' So the eldest son said, 'I think the man that sent the woman to him to whom she was pledged, was the honest, generous man: he did well.' The second said, 'Yes, but the man to whom she was pledged did still better, when he sent her to her husband.' 'Then,' said the youngest, 'I don't know myself; but perhaps the wisest of all were the robbers who got the money.' Then the old man rose up, and he said, 'Thou hast thy father's gold and silver. I have kept you here for ten days; I have watched you well. I know your father never told a lie, and thou hast stolen the money.' And so the youngest son had to confess the fact, and the money was got and divided.

E2 'The song of a girl ravished away by the fairies in South Uist'

From Judith Weir, *Songs from the Exotic*, Chester Music, No.4, pp.19–21.

E3 Leonard Bernstein, *Chichester Psalms*

From the score of Leonard Bernstein's *Chichester Psalms*, published by
G. Shirmer, New York.

Bernstein began his musical career as a conductor, working with the New
York Philharmonic Orchestra from 1944, and then going on to work with
most of the world's leading orchestras. Bernstein's compositions include a
number of stage works, such as the ballet *Fancy Free* (1944), the Broadway
musical *On the Town* (1944) and his most popular work, *West Side Story*
(1957). He also wrote symphonies, choral works and chamber music.

This work was commissioned by the Reverend Walter Hussey, Dean of
Chichester Cathedral, West Sussex, for the 1965 Chichester Festival.

Words:

Ps. 108, vs. 2	*Urah, hanevel, v'chinor!*	Awake, psaltery and harp!
	A-irah shahar!	I will rouse the dawn!
Ps. 100, entire:	*Hariu l'Adonai kol haarets.*	Make a joyful noise unto the Lord all ye lands.
	Iv'du et Adonai b'simha.	Serve the Lord with gladness.
	Bo-u l'fanav bir'nanah.	Come before His presence with singing.
	D'u ki Adonai Hu Elohim.	Know ye that the Lord, He is God.
	Hu asanu, v'lo anahnu.	It is He that hath made us, and not we ourselves.
	Amo v'tson mar'ito.	We are His people and the sheep of His pasture
	Bo-u sh'arav b'todah,	Enter into His gates with thanksgiving,
	Hatseirotav bit'hilah,	And into His courts with praise.
	Hodu lo, bar'chu sh'mo.	Be thankful unto Him, and bless His name.
	Ki tov Adonai, l'olam has'do,	For the Lord is good, His mercy is everlasting,
	V'ad dor vador emunato.	And His truth endureth to all generations.

E4 *White Man Sleeps*

From the score of *White Man Sleeps*, published by Chester Music, 1995, CH 61123, p.2.

String Quartet No. 1 (*White Man Sleeps*) was written for the Kronos Quartet and first performed by them on 13 July 1986 at the Institute of Contemporary Arts, London.

Sources

In composing this piece I drew from the following sources: the first movement owes something to the style of Basotho concertina music; the second and fourth movements are drawn from traditional Nyungwe music played by Makina Chirenje and his Nyanga panpipe group at Nsava, Tete, Mozambique, recorded and transcribed by Andrew Tracey (to be found in an article entitled 'The nyanga panpipe dance' in *African Music*, Vol. 5, No. 1 (1971)); the third movement derives from the San bow music (recorded by Tony Traill of the University of Witwatersrand) and from Basotho lesiba music, transcribed by myself; in the fifth movement I added my own invented folklore. My approach to the original music was anything but purist – it is played in Western tuning, filtered, slowed down by a few 'time-octaves', cast into non-African metres (like the 13-beat pattern of the first dance) and redistributed between the players in several ways. I also used interlocking techniques where they were absent in the original models and *vice versa*.

The subtitle *White Man Sleeps* comes from a moment in nyanga panpipe music where the performers leave off playing their loud pipes for a few cycles and dance only to the sound of their ankle rattles, to let the white landowner sleep – for a minute or two.

Performance notes

1   The character of this music depends as much on performers following the exact tempo as on playing the correct pitches. Metronome markings must therefore be strictly observed. There should be no variation of tempo or dynamics and vibrato should not be used unless these are marked in the score.

2   The dynamics of *pizzicato* should be marked up as necessary in order to balance with those of *arco*. If *pizzicato* is combined with slurring, the first note of each slur is plucked and any subsequent notes are fingered with the left hand only.

3   Barlines are an aid to counting only, and do not imply any particular rhythmic emphasis.

4   Slurs indicate phrasing, not necessarily bowing.

5   The markings x2, x3, x4 etc. in repeated sections indicate the total number of times the passage is to be played (i.e. twice, three times, four times, etc.)

6   Players should not move during pauses within movements, or when tacet.

E5   Penny Clough, 'A survey of the younger generation of South African composers'

From P. Klatzow (ed.) (1987) *Composers in South Africa Today*, Oxford and Capetown, Oxford University Press, pp.218–21, footnotes edited.

Kevin Volans was born in Pietermaritzburg on 26 July 1949. He started piano lessons at the age of 10, but otherwise was self-taught musically until after he left school. Awarded a scholarship for science, he enrolled in the engineering faculty at the University of Natal.

He changed to architecture during the year but a persistent interest in music persuaded him to start studying music the following year at the University of the Witwatersrand. There, he became interested in musicology, and later on, in composition. After graduating in March 1972, he completed one year of post-graduate study at the University of Aberdeen, Scotland.

Thereafter, from August 1973 to 1976, he was a pupil of Karlheinz Stockhausen, at the Musikhochschule in Cologne. As one of an exceptionally gifted class of composition students, Volans became Stockhausen's teaching assistant, conducting many seminars and master classes in composition and analysis. As a guest lecturer, he also gave two courses in serial composition at the University of Cape Town Summer School in 1976, and, on later occasions, lectured in a similar capacity at universities in England, Germany and the United States.

Simultaneously with his studies with Stockhausen, Volans studied music theatre under Mauricio Kagel, piano with Aloys Kontarsky and improvisation, electronic music analysis, media aesthetics, music and speech under Johannes Fritsch.

From 1976 to 1979 he studied electronic music composition at the Musikhochschule electronic music studio. During this period he made four field recording trips to South Africa, commissioned by West German Radio, resulting in authoritative collections of traditional Zulu Basutho music. A number of programmes based on this research were broadcast.

As a pianist and harpsichordist, Volans appeared in many festivals of contemporary music in Europe and the United Kingdom, and some of his own compositions were premiered on such occasions.

After nine years of very successful and productive musical life in Europe, he returned to South Africa in 1981 and lectured in composition at the University of Natal in Durban. Volans left the University at the end of 1984 to leave himself open for freelance work.

International recognition of his talent won him an invitation to join the board of professors of the 1984 Darmstadt International Summer School which took place in the second half of July. The school is devoted to the study of the composition and performance of contemporary music. Also on the board of teachers was John Cage.

Two concerts of Volans works have been performed recently in Frankfurt and Cologne as part of a six-week festival of twentieth-century music called *Music of the Future*.

Considering the comparatively impoverished musical environment in South Africa it seems remarkable that this talented multi-faceted musician ever left Europe. Volans explains that it was in part due to a growing interest in African music, which ironically, only developed in Cologne. 'Feedback Studios had done a survey of street music in Cologne which impressed me tremendously. I discovered that I missed the sound of Zulu being spoken, of Zulu guitar music ... so I embarked on a study of African music through the literature and records that were available and put together a lengthy document on the subject which I presented to the West German Radio Station. They were interested in further research and sponsored four trips in all to Zululand, Lesotho, etc.'

Apart from the extensive material he collected, Volans became very interested in music for the family of plucked reed instruments called *mbira*, and on one of his trips, he bought a pair. However, as with any instrument, playing the *mbira* properly required practice and there were practical problems like having long finger-nails which interfered with piano playing. Volans solved the problem by using a harpsichord, not only for its similarity of sound, but primarily because it could be retuned to one of the several tuning systems (roughly seven equal steps to the octave) used for *mbira* music.

For a concert sponsored by the Kulturamt in Cologne he wrote two pieces, *Mbira*, for two retuned harpsichords and rattles and *Matepe*, for the same combination augmented by a viola da gamba. Both works are fairly strict realizations of pieces originally composed by Shona musicians (Zimbabwe), which have been researched and documented by Andrew Tracey. Public response to these two works, as on later occasions, was overwhelmingly enthusiastic, from audiences and critics alike, and Volans went on to write further pieces which he called 'African Paraphrases', amongst them *White Man Sleeps*.

This is a set of five dances drawn freely from San Bow music (which depicts the gaits of animals – hyena and elephant in this instance), Tswana panpipe music (researched and documented by Christopher

Ballantine), Basotho *lesiba* music (an instrument with a single string which is blown rather than bowed or plucked), Nyanga panpipe music (researched and documented by Andrew Tracey) and Basotho concertina music. The African atmosphere is vividly evoked by the intricate interweavings of rhythms and melodies, endlessly inventive in the effects they obtain from the same limited ensemble – two retuned harpsichords, viola da gamba and percussion – communicating enormous energy and what one critic has referred to as 'a hard spiritual beauty' [Musica Volans, *The Daily Telegraph*, London, July 20, 1982].

Also included under the heading 'African Paraphrases' are three taped pieces: *Cover him with Grass*, a seventeen-minute, straightforward reproduction of the people of Lesotho going about their business, *Kwazulu Summer Landscape*, a sixty-four-minute tape of untreated natural sounds, and *Studies in Zulu History*, which combines electronic and natural resources, the former deliberately imitating the latter in line with the paraphrase idea.

While South African audiences are generally unprepared for the lengthy soundscapes which these taped pieces create, Volans' most recent work, *Journal Walking Song*, commissioned for the 1983 Durban Arts Festival, was performed to enthusiastic acclaim. As the eighth in his set of African paraphrases, *Journal* (implying journey) is a personal response of the composer to African music. Whereas in previous works, Volans had 'allowed (himself) the liberty of adopting an African attitude to a Western instrument', *Journal* represents more a separation of the two cultures and a denial of their integration.

The chamber ensemble of two pianos, two flutes, clarinet, bassoon, trumpet, trombone, violin and double bass maintains Western equal temperament, signifying an alienation of the two elements – Western and African – which, formally, are also presented quite separately. The work is divided into two main sections, A and B, with three Interludes and a Coda. The African element only enters definitively in the B section in the form of an Ethiopian march tune. The second Interlude is based on *Mbira*, while the Coda consists of reworkings of early versions of *Monkey Music* (1977 and 1981).

The two pianos carry the main body of the material, with the other instruments often filling in or highlighting different motivic or rhythmic features of the two keyboard parts.

Though Volans describes his African paraphrases generally as successful 'middle-brow' music, his works in this field must be seen as a significant and pioneering contribution to contemporary South African repertoire. Whether or not wholly successful blending of Western and African music can be achieved is debatable, and Volans himself feels it is perhaps unattainable.

However, his aims to put local (African) music into a Western context –
which some unfairly regard as cultural banditry – are not intended as
mere exoticism but rather as a vital drawing on a sadly neglected and
infinitely rich source of indigenous musical culture. In so doing, he not
only brings such music to the attention of an appallingly unaware
listening public, but he also effects a reconciliation of musical cultures, a
reconciliation of both musical value and integrity.

E6 Benjamin Britten, *Serenade for Tenor, Horn and Strings* (1943)

From sleeve notes for the recording by Robert Tear/Alan Civil/Northern
Sinfonia/Sir Neville Marriner, EMI CDM7 69522 2 (1971/1988).

Words:

4 Dirge

This ae nighte, this ae nighte,
Every nighte and alle,
Fire and fleet and candle-lighte,
And Christe receive thy saule.

When thou from hence away art past,
Every nighte and alle,
To Whinnymuir thou com'st at last;
And Christe receive thy saule.

If ever thou gav'st hos'n and shoon,
Every nighte and alle,
Sit thee down and put them on;
And Christe receive thy saule.

If hos'n and shoon thou ne'er gav'st nane,
Every nighte and alle,
The whinnes sall prick thee to the bare bane;
And Christe receive thy saule.

From Whinnymuir when thou may'st pass,
Every nighte and alle,
To Brig o'Dread thou com'st at last,
And Christe receive thy saule.

From Brig o'Dread when thou may'st pass,
Every nighte and alle,
To Purgatory fire thou com'st at last,
And Christe receive thy saule.

If ever thou gav'st meat or drink,
Every nighte and alle,
The fire sall never make thee shrink;
And Christe receive thy saule.

If meat or drink thou ne'er gav'st nane,
Every nighte and alle,
The fire will burn thee to the bare bane;
And Christe receive thy saule.

This ae nighte, this ae nighte,
Every nighte and alle,
Fire and fleet and candle-lighte,
And Christe receive thy saule.

Anon. 15th century

E7 John Culshaw, '"Ben" – a tribute to Benjamin Britten'

From C. Palmer (ed.) (1984) *The Britten Companion*, London, Faber, pp.62–6, first published in *Gramophone*, February 1977, footnotes omitted.

'Our job', he once said, 'is to be useful, and to the living.' And he was. He was a consciously practical composer in that, so far as I can recall, he never wrote a note unless it was going to be useful to someone. He liked to write with specific people in mind, not just because of their professional skills but because of their qualities as human beings: Peter Pears, Kathleen Ferrier, Joan Cross, Owen Brannigan, Janet Baker, Dietrich Fischer-Dieskau, Mstislav Rostropovich and a host of others. *Owen Wingrave* was cast before it was written, because he wanted to think about human beings rather than dramatic abstractions. I am writing this in Adelaide, South Australia, on 7 December 1976, the day of his funeral in Aldeburgh, and it is hard to collate memories of the twenty-five years or so that we worked together in recording or television, partly because there are so many and partly because it is too soon to accept that, at 63, he is dead. The happiest hours I have spent in any studio were with Ben, for the basic reason that it did not seem that we were trying to make records or video tapes; we were just trying to make music.

He was a complex character, and superficially full of contradictions. He was world famous but he did not care for the trappings of fame. He was a marvellous pianist and conductor, yet he did not enjoy performing and the prospect of a concert sometimes made him literally sick. As he grew older, he seemed to harbour increasing doubts about his own works – doubts which were not shared by his colleagues or by the public: witness the triumph of *Death in Venice* at the Metropolitan, New York, in the autumn of 1975. He could be very stern with an undisciplined orchestra or chorus. Professional musicians of the toughest order revered him all the same, and after a difficult session would retire to the nearest pub, and drown their misbehaviour in pint after pint while speaking in awe of his professionalism. He was a gentle person, and loved gentle pictures like those painted by his neighbour Mary Potter. But then he also loved fast cars, and before his illness he would drive brilliantly through Suffolk lanes narrow and twisty enough to frighten a cyclist, let alone his passengers, although there was no need for fear because he knew every tree and every curve and every place where a stray cow might be lurking; and he knew his stopping distance. When he found out that I held a private pilot's licence he hired a Cessna for a Sunday morning joyride up and down the Suffolk coast, a prospect which didn't seem to frighten him or Peter Pears one little bit.

There are several ways of driving from Aldeburgh to London, but whenever I drove him to the city we took a scenic route which he had worked out in order to pass through some of the most exquisite parts of Suffolk and Essex, and hit the sprawl of north London as late and as deviously as possible. If we left the Red House shortly after nine in the morning we would arrive at the last genuinely country pub in time for a Bloody Mary around noon and still reach his London home for lunch. He did not like London; I don't think he liked any modern cities. He was really at peace only in Aldeburgh (and, perhaps, some years ago in Bali). To be a weekend guest at the Red House was to relax completely; although, before his illness, Ben's own ideas about relaxation might not totally coincide with those of a city-dweller. Of course nothing was obligatory, and I enjoyed the long country walks, not least because he was an expert ornithologist, whereas I cannot tell a curlew from a duck; but I confess that more often than not I dodged the early morning swim before breakfast because I had been awakened hours earlier by the dawn chorus of birds which those who live in the country never seem to hear. By the time the birds had shut up I would be fast asleep again, and Ben and Peter would be in the pool or walking the dogs in the garden or at breakfast. One of the cruellest ironies of Ben's early death is that he had kept himself so fit. He was no health fanatic, but until the final illness he enjoyed the outdoor life: he walked regularly, he swam, he played tennis. He did not smoke, but he enjoyed a drink if there was conversation to go with it. He loved good food, and the best food of all was at the Red House because it was fresh, like fish straight out of the sea with vegetables from the garden. The last time we had a meal together there we had grilled sprats which, he remarked, 'really are worth the awful smell they make in the kitchen'. Maybe it seems trivial to mention such things, but I don't think so, because they show the other side of a shy public figure. However well read, however sensitive, however concerned about the state of music and indeed the state of man, he was at heart, like Elgar with whose music he eventually came to terms, a countryman. A deceptive simplicity, an earthiness, lies behind all his music, just as it lies behind the music of his beloved Schubert.

He was a reluctant performer both in public and in the studio, and yet he never lost command of his forces. In concert performances of the *War Requiem* he chose to conduct the chamber ensemble and thus relinquish overall control to another conductor; but in the recording he conducted everything, and I have still to hear a better performance. It was made in January 1963 in Kingsway Hall and because of the importance of the occasion, and without Ben's knowledge, my colleagues at Decca 'wired' the hall and the control room in such a way that we were able to record every word of the rehearsals and the comments during playback in the control room. Had we told Britten what we were up to he would, at worst, have refused to proceed or, at best, have been inhibited by the cunningly hidden additional microphones. But there was a friendly purpose in this exercise, for over the coming months the hours and hours of rehearsal tapes were reduced to just under one hour; a major security clamp was placed on both the extracted and the residual material; and eventually one record was produced bearing a properly printed Decca label with the serial number BB50. It was then packed in an embossed leather sleeve and presented to Britten for his fiftieth birthday – 22 November 1963 – by Sir Edward Lewis. When he left the office Ben said to me, with a mischievous grin, 'I shan't forgive you quickly for this!' But he did.

Apart from anything else, the *War Requiem* rehearsals revealed all over again his amazing ability to control and communicate with children. He loved writing for children, and he loved working with them. He always wanted them to understand just what they were doing, and just what the music was meant to convey. When it came to boys' voices, he preferred a rougher quality than the 'pure' sound of the cathedral choirs, which in his view put the emphasis in the wrong place. It was a view that he applied generally. 'Frankly', he once said to me when we were discussing a casting problem, 'I'm not very interested in beautiful voices as such. I'm interested in the person behind the voice.' In other words, a beautiful voice controlled by a mind was a blessing indeed, whereas a mindless beautiful voice was of no interest to him. The same, of course, went for instrumentalists and, not unexpectedly, other composers, although in the last fifteen years or so of his life his tastes broadened, and sometimes in unexpected directions.

I don't think he ever came round to Wagner, though many years ago when he was going to India he told me he was taking a score to study (I think it was *Götterdämmerung*). He was invited to conduct at Bayreuth, but declined (if he was going to conduct Wagner anywhere for the first time, Bayreuth would be the last place). His love for Purcell, Bach, Mozart and Schubert was evident whenever he conducted or played a note of their music. He didn't care for the florid school of Italian opera, which he wickedly lampooned in *A Midsummer Night's Dream*, but he was passionate about mature Verdi. He was, I think, unsure about Tchaikovsky as a symphonist, but he loved the ballet music. Then there were the personal enthusiasms: the music of Frank Bridge, and not just because Bridge had been Britten's teacher, and of Percy Grainger, because Grainger's music had a simplicity which spoke to him directly. Elgar did not appeal to him until late in life, and it would have been unimaginable in the 1950s to suggest that one day he would record *The Dream of Gerontius* and the *Introduction and Allegro*.

In the summer of 1965 Ben and Peter invited me to go and explore an old building at Snape which might, by a considerable stretch of the imagination and a lot of money, be converted into the kind of multi-purpose hall that was so urgently needed by the Aldeburgh Festival. We walked round the Maltings and then clambered inside. It was all but impossible to imagine what it would be like when gutted, because it consisted of floor upon floor with no through sight-line. We kept on descending until we reached the ovens in the basement. And yet ... there was a feeling about the place, about its setting by the river with the view of Iken Church through the reeds and across the marshes, that made it right. If Ben was to have a concert hall on his doorstep, this was it; and in 1967, thanks to a superb conversion job by Ove Arup and Partners, who joined in close acoustical collaboration with Decca and the BBC, the Maltings at Snape was opened by the Queen. Two years later it burned down to a cinder, yet in 1970 it was open again and, if anything, better than ever.

The Maltings is Ben's monument, although I am not sure he would have liked me to put it that way. It is not a monument in the sense of Bayreuth, because it was not built to serve the music of one composer: it was built to serve all music. It has proved to be a marvellous concert and recital hall; it can accommodate opera without strain; the many Decca recordings made there prove its quality as a recording location; and on at least three occasions – for *Peter Grimes*, *Winterreise* and *Owen Wingrave* – the BBC turned it literally into a television studio. But, most important of all, its existence encouraged Britten to make many recordings which might otherwise never have been made, since they would have involved him in prolonged trips to London. At the Maltings he could work in peace, and in the environment that inspired so much of his work; the warmth and welcome of the building were, and will remain, a reflection of the man.

The first music of his that I ever heard was the *Serenade* for tenor, horn and strings. I was a serviceman at the time; it was towards the end of the war; and it was the original Decca recording. No other piece of contemporary music had spoken so directly to me or meant so much. I had no reason to suppose that within five or six years I would be working with Ben and Peter in Decca's No 1 studio in West Hampstead. at the start of a long relationship which was to involve a lot of hard work, but also some fun. There was one evening when, after two *Lieder* sessions, they tried to remember a couple of cabaret numbers Ben had written years earlier to words by W.H. Auden [now published as *Four*

Cabaret Songs, Faber Music, 1980], until both the words and the music ran out. Then there was the seemingly impossible problem of making David Hemmings in *The Little Sweep* sound as if he were up a chimney; the solution was to get him to sing into a globe rather like a goldfish bowl, of which there was only one, and which he promptly dropped.

I believe Ben's doubts about recording have been exaggerated or at least misinterpreted on the basis of the speech he made at Aspen, Colorado, in the 1960s. Nobody who actually disapproved of recording could have made as many records, and with such enthusiasm, as he did; but he sounded a warning with which few, I imagine, would disagree. Nothing in musical performance is ultimately definitive, and to that extent a recording is only representative of the artist's approach at the time of recording. His approach to *Peter Grimes* when he conducted it for the BBC television production in 1969 was quite different from the one he brought to the Decca recording ten years earlier. His playing of *Winterreise* darkened and deepened over the years, magnificent though it was from the start. He could never be stale or complacent.

I saw him for the last time during the 1976 Aldeburgh Festival. He was very frail, but he made a massive and perhaps damaging attempt to attend as many events as possible. It was the right thing for him to do, whatever the risk, because it was not in him to admit defeat. I am glad that he was present in the Maltings to witness the triumph of his cantata, *Phaedra.* The audience may have marvelled at how, under such adversity, he could have written such a piece, and it was an emotional moment when he rose to acknowledge the applause; but finally it was the music that was being applauded, because it had communicated, and for Ben, communication was what music was all about.

E8 Dmitri Shostakovitch, *Testimony*

From D. Shostakovitch (1981) *Testimony: The Memoirs of Dmitri Shostakovitch,* as related to and edited by Solomon Volkov, London, Faber, pp.156, 140–41.

The majority of my symphonies are tombstones. Too many of our people died and were buried in places unknown to anyone, not even their relatives. It happened to many of my friends. Where do you put the tombstones for Meyerhold or Tukhachevsky? Only music can do that for them. I'm willing to write a composition for each of the victims, but that's impossible, and that's why I dedicate my music to them all.

I think constantly of those people, and in almost every major work I try to remind others of them. The conditions of the war years were conducive to that, because the authorities were less strict about music and didn't care if the music was too gloomy. And later all the misery was put down to the war, as though it was only during the war that people were tortured and killed. Thus the Seventh and Eighth are 'war symphonies.' [...]

I doubt that Stalin ever questioned his own genius or greatness. But when the war against Hitler was won, Stalin went off the deep end. He was like the frog puffing himself up to the size of the ox, with the difference that everyone around him already considered Stalin to be the ox and gave him an ox's due.

Everyone praised Stalin, and now I was supposed to join in this unholy affair. There was an appropriate excuse. We had ended the war victoriously; no matter the cost, the important thing was that we won, the empire had expanded. And they demanded that Shostakovich use quadruple winds, choir, and soloists to hail the leader. All the more because Stalin found the number auspicious: the Ninth Symphony.

Stalin always listened to experts and specialists carefully. The experts told him that I knew my work and therefore Stalin assumed that the symphony in his honor would be a quality piece of music. He would be able to say, There it is, our national Ninth.

I confess that I gave hope to the leader and teacher's dreams. I announced that I was writing an apotheosis. I was trying to get them off my back but it turned against me. When my Ninth was performed, Stalin was incensed. He was deeply offended, because there was no chorus, no soloists. And no apotheosis. There wasn't even a paltry dedication. It was just music, which Stalin didn't understand very well and which was of dubious content.

People will say that this is hard to believe, that the memoirist is twisting things here, and that the leader and teacher certainly didn't have time in those difficult postwar days to worry about symphonies and dedications. But the absurdity is that Stalin watched dedications much more closely than affairs of state. For this was not only happening to me. Alexander Dovzhenko told me a similar story. He made a documentary film during the war and somehow overlooked Stalin in some way. Stalin was livid. He called Dovzhenko in, and Beria shouted at Dovzhenko in front of Stalin, 'You couldn't spare ten meters of film for our leader? Well, now you'll die like a dog!' By some miracle, Dovzhenko survived.

I couldn't write an apotheosis to Stalin, I simply couldn't. I knew what I was in for when I wrote the Ninth. But I did depict Stalin in music in my next symphony, the Tenth. I wrote it right after Stalin's death, and no one has yet guessed what the symphony is about. It's about Stalin and the Stalin years. The second part, the scherzo, is a musical portrait of Stalin, roughly speaking. Of course, there are many other things in it, but that's the basis.

E9 J.S. Bach, Brandenburg Concerto No. 2

From J.S. Bach, Brandenburg Concerto No. 2, Kalmus Study Score 741, New York, 1968, pp.33–40.

CONCERTO II.

E10 Howard Mayer Brown, 'Pedantry or liberation? A sketch of the historical performance movement'

From N. Kenyon (ed.) (1988) *Authenticity and Early Music*, Oxford University Press, pp.27–30, footnotes omitted.

One central question about 'authentic' performance of early music can be formulated very simply: should we play music in the way the composer intended it, or at the very least in a way his contemporaries could have heard it (bearing in mind that these are not always the same thing)? A whole host of subsidiary questions immediately come to mind. How do we know what the composer intended? How fixed were his intentions? However fixed they were, how closely should we feel obliged to follow them? How should we deal with those elements which the composer himself would have taken to be variable? And how should we deal with those aspects of performance that are not documented (and in many cases not documentable)?

Even if it could be shown that authenticity is the highest ideal to which we can aspire, we cannot reproduce every aspect of past performance, and most musicians probably have no real desire to do so. We know too little about a number of the variables that went into making particular performances: the precise character of the available instruments at a particular time and place, the particular pitch level the musicians used, the vocal technique of a particular set of singers, the kinds of strings or reeds, the precise tempos, and so on. In any case, performers can scarcely buy and learn to play a new instrument for every composition they present in public. And even if we did know all the myriad details about a particular set of performances, the venue and the reasons for performing music in the late twentieth century will almost certainly be different from those prevailing in earlier times. Which compromises are tolerable, and which not, will clearly always be an area where musicians will disagree.

Moreover, performing styles and techniques change rapidly, as we can all now easily hear on recordings made in the course of the present century. The sound of a particular symphony orchestra, for example, evolves and may be quite different from one decade to the next. Unwritten conventions of instrumental playing and even the vocal techniques of the best singers at the beginning of this century differed radically from what is considered ideal today. Technological changes (such as using wire strings on violins) have transformed, though not necessarily improved, the sound of many kinds of instruments. And recordings, such as those by Igor Stravinsky of the same works conducted at various times in his life, should teach us to be cautious about accepting at face value the strictures concerning fixed intentions of even the most articulate and demanding of composers. In short, musicians in the twentieth century can be shown to have changed their styles of performance frequently. There is no reason to suppose that musical life was ever any different. Moreover, the irrational force of fashion has played as influential a role in the performance of early music in our own time as it has in the performance of the symphonic or operatic repertory.

Some repertories can scarcely be played at all in a convincing way unless musicians use techniques or instruments different from those in current use. Performers in these areas have no choice at all about whether or not to try to revive old instruments and old styles and techniques of playing and singing. Anyone dedicated to the proposal that the music of the thirteenth, fourteenth, and fifteenth centuries merits revival in performance, for example, is virtually forced to take a position on the question of authenticity, since it is clear that such music can hardly be played effectively on modern instruments, or sung to good effect using the sort of vocal technique appropriate for twentieth-century opera-houses. Machaut's music can barely be understood without some attempt to use styles and techniques of performance different from those in current use. In the case of medieval music, it is actually easier and certainly more logical to try to find out how the music was performed at that time rather than attempting some sort of translation of very old sounds into modern terms. However, problems immediately arise because the evidence used for documenting medieval performance practice is almost all highly ambiguous and any attempt to duplicate precisely the original performing conditions will inevitably fail for lack of secure information and because of the vast cultural differences between medieval society and our own.

Less obviously, some repertories of much later music will inevitably be lost to us unless we revive the instruments for which they were originally conceived. A particular case is that of the music written in France during the seventeenth and eighteenth centuries – by Lully, Rameau, Couperin, Marin Marais, Forqueray, and others – in which nuances of sonority and a very particular balance among instruments play an essential role in the character of the works. But many other repertories as well from after 1600 seem by their nature to demand some attempt at reconstructing the precise sounds their composers imagined.

It would be fascinating, and perhaps even instructive, to hear symphonies by Schumann, Brahms, Bruckner and Mahler as their contemporaries heard them, but that is a long way from saying that from now on we should only hear such music in period-style performances. To argue that all music should be performed as close to the way the composer conceived it as possible means that we should not tolerate a performance of a Mahler symphony, unless it is played with Viennese winds, extensive use of portamento string playing, and with precisely the size and dimensions of orchestra that Mahler conducted. Surely, most of us would consider such restrictions as unacceptable pedantry, comparable to that of a friend of mine who rejected Peter Maxwell

Davies's opera *Taverner* because the stage band used baroque rather than Renaissance violas da gamba. And if we took that attitude, what then would become of our great symphony orchestras? Indeed, if we had so radical a view of authenticity, we could well ask what should be the proper repertory for the Chicago Symphony, born almost at the end of the symphonic age? The truth – although it may seem controversial to say so now – is that it is more acceptable to play Bach's music on modern instruments than Rameau's, for it can be argued that authentic sonorities and old playing techniques are less important in the one than in the other, and that therefore the essential nature of Bach's music can emerge in a performance that translates the original into modern terms. In short, it is possible to defend what might be described as a woolly-headed liberal approach to the question of repertory: we may well be enlightened in unexpected ways by performances on original instruments of much music written in the late eighteenth and nineteenth centuries, and we should keep an open mind about the interest and importance of such performances. But at the same time we should encourage rather than discourage our major cultural institutions – symphony orchestras and opera companies – to broaden their repertories even though such organizations may perform this music in 'inauthentic' ways. This is a more positive approach than that of declaring off-limits to any but the specialists more and more of our musical heritage.

E11 John Duarte, 'Edward Elgar'

From sleeve notes for a recording by Beatrice Harrison/New Symphony Orchestra/Elgar EMI 7243 555221-2 (1928/1994), pp.5, 6, 8.

Amongst the many friendships that were of key importance to Elgar's musical career were those with A.J. Jaeger, the Publications Manager with Novello & Co. and the 'Nimrod' of the *Enigma Variations*, and Fred Gaisberg of the Gramophone Company, the pioneers of electrical recording in England, which paid Elgar handsomely (by the standards of the day) and gave him the freedom to record when and what he chose. It is due to the latter that we are still able to hear Elgar conducting his own works, an acoustical archive such as was not possible prior to the present century. [...]

The recording speaks of the performing practices of the time and of Elgar's way with them. String vibrato was minimal (today's more generous kind may owe much to Hollywood!), *portamenti* were commonly used, and there was less concern with fine detail – even that of the observance of written note-values. Marked changes of tempo, *accelerandi* and *rallentandi*, and the use of *rubato* were characteristic of chamber and solo-instrumental music, but when they were introduced into orchestral music by Elgar, wearing his conductor's hat, they caused problems for both performers and critics, one of which latter described

Elgar's beat as 'uneasy' and 'wilful'. He was not concerned, as modern conductors are, to maintain a steady tempo, but allowed it to vary with the tension of the music, and his tempos in quick movements were faster than we are now accustomed to hearing.

Exactly what stimulated Elgar to write a cello concerto is not known, though efforts to interest him in such a project were made as early as 1900 by the eminent cellist Carl Fuchs, in whose autograph album Elgar's is one of many now-famous names. Elgar sketched the opening theme in March 1918 but without indicating for what kind of work it was intended, but within a year all was revealed. Albert Coates, a cellist who had turned to conducting, was extremely enthusiastic about the concerto and when it was premièred in the Queen's Hall on 27 October 1919, with Felix Salmond as soloist, it was Coates who conducted it. Unfortunately the rehearsal went badly, for which Coates was to blame, the performance fared no better, and good relations between Elgar and Coates ended abruptly. Again it was Fred Gaisberg who came to the rescue, introducing Elgar to Beatrice Harrison, a cellist who was associated with contemporary music, and arranging for her to record the work under Elgar's baton. The first (acoustical) recording was made in 1919 and remade in 1920; the second (electrical) made in 1928, is the one presented here.

The Cello Concerto, dedicated to Sidney and Frances Colvin (friends who were not musicians), was Elgar's last major orchestral work; after the death of his wife in April 1920 he maintained his jovial exterior, but if his creative Muse spoke to him he listened with little enthusiasm. The work encapsulates the extremes of Elgar's character, in the skittish *Scherzo*, the proud opening and the humorous episodes of the final movement (described by Tovey as 'dignity at the mercy of a banana-skin'), and the dignified sadness of the *Adagio*. Near the end of the last movement of both of these concertos, themes from previous movements are recalled: in the case of the Violin Concerto it is those of the first movement, recalled with wistfulness and passion in a cadenza; in the Cello Concerto it is the theme of the *Adagio*, fading into silence with heart-rending pathos, followed by a defiant restatement of the bold theme with which the work began – sad reflections on a life that had not always treated Elgar kindly or even with justice?

John Duarte is a journalist and critic and a long-time lover of Elgar's music. He is the composer of over 100 original works, 32 of them commercially recorded, and is a leading authority on the classical guitar and its music.

E12 R. Philip, 'Implications for the future'

From R. Philip (1992) *Early Recordings and Musical Style*, Cambridge University Press, pp.229–31.

The most obvious trends in performing style over the first half of the twentieth century are easily summarised. Broadly speaking, early twentieth-century playing was characterised by the following habits: the sparing use of vibrato by string-players, its discreet use by singers, and the general avoidance of vibrato on woodwind instruments by most players except those of the French school; the frequent use of prominent, often slow, portamento by string-players and singers; the use of substantial tempo changes to signal changes of mood or tension, and the adoption of fast maximum tempos; varieties of tempo rubato which included not only detailed flexibility of tempo, but also accentuation by lengthening and shortening individual notes, and the dislocation of melody and accompaniment; and a tendency, in patterns of long and short notes, to shorten the short notes, and to overdot dotted rhythms. Instruments were also different from their modern equivalents in some ways – gut strings (used to a decreasing extent after World War I), wooden flutes (widely used except by the French school), French bassoons (not in Germany and Austria), and, though they have not been discussed in this book, the continued use of narrow-bore brass instruments.

By the 1930s there were clear trends away from these early twentieth-century characteristics: the spread of continuous vibrato on stringed instruments, its increasing prominence among singers, and its adoption by many woodwind-players, including a move towards slower vibrato than the fast tremor sometimes heard earlier in the century; the decreasing prominence and frequency of portamento on both strings and voice; a trend towards stricter control of tempo and slower maximum speeds; more emphatic clarity of rhythmic detail, more literal interpretation of note values, and the avoidance of rhythmic irregularity and dislocation; the adoption of steel on the upper strings of stringed instruments, the increasing use of the metal flute, the German bassoon, and wider-bore brass instruments.

It is possible to summarise all these elements as a trend towards greater power, firmness, clarity, control, literalness, and evenness of expression, and away from informality, looseness, and unpredictability. It is more difficult to draw neat conclusions from them. The problem arises from the very completeness of the evidence. Recordings show in detail how performing styles developed from the early years of the twentieth century up to the present time. This makes it possible to compare our own styles with those of almost a century ago, a comparison which was impossible in previous periods. Enthusiasts for 'authentic' performance may regard this as an opportunity to begin creating reconstructions of early twentieth-century performances. But access to the truth about developing style faces us with some fundamental questions, about the nature of modern style and taste, about the ways in which they have developed, and about the extent to which it is desirable, or even possible, to recreate the performance practices of an earlier period.

The early twentieth century is the earliest period for which the primary source material of performance practice – the performance itself – has been preserved. It lies at the transition between two musical worlds, the old world in which performers were heard only in actual performance, and each performance occurred only once, and the modern world in which a performance (which may not even have been a complete performance) can be heard simply by playing a recording. The recorded performance is available to anyone, including the musician who performed it, and can be repeated any number of times. The recordings of the early twentieth century are themselves transitional in character. They are of the new world, in that they are available and repeatable, but the performances which they preserve are largely of the old world, survivals of a style evolved for unique performance to an audience.

The changes in performance practice over the century have been greatly influenced by this shift of emphasis. Recorded performances from the early part of the century give a vivid impression of being projected as if to an audience. They have a sense of being 'put across', so that the precision and clarity of each note is less important than the shape and progress of the music as a whole. They are intended to convey what *happens* in the music, to characterise it. The accurate reproduction of the musical text is merely a means to this end.

In the late twentieth century the balance has shifted significantly. The accurate and clear performance of the musical text has become the first priority, and the characterisation of the music and its progress is assumed to be able to take care of itself. Of course, this is a crude generalisation. The most admired late twentieth-century performers convey the progress of the music very vividly, and there are some dull and pedantic performances on early recordings. But the general change in emphasis has nevertheless been from the characterisation of musical events to the reproduction of a text. This is particularly true in the recording studio, which has had such a strong influence, good and bad, on performance. Musicians are now used to performing routinely without an audience, and the atmosphere in a recording studio is not like that of a concert-hall. Musicians know that movements and sections can be repeated, and that a finished performance can be assembled from the best parts of different takes. The overwhelming priority is to get each section *right* at least once. One of the most familiar remarks of a recording producer at the end of a session is, 'I think we've got it all somewhere.' There is no need for a complete performance at all.

Recording before the war, and right up to the advent of editable tape in the 1950s, was a very different matter. Rachmaninoff expressed a widespread view of the recording studio:

> I get very nervous when I am making records, and all whom I have asked say they get nervous too. When the test records are made, I know that I can hear them played back at me, and then everything is all right. But when the stage is set for the final recording and I realise that this will remain for good, I get nervous and my hands get tense.

Musicians knew that they had to play at their very best, and that any mistakes would be preserved for ever, unless a side was repeated. Sides were indeed repeated, many times on occasions, but it comes as a surprise to a modern musician to find how many 78 rpm recordings consist of first or second takes. For example, of the nine sides of Rachmaninoff's recording of his third concerto, seven are first takes. Admittedly the division of a long movement into several sides made it impossible to play right through the movement; but in many other ways the atmosphere of recording in the pre-tape period was much closer to that of a live performance than modern recording sessions.

The changes in recording and the recording studio have in turn fed back into the concert-hall. If pre-war recordings are remarkably like live performances, many late twentieth-century live performances are remarkably like recordings. Detailed clarity and control have become the priority in modern performance, in the concert-hall as well as in the studio. No doubt this is partly because musicians have become accustomed to playing in this way, but it is also because audiences, themselves trained by recordings, have come to expect it. Clarity and accuracy are required in modern recordings, because any inaccuracies will be repeated every time the record is played. This has led to a standard which is, in a limited sense, incredibly high. The price is that many modern performances place accuracy and clarity above all other considerations.

E13 Sylvia Olden Lee and Evelyn Simpson-Curenton, 'Scandalize my name'

From sleeve notes for a recording of 'Scandalize my name' by Kathleen Battle/ Jessye Norman/Sylvia Olden Lee, DG 429 790–2, 1991, p.26.

Scandalize My Name

Well – I met my sister the other day,
I give her my right hand.
But just as soon as ever my back-a was turned,
She scandalized my name!

Now, do you call that a sister?
No, no!
She scandalized my name!

Well – let me tell you – I met my neighbor the other day, (You did?)
Give her my right hand. (Go on.)
But just as soon as ever my back was turned,
She scandalized my name!

Now, do you call that a neighbor?
No, no!
She scandalized my name.

Now, wait a minute, let me tell *you*. I met my deacon (No.) the other day,
I give him my right hand.
But just as soon as ever my back-a was turned –
He scandalized your name!

Now, do you call that a deacon?
No, no!
He scandalized my name!

You'll never believe it. But I met my preacher the other day,
Give him my right hand.
But just as soon as ever my back was turned, (Truly?)
He scandalized my name!

Now, do you call that a preacher?
No, no!
Well, do you call that religion?
No, no!
He scandalized my name!

E14 Cherubini Médée (1797), 'Numi, venite a me'

From sleeve notes for the recording of *Médée* (1797) with Maria Callas/
Orchestra e Coro del Teatro alla Scala di Milano/Tullio Serafin EMI CDM
763626/27–2, 1959 and 1990, pp.62–3.

Medea

Numi, venite a me, inferni Dei!
voi tutti che aiutaste il mio voler,
la vostra forza ancor m'assista,
voi l'opra mia compier dovete.
Distenda in ciel la nera morte il velo.
e popol strugga
e re in sua rovina orrenda!

Medea

Gods, come to me, deities of Hell!
All you who aided my will,
let your strength help me again.
You must complete my work!
Let black death spread its veil in the sky.
and destroy people
and king in horrible ruin!

O cari figli, strazio mio supremo,	*Oh, dear children, my last torment,*
ch'io sacro qui	*whom I dedicate here*
dell'odio all'atre Dive,	*to the dark goddesses of hatred,*
non debba io mai il sangue vostro espiar!	*may I never have to expiate your blood!*
Si! Vostro padre fu che v'uccise!	*Yes, it was your father who killed you!*
Reietto in terra il vil,	*Outcast on earth,*
lo sperda il ciel!	*may Heaven reject him!*
S'appressan, ahimè! Quale tormento!	*They are approaching, alas! What agony!*
Un cor di madre batte nel mio petto.	*A mother's heart beats in my breast.*
Natura, or tu invano parli a me.	*Nature, now you speak to me in vain.*
Morir dovran, negata è lor la vita!	*They must die, life is denied them!*
Votati son dell'atre	*They are pledged to*
Erinni al nume!	*the god of the black Furies!*
Il suo volere sol comanda in me!	*Their will is my command.*

E15 Mozart, *Don Giovanni* (1787) 'Finch'han del vino'

From Edward Dent (1946) *Mozart: Don Giovanni*, London, Boocey & Hawkes, pp.107–10.

English version (not a translation)

Finch'han del vino calda la testa,	*Song, wine and women, who'd be without them?*
Una gran festa va preparar.	*I'll have my pleasure, morn, noon and night.*
Se trovi in piazza qualche ragazza,	*These comely wenches, fresh from the country*
Teco ancor quella cerca menar,	*Fill me with rapture, joy and delight,*
Teco ancor quella cerca menar,	*Fill me with rapture, joy and delight,*
Cerca menar, cerca menar.	*Joy and delight, joy and delight.*
Senza alcun ordine la danza sia,	*Ask ev'ry girl you see, make no distinction,*
Ch'il menuetto, chi la follia,	*Ask all the village, ply them with liquor,*
Chi l'allemana farai ballar,	*Set them a-dancing, till it be light,*
Ch'il menuetto farai ballar	*Make no distinction, all I'll invite,*
Chi la follia farai ballar,	*Ask all the village, all I'll invite,*
Chi l'allemana farai ballar.	*All you can capture, all I'll invite!*
Ed io frattanto dal altro canto	*Then while the menfolk drink and are merry,*
Con questa quella vo'amoreggiar.	*I'll play at love's game, safe out of sight,*
Vo'amoreggiar, vo'amoreggiar	*Safe out of sight, safe out of sight.*
Ah, la mia lista doman mattina	*And in the morning, yes, in the morning,*
D'una decina devi aumentar,	*You'll have a dozen names more to write,*
Ah, la mia lista d'una decina devi aumentar!,	*Yes, in the morning, you'll have a dozen names more to write!*

Se trovi in piazza qualche ragazza
Teco ancor quella cerca menar...
Ah, la mia lista doman mattina
D'una decina devi aumentar.
Senz'alcun ordine la danza sia,
Ch'il menuetto, chi la follia,
Chi l'allemana farai ballar ...
Ah, la mia lista doman mattina
D'una decina devi aumentar,
D'una decina devi aumentar,
D'una decina devi aumentar,
Devi aumentar, devi aumentar,
Devi, devi aumentar.

These comely wenches, fresh from the country,
Fill me with rapture, joy and delight ...
Song, wine and women, who'd be without them?
I'll have my pleasure, morn, noon and night.
Ask ev'ry girl you see, make no distinction.
Ask all the village, ply them with liquor,
Set them a-dancing, till it be light ...
And in the morning, yes, in the morning,
You'll have a dozen names more to write,
You'll have a dozen names more to write,
You'll have a dozen names more to write,
Names more to write, names more to write,
Yes, a dozen names more to write.

E16   Maude Valérie White, 'The throstle'

From sleeve notes for a recording by Anthony Rolfe Johnson/Graham Johnson, Hyperion, CDA 66709, 1994, p.16.

The Throstle

'Summer is coming, summer is coming,
I know it, I know it, I know it.
Light again, leaf again, life again, love again,'
Yes, my wild little poet.

Sing the new year in under the blue,
Last year you sang it as gladly,
'New, new, new, new!' Is it then so new
That you must carol so madly?

'Love again, song again, nest again, young again,'
Never a prophet so crazy!
And hardly a daisy as yet, little friend,
See, there is hardly a daisy.

'Here again, here, here, here, happy year!'
O warble unchidden, unbidden!
Summer is coming, is coming, my dear,
And all the winters are hidden.

E17 Anon., 'Kiss me my love and welcome/Drops of brandy'

From sleeve notes of a recording by The Mellstock Band, Saydisc CD SDL 360, 1986.

The works of Thomas Hardy are full of music. Local traditional songs and music are part of the lives of his characters, and portraits of musicians and scenes of dancing abound. The Hardy family were noted local musicians. When they lived in Puddletown, Hardy's grandfather led the church band there and played the cello, and when they moved to Lower Bockhampton he and Hardy's father, playing violin, played for Stinsford church until the band was replaced by a harmonium shortly before Hardy's birth. They continued as before to play for local dances, and Hardy learnt the violin as a boy and played with his father and uncle.

A band of string or wind players formed the usual accompaniment to singing in rural English parish churches from around 1690 to the 1830's. The musicians and choir sat in the west gallery of the church, with the instruments playing the same parts as the singers, to keep them to their parts. The same musicians would be found playing for dances and weddings on other days of the week, and going round the parish singing carols at Christmas.

Like many village musicians in nineteenth-century England, the Hardys could read music, and had a collection of manuscript music books. Hardy's grandfather had been given a compilation of dance tunes and a few songs which had been written out by James Hook (an unknown local musician, not the minor composer). Hardy's father kept a book entitled *Tunes for the Violin*, into which he wrote tunes which took his fancy. Some of these would have been familiar local dance tunes, others would be copied from printed music books or similar manuscript compilations borrowed from other musicians. Many books of this kind survive from other parts of the country, often, like the Hardy manuscripts, with bass or second violin parts for some of the tunes. From these it is possible to build up a good impression of the repertoire and harmonic style of the early nineteenth century village dance bands.

In addition to these, and a manuscript song book, Hardy's father and grandfather each had a manuscript book of carol parts. These were sung and played around the parish on Christmas eve, as described in the opening chapters of *Under the Greenwood Tree*. Similar carol books, some with full four-part settings, survived in the parish church at Puddletown (Hardy's 'Weatherbury'). A few carols are found in both sets of manuscripts, as might be expected from Hardy's grandfather's association with the Puddletown choir. The style of the four-part writing is distinctive and archaic for the period (1820–1840). They were probably initially copied, or adapted and re-arranged, from the music for parish choirs sold on subscription by some London publishers. With one or two exceptions, no composers' names appear. Many copyings and re-copyings must have introduced both corruptions and conscious adaptations to local needs and conventions. As interpreted by the Puddletown and Stinsford choirs, the carols usually have a bass which rarely goes lower than baritone range, a high tenor, trebles carrying the tune, and a very high descant part called the 'counter'. It was not a counter-tenor part, nor were the 'viols' and 'bass-viol' of the Mellstock Quire anything but violins and cello of the usual kind. With one exception the carols are performed here at approximately their original pitch.

As well as strings, Hardy mentions clarinets, flutes, and serpents being used in church bands, and Puddletown church still has the flutes and clarinets used by the old musicians. Dance music also made use of percussion, especially the tambourine. To try to recreate the sound of these bands and choirs, we have used instruments similar or identical to those of the time, playing and singing in the style that has survived in oral tradition in southern England.

Unless otherwise stated, all part-settings of the carols are as found in the manuscripts (transcribed and edited by Dave Townsend), and all part-settings of the dance tunes are by Dave Townsend and The Mellstock Band.

E18 J.O. Urmson, 'The ethics of musical performance'

From M. Krausz (ed.) (1995) *The Interpretation of Music*, Oxford, Clarendon, pp.157–64.

In this chapter I propose to consider what ethical constraints, if any, may be thought to limit the freedom of a performer in playing a piece of music by a composer other than himself. While doing so I shall from time to time consider what seem to me to be closely analogous problems concerning the culinary arts. It has long seemed to me that there are certain formal analogies between music and cookery. For example, the Dundee cake seems to be an abstract entity rather like the 'Unfinished' Symphony, and a Dundee cake seems to be related to the Dundee cake rather as a performance of the 'Unfinished' Symphony is related to the 'Unfinished' Symphony. Similarly the recipe for the Dundee cake and copies thereof seem to play a formally analogous role to that of the score of the 'Unfinished' Symphony and copies thereof. There are also formal disanalogies; a performance of the 'Unfinished' Symphony takes time, whereas a Dundee cake does not, even though it takes time to bake it. I do not propose to defend this view in this chapter; rather I intend to suggest that the ethical considerations involved are also interestingly similar. Readers who find this proposed comparison derogatory to the art of music can, of course, abandon this paper at once or skip the relevant portions.

Before embarking on these questions I may be permitted to utter a word of caution. It may appear that, at the other extreme to those who dissociate art and morality, I regard the performer as predominately faced with ethical decisions when determining questions of interpretation. Nothing is further from the truth. The performer, most of the time, will rightly be concerned with purely musical considerations. But in regard to general policies of performance, particularly professional performance, ethical considerations do, I think, arise. Let us consider one concrete example. Bach's second 'Brandenburg' Concerto is scored for concertante trumpet, recorder, oboe, and violin, with string ripieno and continuo. For a long period in the nineteenth and earlier twentieth centuries a transverse flute was always, and inevitably, substituted for the recorder, since recorders and recorder players were not available. Often, also, a ripieno of a size certainly not contemplated by Bach was used. Is it legitimate nowadays to represent a performance with transverse flute substituted for recorder, or with such a large ripieno, as being a performance of Bach's work? Some performers will say that the balance between trumpet, recorder, and violin is impossibly bad, and a stronger instrument should replace the recorder. Should they not, then, say that this is a badly composed work that should not be performed and represent themselves as playing a new work, based on, and an improvement on, Bach's work? Or is opposition to such a substitution mere pedantry? Personally, I feel defrauded and cheated by such a substitution ethically, and, aesthetically, that such performers should conclude that if they cannot achieve a balance with Bach's scoring then either their technique or their performing practices are at fault. But on this I do not now ask for agreement. I only point out that questions like this do have an ethical as well as an artistic dimension. But the fact that the ethical dimension is almost exclusively considered in this paper should not be taken to imply that it is of exclusive, or even predominant, importance. Even I prefer a well-played transverse flute in that 'Brandenburg' to a badly played recorder.

In considering these questions it would be as well to distinguish three different situations in which a performer or a performing group might play a piece of music. In the first situation the performer plays for himself alone, and not to an audience, whether or not he is overheard by others as he does so. In the second situation the performer plays to an audience, but without any commercial transaction being involved; the audience is not a paying audience but, perhaps, a group of friends. In the third situation the performer plays professionally to a paying audience. Analogously one may bake a cake for oneself, for one's family or as a professional baker. Perhaps ethical questions also will arise in an analogous way.

Now let us ask what ethical constraints might reasonably be thought to apply in any or all of these three situations. Most obviously, it might be suggested that one has a duty or obligation to the composer, to the audience, if any, or, perhaps, to oneself. It might also be suggested that one is constrained by certain abstract principles of morality akin to truthfulness or justice. Beyond these I cannot, myself, think of any other moral constraints which could plausibly be considered to be relevant.

If we consider the first situation, in which the performer plays for himself alone, we can manifestly eliminate at once any duty to an audience. Has one, then, any duty to oneself? I am inclined to answer that the whole notion of duties or obligations to oneself is, unless interpreted very loosely, incoherent. We can, and do, speak of such things as promising oneself a day off tomorrow, if one completes a piece of work today; but since, as promisee, I can forgive myself performance of any promise I make to myself, any such promise has no constraining force. Advertisers tell us that we owe ourselves various luxuries, but we can always forgive any debt that we owe to ourselves; there is no constraint. It is, no doubt, usually foolish and self-stultifying not to try one's best; one may have a duty to try one's best, if, for example, one's musical education is being paid for by someone else. But neither of these considerations involves a duty to oneself, though the latter case involves a duty to one's benefactor. So let us exclude the notion of a duty to oneself as being in principle incoherent, and one that need not be considered further, whatever the situation.

It remains to ask whether the lone performer has a duty to the composer. There are those who hold that one can have no duties to the dead. If that be so, we have the curious situation that whether the performer has a duty to the composer may depend on whether the composer is still alive. For myself, I find it hard to understand why one cannot have duties or obligations to the dead. Certainly there are those who hold that a promise made to a dying person has no weight after his death. If this is claimed as an intuitive certainty, philosophical argument is, obviously, irrelevant; if the claim is made on the ground that the dead cannot benefit from the performance of the promise, or that they cannot know if it is not performed, then the basic moral claim is that promises which do not benefit the promisee are null and void, or that promises the non-performance of which cannot be discovered by the promisee are null and void. Such claims seem to be inherently unacceptable; if made, they render the case of death simply a circumstance which makes the more general principle applicable, not morally significant in itself.

The true reason for denying that the solitary player has a duty to the composer seems to be quite different, and to make the question whether the composer is dead or alive simply irrelevant. If one has, when playing to oneself, a duty to the composer, it will presumably be one of some sort of fidelity to the instructions in his score – I do not now enquire what such fidelity involves in detail since that important question is at present irrelevant. Now let us suppose that the score specifies that the instrument intended is the organ and the piece is in the major mode. Let us suppose that the solitary player decides to play it on the piano and to transform it into the minor. How now do we answer the question whether this is a performance failing in a duty of fidelity to the composer or whether it is a variation, improvisation, or what you will on a theme by the composer, a perfectly respectable activity? Surely in these circumstances, the question of fidelity to the intentions of the composer cannot arise. The questions whether it is, or is intended to be, an accurate performance of the written score certainly do arise, as do such questions as whether the player has produced a worthwhile improvisation based on the score. But that is all. The suggestion that the only legitimate use of a score by the solitary performer is to play it as accurately as one can is surely one that no reasonable person would make and one which, I believe, no composer has ever made. A composer might well complain if a performance that departs in some way from the directions in the score be represented as faithful. But if one intentionally departs from the score in solitary playing, that misrepresentation cannot arise.

If the solitary player has no duty of fidelity to the composer for the reason just given, it would seem to be hard to imagine what general abstract principles might be relevant. No general considerations of truthfulness, honesty, fidelity, and the like seem capable of being relevant. The solitary performer seems to have no relevant duties at all as such. The situation seems to be exactly the same as when one cooks for oneself. Thus, if one decides to make for oneself a loaf of bread and puts before oneself the recipe for what is known as the Grant loaf, as contained in Mrs Grant's *Your Daily Bread*, one reads that one is to include one ounce of salt and one ounce of sugar. What, then, are one's duties? Is one failing in them if one prefers a little more (or less) salt, and uses a yeast that requires no sugar? Or if one decides to add a few raisins or a little grated cheese not specified in the recipe, as an experiment, what then? Why should Doris Grant, or anyone else, complain? It is clear that once again the distinction between a variation on the recipe and lack of fidelity to it is empty in the envisaged situation.

Let us now turn to the case of a performance to a paying audience, leaving aside for the moment the intermediate case of an amateur performance to a non-paying audience. It seems, clear, now, that the performer has duties and obligations. If, as is customary, the performer, or his agent, has published a proposed programme, the performer seems to be in a quasi-contractual situation in relation to the audience of a commercial kind to deliver, for a consideration, the programme promised. I say 'quasi-contractual' since, no doubt, the legal obligation of the performer is tenuously connected to the rights of the audience through a series of agents, concert-promoters, concert-hall owners, and the like, but this complication seems morally irrelevant, and I shall ignore it. Morally, no performer is likely to deny that he has a duty to his paying audience; the problem is to decide just what that duty is.

Let us take it that the performer's duty is to play the advertised programme, unless unforeseen circumstances prevent him from so doing. But how is he to play it? To raise still unclear questions, should he play it in the way that he believes the majority of his paying customers would choose, since the customer is always right? Or should he play it in the way that the composer would have wished (or intended, or liked), since so to do seems to be a near equivalent to obedience to a Trade Descriptions act in the commercial sphere? Or should he play the programme in the way that he thinks sounds best, since so to do is to give the best value for money? These possibilities are unclear, for it would be naïve to suppose that the audience has definite and unanimous desires or that the wishes of the composer are usually known to the performer. But, in any case, they are not necessarily mutually exclusive. The audience is unlikely to be unanimous, but some members, at least, are likely to wish the performer to play it as he thinks it sounds best, others to play it authentically (whatever that may involve), others to play it in the way that they have always heard it before. None of these wishes, not even the last, is altogether unreasonable. For, to a member of the audience, the works in the programme must be such works as he expects them to sound; if some anachronistic conductor who held views on Handelian performance like those held in scholarly circles today had presented such a performance to a late Victorian audience, at least a majority of that audience would surely have been outraged and have thought of themselves as defrauded; that was not what they had paid for. Perhaps a performance in nineteenth-century style, not advertised as such, would cause outrage today.

The condition of the audience is, no doubt, more complicated than so far represented. They wish the performer to perform the work in the way familiar to them, not in preference to correct performance but because they believe that the familiar way is the correct way. They probably also wish the performer to play it in the way he thinks best, in the expectation, or at least the hope, that it will conform to their own view. All their hopes and expectations cannot always be fulfilled.

But, it may be said, we surely cannot expect, or wish, the performer to play the work in any way other than that which he considers to be, aesthetically, best. If we cannot, then are not the wishes and expectations of the audience irrelevant? It is at this point that we can no longer avoid the questions of the identity of a musical work and of authenticity. We must, for example, ask what the name *Messiah* designated to a late nineteenth-century audience: did it designate a certain sound pattern very familiar to them?; did it designate the sound pattern that Handel intended to be designated by that name?; or, since they no doubt took for granted at least a rough identity between the two, does the question perhaps not arise? They might certainly have said 'That's not what I call the *Messiah*'. We must also raise the question how far, mistakes apart, two sound patterns may diverge, and for what reasons, if they are to be accounted as performances of the same work. Is there some norm of authenticity, approximation to which is decisive in determining the identity of a work?

We must raise these questions, though manifestly it would be absurd to try to answer them merely in passing in the present chapter. What is at least clear is that every performer must recognize some bounds of authenticity beyond which he should not go in representing to the audience that it is a performance of a certain work, though we know that not all performers will agree on where those bounds lie. There are some changes which are mere corrections to slips of the pen, which all would agree to be legitimate; some would also agree with, for example, Tovey's opinion (*Essays in Musical Analysis* (London, 1935), i.41) that at one point in Beethoven's Fifth Symphony horns should be substituted for bassoons since, in Tovey's opinion, Beethoven used bassoons at that point only because he 'had not time to change the horns from E flat'; some have even thought it legitimate to add all kinds of instruments to Handel's scores; in the early nineteenth century it was thought legitimate to insert songs by other composers into a Mozart opera – Haydn and Mozart themselves both wrote a number of insertion arias to be used in other people's operas. Where limits of legitimate interpretation lie will, no doubt, never be agreed. They vary from time to time and from performer to performer. But there are limits, and the performer surely has a duty of honesty to the audience not to overstep them, as he understands them. If his views on interpretation differ very widely from those of his intended audience, perhaps he should warn them. I certainly wish that opera houses whose views on the legitimate limits of departure from the composer's directions for staging vary widely from those traditionally held would warn me in advance.

In the end, the performer's duties to his audience seem not to differ widely from those of any purveyor of goods to his customer. There may be other and more important reasons for faithfulness of performance, but one reason is akin to that for obeying the Trade Descriptions Act; people should know what they are buying. To revert once again to the analogy with cookery, while I may legitimately, for my own consumption, introduce any changes I wish to the recipe for the Grant loaf, there are limits to what one may do in producing Grant loaves to be sold to the public; perhaps a little extra or less salt is legitimate, perhaps not; but the introduction of, say, 20 per cent white flour obviously is not; it is cheating, as is unfaithfulness in musical performance. I do not even try now to determine where the bounds of legitimacy or authenticity lie. I merely say that the performer has a duty to his audience not to overstep them, as he understands them.

Thus the professional performer may well be thought to be faced with a number of different and possibly, but not necessarily, competing considerations in determining how he ought to play his programme; no doubt these considerations will include others beyond those that I have mentioned. No doubt compromise will sometimes be thought to be appropriate. If this be so, then the performer's situation will be typical of all departments of life. Doing one's best in the face of possibly competing considerations is the common lot.

But the situation is yet more complicated, for so far we have considered only the performer's relations with the audience; we have not considered other possibly relevant factors. Has the performer not a duty to the composer? It seems reasonable to suppose that the performer has a duty to the composer not to misrepresent him. To avoid the difficulty some feel about duties to the dead, we may for the present limit ourselves to the case where the composer is still alive. It seems hard to deny that avoidance of misrepresentation is a relevant consideration, and it might seem to override others. If this be so, then authenticity as a duty to the audience may seem to be at least reinforced in relation to other duties to the audience. But once again, one's duty to the composer is no more clear than one's duty to the audience without a standard of authenticity. There is no objective, and no intersubjectively agreed standard of authenticity. The performer can only be honest in these matters as he conceives them.

If we ask what the duty of the performer to the composer is, here are some possible answers: it is his duty to interpret it in the way in which he believes the score sounds best in accordance with the understanding of musical notation current at the time of composition; it is his duty to interpret it in the way in which he believes it sounds best, even if this involves some departures from the instructions contained in the score; it is his duty to interpret it according to the known views of the composer on interpretation at the time of composition; it is his duty to perform it in a way that would, to his best belief, be approved by the composer if he heard the performance, however surprising to him. These are some of the possible views; and they themselves must be further complicated if we allow for some uncertainty about the conventions of musical notation at the time of composition and some uncertainty about the views of the composer on interpretation at the relevant time, and total uncertainty about what novelties the composer might approve of if he heard them. Probably, once again, we should say that all such considerations are relevant, but none overriding and exclusive of others. Thus, if there is a recorded performance by the composer himself, it would be cavalier to disregard such wishes on interpretation as clearly emerge from that performance; but, equally, few would hold that subsequent performers should aim merely to duplicate that performance as closely as possible. It is also clear that composers themselves hold different views about the status of their scores in relation to the interpreter. Thus Handel, who included very few indications of dynamics, phrasing, and the like, and occasionally was satisfied to write '*ad libitum*', obviously allowed more freedom to the interpreter than, say, Stravinsky, who plastered his scores with such indications. There can be no universally valid answer to the question how much freedom the interpreter may use without misrepresenting the composer; nor is there a universally valid answer to the question what sorts of departure from the written score count as misrepresentation. Some sorts of departure from the written score have at some times been taken for granted as legitimate and even desirable. The question remains just what departures are legitimate; even the Venetian Ganassi, who wrote 175 different decorated versions of a single five-note cadence, regarded himself as obliged to begin and end on the same notes as the original, a restriction presumably generally accepted at that distant time. There is no universally valid set of rules by which one can answer that question, insufficiently determinate in formulation as it is, for our needs. Perhaps it is not clear what idiom we should adopt in raising it: if Mozart could come back and hear one of his operas played on modern instruments, we do not know whether he would, perhaps, ask why it had been transposed up a semitone or comment that pitch had gone up since his day. Whether he would have liked it is yet another question, and it is not clear how relevant it is, if at all, to the questions under consideration. If a reborn Handel had enjoyed a late nineteenth-century performance of *Messiah*, would that make such an interpretation legitimate? These are questions to which there is no definitive answer. But it does not follow that they need not be raised and considered.

What seems to emerge most clearly from these discussions is that there is a very large number of relevant considerations regarding the legitimacy of an interpretation, unclear in themselves and, in so far as they are clear, often difficult to weigh from lack of information. Myself, I do not think this to be a deplorable situation. I think it is deplorable if the performer does not face these questions, unclear as they are, to the best of his ability and give an honest answer; I think it deplorable that there should be arrogant performers who believe that the satisfaction of their individualities, their artistic visions, or what you will, are of such central importance that all other considerations can be legitimately ignored by them. But we should, perhaps, be glad that we have the opportunity to hear performances of old works in which the performers strive to the best of their knowledge and ability to reproduce the sounds that contemporaries of the composer would have heard, and also performances in which the performers think themselves entitled to make use of the technical resources of modern instruments. We should, perhaps, be glad that we can hear performances of Mozart's Clarinet Quintet both as in the published score and as scholars believe that Mozart originally wrote it.

The issues involved are, as we have seen, too complex for anyone sensibly to be dogmatic on these matters, whatever his personal preferences may be. We may also be glad that, on the whole, we live in a time when performers, unlike operatic and theatrical directors, and far more than composers in other days, do in general take their responsibilities seriously.

The intermediate case of performance by amateurs seems not to raise any serious new issues. They would seem to have the same obligations as professionals, particularly to a paying audience, but somewhat relaxed. They have not the resources that professionals ought to have, and so more licence is justified. In particular, replacement of rare and costly instruments by ones more easily available is easily tolerated. But in general, though amateurs have less knowledge and fewer resources, the same general duties as face professional performers surely remain to be obeyed by them as best they can.

If the general lines of thought expressed in this paper are acceptable, what is clearly missing, and what no effort has been made to supply, is clarification of such notions as authenticity and legitimacy that have been freely used in it. Such clarification is needed, and the problems involved are of great interest and great complexity. They are not the less important because no simple rules are likely to emerge from their discussion. But while such discussions as are contained in this paper are incomplete without such clarification, they are I believe, only incomplete and not useless.

E19   Joachim Kaiser, 'Music and recordings'

From H. Haskell (ed.) (1995) *The Attentive Listener*, London, Faber, pp.365–9; from *Erlebte Musik*, Hamburg, 1977, reprinted in *Suddeutsche Zeitung*, 1 June 1973.

> Kaiser (b.1928) has been one of Germany's most prominent critics in recent years. Writing for the *Suddeutsche Zeitung* in Munich, he first attracted attention with his outspoken reviews of Wieland Wagner's radical opera productions at Bayreuth. A radio and television personality as well, Kaiser here views records as forging an important bond between performers, listeners and scholars – unlike Stuckenschmidt (no. 68), who predicted that recording technology would put an end to live performance.

Have we really stopped to evaluate, quite consciously, how tremendously our whole relationship to music, to the interpretation of music, has changed since the institution of the record came to be taken for granted? ...

We live with records. There are specialists whose only contact with music has been made via records. The record enshrines the one-time performance; it also enshrines a specific mood and interpretation. It has emerged as a call to standards – a threat to standards even – in the most remote village, the most private dwelling. There it is. Anyone concerned with music today must give records a large share of his attention, his interpretive commitment, his capacity for work, and his willingness to record (in both senses of the word) his impressions. Anyone who doesn't do this is letting the reality of our musical life pass him by. But anyone who does must ask himself some questions. Otherwise he turns into the plaything of the record business, the slave of the Bielefelder catalogue. Otherwise he confuses Frau Musica with an industry which is, all in all, honourable. And he doesn't even notice it ....

Even a Karajan, a Friedrich Gulda or an Elisabeth Schwarzkopf can't make a new recording of the masterpieces of the literature whenever he or she wants. When Karajan records Beethoven's symphonies, Gulda Beethoven's piano sonatas, Schwarzkopf her Marschallin, even these world-renowned artists know that they may perhaps have another crack at Beethoven's symphonies and sonatas, or even at *Der Rosenkavalier*, in five or ten years. But they also know that, all in all, the chances are slim. In the meantime – and this is still truer of the interpretations of less renowned artists – the record holds the essence of an artistic existence: this is how fast Gulda plays the *Waldstein* Sonata, this is how slowly Schwarzkopf sings the Marschallin's monologue, this is how lucidly Karajan interprets the Maestoso of the Ninth.

What consequences does this have? Well, the fact that records can't be remade every two years (as, for instance, Horowitz recorded Chopin's *Funeral March* Sonata twice within a few years, because the first version was too undisciplined for him) inevitably leads to a classicism of interpretation. When they commit themselves, artists quite unconsciously choose the middle course. On records they don't risk the extreme or ecstatic interpretations, the captivating blend of manic and depressive which a live but none the less transitory concert sometimes still provokes – under the right, exhilarating circumstances. Records encourage the 'middle way'. Horace, who was no musician, spoke of the golden mean, of course, but Schönberg, a real musician, said that the middle way was the only one which didn't lead to Rome. Thus, one must deal with the fact that records, so to speak, appease us. They encourage care, caution.

Then too, contrary to current belief, only in rare cases does virtuosity make such a spontaneous and compelling impression on records as it does in concert. On records, successes which are merely virtuosic have as weak an effect as a conjuring trick in a film. After all, one must be able to keep a close eye on the conjuror! To put it more positively, only the expression of the compellingly vehement virtuoso makes an impression on the recording, not the flawless facility one naturally expects from the (correctable) electroacoustical product. Perhaps, too, we assume much too thoughtlessly that the recording can 'manipulate' us. I know of no truly first-class, great and important recording which has been produced by a merely second-class, mediocre and unimportant artist. Stature can't be gained surreptitiously, even with ever so many refinements.

In concert there is coughing; your neighbour wears a necklace that tinkles at the slightest movement; the soloist has to warm up; by his second aria, Radames's B natural [in *Aida*] may be no joy to listen to; the stage floor creaks; a cellist drops his bow; and in the middle of a pianissimo an explosion hisses out when a spotlight gives up the ghost. The man who only, 'only' listens to records knows nothing about these live accompaniments. He is alienated from corporeal music making. Half-way through a concert he suddenly longs for the abstraction of his stereo set. In a certain way he's like a living thing in which the sense of public life and presence is dangerously stunted. Late Proust was like that. In hindsight, this has serious consequences for public musical life. It hasn't been made sufficiently clear what it means that every record collector (or borrower) can hold his own ghost-Olympics. He can set the volume on his machine to a specific level, pick up the score and then have ten *Siegfrieds* sung one after another, under conditions which are (so he thinks) completely identical ... If these ten performances are pulled out of the context of their respective *Rings*, if they are isolated, if no consideration is given to what the conductor wanted, what the relation between orchestra and tenor was like, how the protagonist was portrayed, and in what light the silly sot should be seen at just this point, then *playing* records turns into *playing them off* against each other. And in the end one will long for an ideal figure who is a combination of ten tenors. I once read an essay by someone who had heard Schumann's A minor Piano Concerto twenty-two times in a row and then, Arrau, Cortot, Lipatti, Rubinstein and Serkin notwithstanding, decided that if the young Edwin Fischer had made a recording with Furtwängler (which never happened, unfortunately), it certainly would have been the best of the lot.

Certainly? To be sure, one can also run a marriage ad: 'Wife wanted. Specifications: the legs of the young Marlene, Brigitte Bardot's derrière, Marilyn Monroe's bosom, Marcia Haydée's neck, Elizabeth Taylor's eyes and Hannah Arendt's brains.' As far as we know, a woman built like that is nowhere to be found. And if one does turn up, who knows whether she might not be a repulsive monster? In other words, the playing off against each other leads to an ideal type which is far from ideal – it leads to irrefutable smartaleckiness: tenor X's attack isn't quite as light as Caruso's, his change of register isn't as free as Nicolai Gedda's, and Dietrich Fischer-Dieskau is better at penetrating the meaning of the text.

Are we becoming so impossibly hard to please? Answer: no one can simply ignore his hearing experiences, his experience of standards. Often enough famous singers and instrumentalists are afraid not only of being measured against the recordings of their rivals (for they can always fall back on their own individuality) but still more of meeting the spectre of their own recordings on the stage: 'You must be as good and as perfect as you were six years ago in the studio!'

Precisely because I am convinced that only a constant alternation between live concerts and recordings (which are just as serious) makes it possible for us to listen to and partake of music in a reasonably responsible fashion, I must close by calling attention to the various possibilities opened up by recordings. We won't discuss the obvious availability of beautiful things which is now part and parcel of our existence: after the day's trials and tribulations, one can share a glass of red wine with a small group of friends as midnight approaches, listening to a Mozart string quartet, Verdi's Requiem, the Bible Scene from *Wozzeck*, or an aria from *Norma* in peace and quiet (and one probably gets more of such music that way than under any other conditions whatsoever). So far, so good.

But one can also – and this is the record's pedagogical function – learn to experience the complex masterworks. No one who doesn't know how to read scores like a professional, even if he's a diligent concertgoer, can do a reasonable job of internalizing Bruckner's Sixth Symphony or Schönberg's Violin Concerto or the complete works of Webern or Messiaen, unless he studies music and records equally seriously. The Lasalle Quartet's Schönberg-Berg-Webern cassette must have been epoch-making. And our descendants will be able to hear how Strauss or Stravinsky or Boulez saw themselves as interpreters of their own music.

The third possibility which recordings open up is much too seldom perceived, astonishingly. At the moment we have a culture of musicological analysis (one professor refers to others, and they all refer to the music) as well as an active culture of interpretation. (The great pianists of our time plunge into the Op. III Sonata [of Beethoven] and bring to light, often after a labour of decades, connections, gestures, interpretations and insights.) Doesn't it stand to reason, for example, that a bond will eventually be forged between the professor's and the pianist's image of Beethoven? Doesn't it stand to reason that everyone who thinks about our culture's supreme musical works will also give thought to the ineffable insights of these interpreters, who are certainly no stupider or more unmusical or poorer in experience than the professors of musicology? Nothing, however, can be more beneficial to such a broadened outlook on works and tendencies than the careful and urgently comparative consideration of recorded interpretations.

E20 Hugh Aldersey-Williams, 'Sound designs that release the music of architecture'

From *The Independent on Sunday*, 29 April 1990, p.43.

When Simon Rattle lifts his baton to command the strings of the City of Birmingham Symphony Orchestra on 12 June next year, the first ominous chords of Mahler's Second Symphony will ring out in a concert hall unlike any other in Britain. The inaugural concert at the city's new Symphony Hall will test an acoustical system that can be adjusted to suit works ranging from the vast sonorities of a Mahler symphony to the crispness of a song recital.

The adaptability of the Birmingham hall is the result of the latest developments in acoustics. It has been fitted with easily moved devices to alter the quality of the sound: from high-reverberation, 'blended' sound for works on a grand scale and organ recitals to cleaner, clearer sound for voices.

Central to the building's acoustical design is the shoebox-shaped main section of the hall, explains Russell Johnson of Artec, the New York design consultants on the project. 'When the side walls are close together and roughly parallel, a lot of sound energy reaches listeners from the sides. That's a very favourable direction for the ear.' The narrowness of the hall ensures that the sound reaches the ear fast enough to still be relatively loud and clear.

Nicholas Edwards, Artec's senior consultant at Birmingham, says the hall has the best attributes of a shoebox shape. In addition, the orchestra sits in an area where the walls fan out to project the sound forward, whereas the audience at the back of the hall sits in an area where the walls are set at an angle – like a fan in reverse – which sends the sound inwards from the two sides at the rear.

Greater sound energy coming to listeners' ears from the sides increases a phenomenon important to audience appreciation, but only recently recognised in acoustics – that of 'binaural dissimilarity', The effect is similar to that of stereophonic sound. But whereas two or more sound sources are required for stereo, a single point source of sound will produce the effect, provided the listener is sitting nearer one side of the hall than the other. The dissimilarity is caused as the sound arrives directly at one ear but must bend around the head to reach the other. This diffraction is more pronounced with lower frequencies and leads to a feeling of being enveloped by sound. 'If there's been a discovery in the last 10 years in concert hall design, it's that we have realised that people have two ears,' says Mr Edwards.

At Birmingham, reverberation (the degree to which a sound lingers in an enclosed area) is altered in two ways. There are 50 concrete doors to a horseshoe-shaped empty chamber around the concert hall. When they are opened, the extra space effectively makes the hall bigger, and this increases reverberation to give it an almost cathedral-like quality. A sound that previously took around a second to fade away would now take three or more seconds, according to Artec.

The reverberation can be reduced by positioning sound-absorbing panels along the hall walls. During rehearsals, conductors like to get music sounding as if an audience is present, so these panels are pulled out to mimic the sound-absorbing effect of the bodies of the audience.

The height of a sound-reflecting canopy above the orchestra can be adjusted for different types of music. It can be lowered for chamber music to give a feeling of intimacy, and raised for a more robust work.

Although Artec used the same ideas in a number of new American halls, the architects, physicists and musicians that make up the company do not see themselves as purveyors of high-tech gadgetry. They embrace the traditional and the intuitive. During 40 years of going to concerts and talking to musicians, Russell Johnson has established surprisingly *ad hoc* rules for the design of performance spaces. In his experience, most of the best halls date from before 1912 – before the dawn of acoustics as a modern science.

The architects of these halls were working under constraints that almost automatically produced good-quality sound. They used massive materials instead of light frame construction, and this conserved sound energy. The engineering of the time limited the maximum spans, keeping down the width of the halls. Given the technology to produce light-frame, large spans, architects today can unwittingly ruin the acoustics of a hall.

Just as different concert pieces demand different acoustics, so do different operas. Derek Sugden of Arup Acoustics is the consultant on the new Glyndebourne opera house project, for which plans are expected to be unveiled early this summer. His problem is to reconcile the contrasting demands of, for example, a small-scale Haydn opera played on original instruments and the huge forces demanded by a production of Wagner's *Ring* Cycle.

Mr Sugden hints of his design: 'If I chose to do an opera house which tries to fit in most of the classical and modern repertoire [which Glyndebourne does], I think it has to be so conceived as to see the singers' eyes. I would never build an opera house bigger than 1,200 seats.' The new Glyndebourne house sneaks in with a capacity of 1,150, up from its present, tiny 830. The reverberation properties cannot be changed. Mr Sugden feels that building in adjustable features can be a wasted effort. People become accustomed to a hall's acoustics.

Artec nevertheless claims that good acoustics in a new regional concert hall can serve as a magnet, drawing away performers and audiences from less-perfect big-city venues. Londoners should take note.

E21 Ailie Munro, 'Setting the scene'

From A. Munro (1996) *The Democratic Music: Folk Revival in Scotland*, Aberdeen, Scottish Cultural Press, pp.1–8, footnotes edited.

Once you accept that the model of literature is based on universal equality of human existence, past and present, then you can travel in literature, as a writer or a reader, wherever you like ... No caste has the right to possess, or even imagine it has the right to possess, bills of exchange on the dialogue between one human being and another. And such a dialogue is all that literature is.

[Tom Leonard, 1990, pp.xxx–xxxi]

That the above comments are true for music, as well as for literature, is the assumption on which the present book is based. Tom Leonard really means it when he says 'you can travel ... wherever you like', for he claims the freedom to talk about Anton Bruckner (not one of the more accessible of nineteenth-century composers) 'without being called 'élitist': I happen to like his music a lot'. This proves Leonard's truly democratic, all-embracing approach to the arts, for the poems in his book have all been rescued from the nether regions of Renfrewshire public libraries – and most of them have been out of print for over a hundred years: they had not been considered part of the *canon* or *code* of literature. A broadly similar attitude has obtained in the world of music, especially in the oral tradition.

The musical renaissance in Scotland since 1945 is usually taken to mean certain major developments in the world of art music. These include the establishment of the annual Edinburgh International Festival; the continually growing reputation of the Scottish National Orchestra, now the Royal SNO; the birth of Scottish Opera and its rise to such excellence that audiences are drawn from London and farther afield; and lastly the increasing number of composers who have chosen to live and work in Scotland, and the quality of music they have created here during this period.

There is, however, another equally important phenomenon in this musical renaissance: part of a movement embracing the whole world, yet with deeper native associations than any of the four mentioned above. This is the folk music revival.

'Traditional' is sometimes a better word for this music than 'folk'. Although neither is completely satisfactory, and both will be used here *faute de mieux*, the latter is still the most widely used term; it was also used by the predominantly English revivalists of some 50 years earlier and by their supporters.

The forerunner of our revival was the folk song collecting of S. Baring-Gould, Cecil Sharp, the Broadwoods, and others during the late nineteenth century and the early twentieth. Although Lucy Broadwood made a fine contribution to Scottish Gaelic song, Sharp and his associates were concerned with collecting English folk songs from rural districts; but their influence was felt throughout Britain. Hundreds of these songs were published, the music consisting of the basic shape of the verse tune. The melodies were to have an enormous influence on the new English school of art music composition led by Vaughan Williams (himself a collector), Gustav Holst and later Alan Bush. A much-needed, definitive account of this first revival can now be found in *The imagined village*, subtitled

'Culture, ideology and the English Folk Revival', by Georgina Boyes. As the title indicates, this author's approach is critical and myth-debunking, setting the movement firmly in its social/historical context and charting, by the thirties, its declining hold on public imagination.

In Scotland at the turn of the century, Gavin Greig and James Duncan, contemporaries of Sharp, collected over three thousand song versions in Aberdeenshire and the surrounding counties. Most of these songs were not published: those that did appear were among the chief printed sources for enthusiasts several decades later, but publication of the entire Greig-Duncan collection did not start until 1981.

With the basic shifts in opinion which occurred after the Second World War, the time was ripe for a major revival of this music:

> The 1945 election saw a massive Labour victory ... the heroic struggle of the Soviet Union gave the left a tremendous credibility among working people. In this moment, songs ... which celebrated ordinary people in all aspects of their lives spoke to the hopes and fears of a generation.
>
> (A. Howkins, review, WMA Bulletin, no. 19, February 1985)

The idea of folk music as a separate category is a concept found chiefly in Europe and America – it does not exist in many other parts of the world. The only attempt at a definition by the International Folk Music Council was made in 1954, whilst after 1980, when the IFMC changed its name to the International Council for Traditional Music, it was recognised that a universal, single definition would be difficult to sustain. But 'traditional music hardly seems more precise than folk music. Yes, folk music forms traditions, but so do other genres of music.' To oral transmission had been added transmission by print, both of words and music, and also transmission by disc and tape. The print factor is especially important here because folk or traditional music in Scotland has been assiduously collected and printed for over 300 years: by Allan Ramsay, James Oswald, James Johnson, Robert Burns, William Dauney, Patrick Macdonald and many others. This exceptional richness of collection and publication is connected with the loss of nationhood experienced by many Scots after the unions with England; they felt preserving their native music in this way might help to preserve their national identity. This applied more to the literate urban-dwellers, who had been cut off from the living tradition still continuing in the countryside. How important were these collections in keeping the music alive? And was this music *heard* by the people who studied the collections?

There is some evidence that nobles of the seventeenth century included grassroots as well as courtly musicians in their country house music making. 'The *Mar Account Book*, to take only one of several such, records within a few months gifts to "a blind singer at dinner", "a Highland singing woman", "Blind Wat the piper" and "ane woman harper".' In the eighteenth century, when public concerts first started in

Edinburgh, Glasgow and Aberdeen, traditional Scots songs and fiddle music were often included alongside Italian and German art music. As regards fiddle music, a supreme exponent, Niel Gow, was often asked to play at these events, and the craze for dancing ensured its continued hearing. But the songs were sung by singers with trained voices, so that, in the towns at any rate, traditional singing styles were seldom heard. As for drawingroom music making, folk enthusiasts, such as Walter Scott's daughter Sophia in the early nineteenth century, although singing in a simpler manner, would still be far from traditional in style; they probably sang in a style midway between traditional and art. And the folk-based songs of Robert Burns were, and still are, adapted in style when performed in the drawingroom or concert situation. Bagpipe music, played by the town piper or pipers, was heard at ceremonial occasions of various kinds.

The nineteenth century saw a veritable explosion of amateur music societies, at first mainly choral but soon extending to orchestras and chamber music groups; these practised and performed church music, glees and madrigals, and classics by Handel, Beethoven, Mozart, Spohr, J.C. Bach and others. Members of these societies, and those who attended the growing number of public concerts following the breakdown of the old system of aristocratic patronage, were not only the middle classes: 'the masses also became largely the inheritors of what had hitherto been the possession of the privileged few.' After the Industrial Revolution these masses were mainly in urban areas. Some of them would still sing 'the auld sangs' in their homes, and in rural areas these songs still flourished, especially in the Gaelic North-West and in the rich ballad and bothy-song parts of the North-East. Even as early as 1826 this difference between the industrialised South-West and the North-East had been remarked on by the ballad collector and editor, William Motherwell, writing from Paisley to Peter Buchan in Aberdeenshire:

> I sincerely rejoice in your good luck in being so fortunate as every other day to meet with venerable sybils who can and are willing to impart to your thirsting soul the metrical riches of 'the days of other years'. I wish I were at your elbow to assist in the task of transcription. I cannot boast the like good fortune. This part of the country if it ever did abound in this *Song of the people* is now to all intents utterly ruined by every 3 miles of it either having some large town or public work or manufactory within its bounds which absorbs the rustic population and attracts strangers – corrupts ancient manners – and introduces habits of thinking and of living altogether hostile to the preservation and cultivation of traditionary song.
>
> *(Letter of 5 September 1826, Glasgow University Library, Robertson MS 9)*

The members of amateur societies in towns did not meet to sing traditional songs or to play traditional music: the desire to better themselves culturally led quite naturally to music of the upper sections of society, to 'music of learned origin'. Traditional song and the style of singing it came to be despised as lower class and uncouth. (Although class divisions in Scotland were never as rigid as, for instance, in England, they certainly existed.)

For several hundred years the singers and players who had inherited this music orally from generations of their forebears, the grassroots tradition bearers, were rarely heard in those centres where only one kind of music flourished. Although a great and highly developed form, this music of concert hall, salon and conservatoire is just one of the many kinds of world music. Only as the value and beauty of these other musics come to be recognised are 'educated folk' realising that on their very doorstep they have their own other kind: unvarnished rather than rough, unfamiliar (to ears used to learned music) rather than unsophisticated, stoical rather than harsh, with different assumptions of form and of timing, and with melody far more important than harmony. Music of a different genre, yet still within Western tradition.

Where can this different genre, folk or traditional music, be heard? You can hear various forms of it in any large concert hall: Scottish groups such as Runrig and Capercaillie; Gordeanna MacCulloch with the Eurydice women's choir; Dick Gaughan; Jean Redpath; English – Martin Carthy; Irish – Mary Black or Christy Moore; the Reel and Strathspey Societies – these and many more can fill such a hall. But the best places to hear it are smaller, and more intimate – certain folk clubs, especially in the smaller towns; certain folk pubs and festivals; and, in some ways best of all, gatherings of friends in each other's houses, where you will find something nearer the original ceilidh situation.

The Gaelic word *ceilidh* means literally 'a visiting', a group of friends in a room. Originally such gatherings do not include music, but gradually the new kind develop at certain houses or occasions. No-one is a star, although some can sing or play better and some can tell stories well, while others may be gifted conversationalists or simply agreeable companions whose presence enlarges and helps to knit the pattern of the evening together. For these were essentially evening, and winter, events, often extending into the small hours of the morning. Originating in rural parts of the country, after the day's darg was over, the housewife, shepherd, fisherman, ploughman, laird, factor, village teacher and sometimes the local minister or priest, foregathered for company and for an extension of this fellowship. The old songs and ballads, with their images and archetypes of human behaviour and their melodies shaped by generations of singers long since dead; the wordlessness of instrumental music, as the fiddler played a slow air or march and then broke into a strathspey and reel which set feet tapping and often started an impromptu dance session; the symbolism of the stories too, the age-old art of suspension of disbelief – all these would inform the unconscious by stretching tentacles far back into the past and bringing it forward, making it relevant to the fleeting and ever stressful present. These sounds fed mind and spirit, refreshing them anew from the wellsprings of human existence with its joy and its pain, bringing order out of chaos and beauty out of ugliness.

A.E. Housman once said that when he was shaving, if he thought of certain lines of poetry, he could feel the bristles stiffen. Then there is Sydney Carter's criterion for recognising the traditional: 'What alerts me is a sort of shiver.' You could say that both these psycho-physical reactions describe human response to all great art, and I would agree; but with folk poetry, music and story one's reaction seems somehow more immediate, almost more ... atavistic. This is chiefly due to the content of what one hears, but it is also due to the more intimate and unified nature of a situation where the singer, player and storyteller *are* the audience and vice versa.

A more public approximation to this can be found in the folk clubs which have appeared over the last 30 years or so. There are close on 40 of these in Scotland at the present time, meeting weekly, fortnightly or in some cases monthly. Clubs tend to be in cities and large towns, with only a few in small country towns. Predictably there is much diversity in content and style, ranging from clubs with a strong bias towards the traditional, through those which encourage newer songs and other music in the folk style (a significant development), to those which present a kind of folk-pop.

The following is a description of a folk club evening in the late seventies, typical of many during that period and still the model for the more informal kind of club – The Edinburgh Folk Club was founded in 1973 by a journalist, a policeman, a technician and a physicist.

> People sit facing a part of the room where the soloist or group will be performing. This modification of the true ceilidh situation is dictated by the pressure of numbers (between sixty and a hundred) and by the need for good acoustics.

So what is different here from the ordinary concert, with its 'them' and 'us' separation of performers and audience? First, the audience always contains a considerable proportion of performers, called floor singers or players. These are club members who contribute to the evening's music making, more particularly when there is no guest singer or group. Second, when guest performers are present (usually professional or semi-professional artists, professionalism being bound to appear within this mainly amateur movement) they invariably mingle with the rest of the company, not only during the interval and at the close of the evening, but often during breaks between their own items, to chat and to listen to the other singers or players. Last, and most basic, is the music itself.

> Members of a recently established folk club in a country town are the non-professional guests tonight. The compère welcomes the company, and announces the artists as they appear. Irish jigs, on fiddle and guitar, are followed by two American songs: in the second of these, Tom Rush's 'Honey I'm a jazz-man, tryin' a trick or two', the fiddler weaves a beautiful

obbligato round the voice line. An expatriate Highlander gives a spirited unaccompanied version of 'The Muskerry Sportsmen', but his second, Gaelic, song about Loch Leven, with its tender lyricism and delicate ornamentation, shows where his true roots lie. Next comes concertina music, and more songs: an Ulster march, 'O'Neill', followed by two jigs; a haunting ancestral folk version of 'Down by the Sally Gardens'; and two mining songs, 'The old miner' ('me hair's turning grey') and an account of a mine closure. Two young women provide some fine two-part unaccompanied singing, with lots of lovely bare fourths and fifths, and with every word audible: two songs on a similar theme – a girl follows her sailor to 'the watery main' – with a modern song, plus guitar accompaniment, sandwiched between.

Then appears the most consistently traditional singer as yet, again with guitar. His songs include 'Corachree', as learned from the Aberdeenshire itinerant singer Jimmy Macbeath, and Jeannie Robertson's 'The twa recruitin' serjeants' with a chorus which everyone joins in. The last of his group of songs is on a familiar theme in Western folk tradition: that of the deserted woman. A Shetland woman sings an exquisitely sad song to an Irish tune, explaining first that it enshrines the belief 'if you mourn too long for the dead, they can't lie easy', and concludes with a version of the much-loved 'She moved through the fair'.

During the interval, over drinks, people meet and talk – no formal introductions are needed – and you find visitors from England, Ireland, the Continent and farther afield.

The second half of the programme presents more instrumental music, with a tin whistler from Somerset plus a famous Border fiddler, the winner of the Kinross Festival's men's singing class in a group of songs with guitar, and two more Border singers to end with, one giving a particularly fine version of 'The rigs o'rye'.

An evening well spent, you feel as you go home or on to a friend's house for more company or music. There are always some bits, both words and music, which give you that 'sort of shiver', which go on singing in your head and seem to illumine the next day.

An even more informal setting for different kinds of folk music can be found in the folk pubs. It would be difficult to assess how many exist throughout Scotland; Edinburgh alone has around 40, the uncrowned king among them being Sandy Bell's Bar (officially, the Forrest Hill Bar – Bell was the name of a former owner). It is situated little more than a stone's throw from the Royal Infirmary, from various centres of Edinburgh University, from Moray House Institute of Education, the College of Art and the Dental Hospital. Some thirty years ago, before many old tenement blocks were knocked down to make way for new academic buildings, this was still a residential area with a largely working class community. Members of this community still return to Sandy Bell's and you find a fair cross-section of society there.

According to several authorities with long memories of the Scottish Revival, Sandy's was 'where it all started', way back in the late forties;

through music, discussion and the making of plans, it became in one sense the first unofficial folk club of Scotland. It is still a centre for information and for meeting other enthusiasts, whether from Edinburgh and outlying districts or simply passing through.

What is it that draws people like a magnet to Sandy's, to crowd into the single room with its Edwardian decor and its awkward shape – long and narrow? The friendly atmosphere, of course, and the social drinking, but one of the chief attractions over the last 40 years has been the hope of hearing some music, spasmodic and extempore though it may be: the exciting possibility that a good music session may erupt, like a volcano from the seething, molten flow of that 'submerged world'. You may be having an engrossing conversation (and these four old walls seem to encourage, to draw out good talk) with a miner, a tapestry weaver from an old town studio, a doctor from the nearby infirmary, an Irish traveller, a university lecturer escaping from academia, a mother relegating for a while the awesome responsibility of young children, a labourer, an unemployed teacher, a visiting world-famous authority on some esoteric subject, or a well-known alcoholic on whom the management keeps a watchful eye, when suddenly, right beside your ear or at the farthest corner of the room, you hear it. At first only just audible in the hubbub: a jig, hornpipe or reel on the fiddle or penny whistle, or from a group of players; a voice raised in an old familiar ballad or a song written last week; a rollicking, ranting ditty belted out by a trio of young men; the dancing irresistible lilt of an accordion, or the moan of the concertina now enjoying renewed popularity. But what happens after those first strains percolate depends on two things: the quality of the music, both content and performance, and the kind of people who happen to be present, for without the right mixture and vibrations nothing worthwhile will happen.

If both these factors are right then you are in luck. The babble of talk will gradually or with miraculous speed die down, movement will be stilled, the next drink ignored or unordered, and while the music lasts the varied company will be united in its thrall. On the other hand if you are unlucky, if voices rise in pitch and volume to compete with the music, the result can be cacophony.

A more spacious establishment, in the Royal Mile nearby, is gradually overtaking Sandy Bell's as the city's leading folk-bar centre. Cy Laurie had already initiated the ceilidh dance upsurge at Glasgow's Riverside Club; in 1991 he looked Edinburgh-wards and took over what has become the Tron Bar and Ceilidh House. It has several rooms – in particular the lowest basement room, the 'dunny', is sacred to music on Fridays and Saturdays. It is one of the main regular clubs for the city's jazzers; poetry and stories are also creeping in.

At a festival you experience a distillation of the folk clubs and the folk pubs scenes, with several added ingredients. Usually a weekend event, lasting from Friday to Sunday evening (with the quieter Monday aftermath if you have sufficient stamina and do not have to be at work), there is more time to enjoy the familiar and to absorb the new. Impromptu ceilidhs spring up everywhere – in hotel lounges and bedrooms, in the streets, on the steps of a hall, in pubs, in fields, in tents and caravans – from morning to midnight and long past. There is often the drama of competition classes on the Saturday. Classes include such sections as: women's singing and men's singing, usually unaccompanied (and at some festivals combined in one class); solo folk instruments such as fiddle, accordion, melodeon, tin whistle, concertina, jew's or jaw's harp, and mouth organ; ceilidh bands (combinations of three or more instruments – sometimes including piano, guitar or pipes) playing traditional music for dancing; oral whistling; diddling, (singing to nonsense syllables) which has connections with *canntaireachd;*[1] and lastly storytelling, a more recent development at several festivals. There is an opening concert on the Friday evening, a prize winners' concert on Saturday, and several more official ceilidhs with a compère and invited artists. Many local residents take part.

If there is a local pipe band, it may pipe in the festival with a march, strathspey and reel; but both solo pipers and pipe bands have their own festivals and competitions which flourish separately from folk events. Accordion and fiddle clubs also run separate festivals.

There are around 60 folk festivals in Scotland now, most of them held annually, with locales ranging from Shetland in the far north to Newcastleton near the English border. Emphasis and organisation vary from place to place, but those affiliated to the TMSA (Traditional Music and Song Association) lay special emphasis on the traditional. Several longer festivals include those at Edinburgh (ten days) and Glasgow (a week).

The supreme value of festivals is that enthusiasts from widely distant parts can meet, listen to each other and exchange news and views. The atmosphere is one of relaxed celebration.

[1] *Canntaireachd* – chanting. Now used to denote the vocal method used in teaching bagpipes.

E22 Arnold Schoenberg, 'Musical dynamics 1929'

from A. Schoenberg (1984) *Style and Idea*, London, Faber, p.341, footnote omitted.

In indicating loudness, part of what the author writes is meant *absolutely*, part *relatively*. At times, that is to say, it is a matter of 'however loud *forte* means on your particular instrument's scale of dynamics, play that loud' (from the point of view of the instrument, an absolute dynamic). But at other times the same *forte* will simply mean 'loud compared with what is going on around you' (as loud or louder; absolute in relation to the sound as a whole, then, but relative as far as the instrument is concerned).

Now, it would be best to indicate a degree of loudness for the total sound, since on individual instruments the degree of loudness is a variable factor, not only from one player to another but also changing to match technique and also the taste of the time or country.

A marking of this kind (such as I myself have used for the most part) matches the kind found in the classics and arose, in the latter, from the erroneous belief that loudness will remain forever the same. In my music, however, the basis is a desire always to use the particular instruments on which the prescribed loudness fits correctly into the total loudness. A marking of this kind has the disadvantage that if my procedure is not adhered to, and also if loudness alters, the conductor is obliged in each case to give the player special instructions about loudness.

Perhaps the following is a way out:

To show, in one's markings, whether the total loudness is meant or the instrument's own degree of loudness.

E23   Arnold Schoenberg, 'Vibrato c.1940'

From A. Schoenberg (1984) *Style and Idea*, London, Faber, pp.345–7.

In my youth vibrato was called tremolo, a fitting expression since tremolo means trembling. It was one of the ways of giving life to a note that was dying out or losing its colour – one could strike it over and over again, as in the case of the *Bebung*, also of the mandolin; or, in the case of a broken tremolo on piano or strings, one could repeat it as rapidly as possible; or, as in flutter-tongueing, break it down into a large number of single short attacks. Lastly one should also include here the trill, which indeed serves the same purpose.

All musical instruments except the organ have difficulty with a sustained note. Whether it is the length of breath, or of the bow, or its steadiness, evenness, or the shortness of the note itself (as on the piano, harp, guitar, etc.) – the musician is constantly concerned to divert attention from the imperfection of the sound. In many cases dynamics are enough; swelling out and dying away, or one of the two. One may forgive it in the case of trumpets, horns, trombones, saxophones and most woodwind instruments, for the same reason, even though it does harm to a certain 'worthiness', chastity, clarity, and unsentimentality and objectivity in the sound of these instruments. A tremolando of that kind is entirely ludicrous on instruments of the organ family, since there the wind-strength can be maintained without limit.

Many of the vibrations produced by tremulant stops resemble the vibrato of strings and singing voice. As with trills, here too the main note, the true note, alternates with one or more subsidiary notes. But whereas the trill uses subsidiary notes that are in themselves pure, the subsidiary notes in vibrato are from every point of view impure.

Vibrato has degenerated into a mannerism just as intolerable as portamento-legato. Even though one may at times find the latter unavoidable, and admissible for purposes of lyrical expression, its almost incessant use even for intervals of a second is as reprehensible technically as from the point of view of taste.

But I find even worse the goat-like bleating used by many instrumentalists to curry favour with the public. This bad habit is so general that one could begin to doubt one's own judgement and taste, did one not occasionally have the pleasure, as I did recently, of finding oneself supported by a true artist. I listened on the radio to Pablo Casals playing the Dvořák Cello Concerto. Extremely sparing vibrato, exclusively to give life to long notes, and carried out with moderation, not too quickly, not too slowly, and without detriment to intonation. *Never* that sentimental portamento. Even intervals not easy for the left hand to join smoothly are bridged without adventitious help, simply by the artistry of his bowing. And when the occasional portamento does occur, it is only to lend a lyrical *dolce* passage the tender colouring that expresses the mood of such a passage all the more piercingly.

About the same time I heard on the radio a French woman singer performing Gluck's *Orpheus* perfectly, as I had never heard it before. It would be wrong to try to characterize this ideal performance in any other way than by the word 'perfect'. Such a performance places the inferiority of technical palliatives in its true light and, at the same time, shows who is able to do without them.

ACKNOWLEDGEMENTS

Grateful acknowledgement is made to the following sources for permission to reproduce material in this book:

A2: Denniston, D. and McWilliams, P. (1975) 'What TM is Not', *The TM Book: How To Enjoy The Rest Of Your Life*, Versemonger Press.

A3: this extract is from *Worlds of Faith*, pp.24–48, by John Bowker, 1983, with the permission of BBC Worldwide Limited.

A4: Barker, E. (1989) Appendix II, 'New religious movements: definitions, variety and numbers', pp.145–8, 149–150, © Crown Copyright.

A5: Smart, N. (1989) *The World's Religions: Old Traditions and Modern Transformations*, pp.10–25, Cambridge University Press.

A6: *Hinduism: A Cultural Perspective* by D.R. Kinsley © 1993. Reprinted by permission of Prentice-Hall, Inc., Upper Saddle River, NJ.

A7: Chaudhuri, S. (ed.) (1990) *Calcutta: The Living City, Volume II: The Present and The Future*, pp.331–3, 335–6, Oxford University Press, New Delhi.

C2: Pedersen, L. (1977) 'Shakespeare's *The Taming of the Shrew* vs. Shaw's *Pygmalion*: male chauvinism vs. women's lib?' in R. Weintraub (ed.) *Fabian Feminist: Bernard Shaw and Women*, pp.77–85, by permission of Rodelle Weintraub.

D1: de Jongh, J. (1986) 'Medea', *The Guardian,* 1 June.

D1: Review, *The Observer,* 8 June 1986.

D1: 'Medea, Lyric Hammersmith, London', *Today,* 4 June 1986, Rex Features.

D2: Hazel, R. (1994) 'Monsters and stars: *Medea* in a modern context', Dr J. March (ed.) *C.A. News*, 11 December, pp.2–3, Classical Association News.

D6 and D7: Translated by K. McLeish, 1993, excerpts from 'Festival Time' and 'Frogs', *Aristophanes Plays: Two,* Methuen, by permission of Random House.

D8A: translated by J. Morwood (1997) *Medea*, pp.26–7, by permission of Oxford University Press.

D8B: translated by D. Stuttard (1996) *Medea*, p.5, Actors of Dionysus.

D8C: translated by D. Wiles (1986) *Medea*, p.7, Royal Holloway and Bedford New College.

D9: Williamson, M. (1990) 'A Woman's Place in Euripides' Medea' in A. Powell (ed.) *Euripides, Women and Sexuality*, pp.16–31, Routledge.

D10: Easterling, P.E. (1977) 'The Infanticide of Euripides' Medea', *Yale Classical Studies*, pp.177–91, Yale University.

E2: Weir, J. (1991) 'The song of a girl ravished away by the fairies in South Uist', *Songs from the Exotic,* pp.19–21, © Copyright 1991 Chester Music Limited. Reproduced by permission.

E5: Clough, P. (1987) 'A survey of the younger generation of South African composers' in P. Klatzow (ed.) *Composers in South Africa Today,* pp.218–21, Oxford University Press, by permission of Professor P. Klatzow.

E7: Culshaw, J. (1984) '"Ben": a tribute to Benjamin Britten' in C. Palmer (ed.) *The Britten Companion,* pp.62–7, Faber & Faber Limited.

E10: Brown, H.M. (1988) 'Pedantry or liberation? A sketch of the historical performance movement' in N. Kenyon (ed.) *Authenticity and Early Music,* pp.27–30, Oxford University Press.

E11: Duarte, J.W. (1994) sleeve notes for *Composers in Person, Edward Elgar,* a recording by Beatrice Harrison and the New Symphony Orchestra, pp.5–8, EMI Records Ltd.

E12: Philip, R. (1992) 'Implications for the future' in *Early Recordings and Musical Style,* pp.229–31, Cambridge University Press.

E13: Lee, S.O. and Simpson-Curenton, E. (1991) 'Scandalize My Name' from sleeve notes of *Scandalize My Name,* recorded by Kathleen Battle, Deutsche Grammophon Gasellschaft mbH.

E17: Sleeve notes from *The Mellstock Band,* 1986, Saydisc Records, Chipping Manor, The Chipping, Wotton-under-Edge, Gloucestershire, GL12 7AD.

E18: Urmson, J.O. (1995) 'The ethics of musical performance' in M. Krausz (ed.) *The Interpretation of Music,* pp.157–64, Clarendon Press, by permission of Oxford University Press.

E19: Haskell, H. (ed.) (1995) *The Attentive Listener,* pp.365–9, Faber and Faber Limited.

E20: Aldersey, A.W. (1990) 'Sound designs that release the music of architecture', *Independent on Sunday,* 29 April 1990, p.43.

E21: Munro, A. (1996) *The Democratic Music: Folk Music Revival in Scotland,* pp.1–8, Scottish Culture Press.

E22 and E23: Schoenberg, A. (1984) *Style and Idea,* pp.341, 345–72, Faber and Faber Limited.